Digital Futurama

Michael Korolenko
Bruce Wolcott

Bellevue Community College

KENDALL/HUNT PUBLISHING COMPANY
4050 Westmark Drive   Dubuque, Iowa 52002

CONTENTS

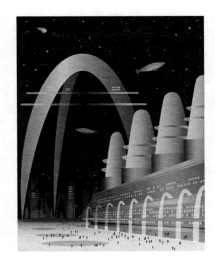

Introduction
The Gernsback Continuum

"The future isn't what it used to be"

Attributed to both Yogi Berra and Arthur C. Clarke

"We're all in science fiction now"

Attributed to Allen Ginsberg, 1975

"There are two futures, the future of desire and the future of fate, and man's reason
has never learnt to separate them"

J. D. Bernal, 1929

"Think of it," Dialta Downes had said, "as a kind of alternate America: a 1980 that never happened.
An architecture of broken dreams." from William Gibson's "The Gernsback Continuum"

Over twenty five years ago, speculative fiction author William Gibson wrote a fascinating and brilliant short story titled "The Gernsback Continuum". In it, a man named Parker is given a magazine assignment to photograph what was once considered futuristic architecture in the 1930s and 1940s: fading masterpieces from the era of Art Deco and the great World's Fairs that prophesized a future made utopian by technology. The "Gernsback" of the title refers to Hugo Gernsback, one of the fathers of modern science fiction. Gernsback loved technology and felt that it would make our world a much better, and cooler place, for man.

At one point in the story, Parker, while heading back to Las Vegas, finds that he's crossed over through some rift into an alternate universe where the future as predicted during those streamline decades has come to pass. He sees a city with soaring, impossibly gigantic art deco-style architecture, mile-long dirigibles and gigantic wing airliners. The people of this world are handsome, blonde, and blue-eyed, driving teardrop shaped automobiles and swallowing food pills. To Parker (and Gibson) "It had all the sinister fruitiness of Hitler Youth propaganda."

Later, Parker is in San Francisco, when he once again sees imagery from his dream, or warp trip into an alternate present, although, this time, the flying wing he sees seems "tenuous". Parker picks up a newspaper with headlines about a gas crisis and the hazard of nuclear energy.

"Hell of a world we live in, huh?" The proprietor (says to Parker).
"But it could be worse, huh?"
"That's right," (Parker says), "or even worse, it could be perfect."

A few years after this story was written, Gibson would go on to write some of the seminal cyberpunk novels of the 1980s and 1990s, including "Neuromancer" where, in a near future dystopia, people literally plug themselves into a virtual computer world.

One of the purposes of this book is to show how the past thought about and forecast the technological future, and compare it to how we see the future today, in the 21st Century.

Before the advent of the Industrial Revolution, the "future" was not something men often thought about. There were stories of the fantastic—of heroes and monsters and strange cities. But the future was something that was not discernable—no different from the "present" or, for that matter, "the past". Think of the ancient Romans in Shakespeare's "Julius Caesar" looking up to consult a clock that wouldn't be invented until the 13th Century AD.

Since those early days when men first looked at the stars in wonder, time has been seen as cyclical, following the four seasons, the movement of the earth (or, rather, the sun when the earth was perceived to be the center of the universe in pre-Copernican times). All was a cycle of birth, aging, death, and renewal. Like the four seasons, man would be born, live and die only to be born again.

For century upon century, Time was looked upon as circular, in concert with the rhythms not only of life and the twenty-four hour day, but of the heavens themselves.

With the coming of the Industrial Revolution, the very idea of Time began to change. With electricity, people no longer needed to depend on the light of sun or the dim flicker of candles and gaslights. People could soon work nights and sleep days. The landscape of our culture changed radically and, by the middle of the 19th Century, the idea of change both in one's life and in one's world was seen as not only natural, but necessary. New technology equaled freedom and convenience for many. But there was a downside to progress as well.

Since the Industrial Revolution, humanity has become increasingly alienated from the soil and from the seasons. The "simple life" with its rituals and rhythms connected to agricultural cycles as well as the cyclical nature of the earth's rotation every day and every year has been largely abandoned in the western world. The traditional notions of renewal and harmony have been replaced by a drive toward expansion and development. For the first time, people must deal with a rapidly changing culture in which values and traditions are shed whenever they do not fit emerging economic and social frameworks. The meaning of time has changed in both religious and scientific cosmological models. The universe is no longer seen as static and clock-work; the "city of man" is no longer considered to be permanent. Time is now seen as dynamic.

New metaphors became necessary for this new outlook on Time. No longer was time circular: in fact, the old pocket watch, so often used as a metaphor for the circular nature of time, was suddenly replaced by digital numbers; yellow and green light points winking forever onward into the future. It is inherently ironic that philosophers have called digital time "linear" as opposed to circular or cyclical time.

With new discoveries and inventions, people realized that with time, comes change! It was no accident that, by the early 19th Century, as the first seeds of the Industrial Revolution began to bear fruit, the first science fiction began to appear. We were no longer passive vessels being carried along the current of time, but were now becoming, technologically speaking, the "master of my fate, the captain of my soul." With the advent of the 21st Century we now have increasingly within our grasp, the ability to engineer biological processes, build materials from the atom up—molecule by molecule, and augment our thinking capacities through an intimate relationship with machines that possess their own kind of intelligence.

"I saw the pale student of unhallowed arts kneeling beside the thing he had put together. I saw the hideous phantasm of a man stretched out, then, on the working of some powerful engine, show signs of life . . . His success would terrify the artist; he would rush away . . . hope that . . . this thing . . . would subside into dead matter . . . he opens his eyes; behold the horrid thing stands at his bedside, opening his curtains. . ."

Mary Shelley on the vision that inspired her creation of Frankenstein

1818 saw the publication of Mary Wollstonecraft Shelley's "The Modern Prometheus", better known as "Frankenstein."

By 1863, Jules Verne had published "Five Weeks in a Balloon", in 1865 "From The Earth To The Moon". 1868 saw the Frank Reade dime novel "The Steam Man of the Prairies" (about a steam powered mechanical man who helps the hero fight Indians) by Edward F. Ellis. The following year saw Edward Everett Hale's "The Brick Moon" (about an artificial satellite). A year after that, came the publication of both Verne's "Round The Moon" and "Twenty Thousand Leagues Under The Sea." In 1871 came Sir George Chesney's "The Battle of Dorking", a tale of future war, which became very popular. And on it went, with story after story, illustration after illustration, describing and showing the wonders of a world not yet here – a world of the future. A world made possible by new technology and technological innovations. 1887 saw Albert Robida's "The Twentieth Century War", with elegant finned airships bombarding cities with chemical and biological bombs, and people watching distant wars in the Middle East on large, high definition screens in their own homes.

In other words, the vision of the future was a child of the Industrial Revolution. Writers and artists in all countries began to write "scientific romances" where man had conquered the air, space, and beyond. Immortality, living under the sea, flying to the moon, no longer seemed in the realm of fantasy. And the literature that investigated such imaginings no longer used the trappings of magic and the supernatural to show how these ideas might come to pass. Now, the heroes of these new tales of the scientific age were able to achieve powers that, in the past, only the gods processed, through technology as opposed to spells and incantations. Men didn't fly to the moon using swans or the spells of dreams but by means of a gigantic cannon or a strange substance not yet invented. Men didn't walk under the sea with the help of mermaids and witchcraft but with great suits and apparatus containing filtered air. And men were no longer made immortal by the whim of a god or a demon, but by an elixir conjured up in chemical laboratory.

As time went on, people began to realize that progress and technology do not necessarily mean utopia. As early as 1909, British novelist E.M. Forster wrote the novella "The Machine Stops", about a future world, a seemingly utopia of airships and virtual reality, where true human companionship has been lost. In 1921, "R.U.R. (Rossum's Universal Robots) by Karel Capek premiered on stage and introduced audiences to a future world where man becomes extinct while human-like synthetic men take over the earth (the play introduced the term "robot").

In 1931, Aldous Huxley's seminal dystopian novel of the future, "Brave New World", was published. He showed a future filled with test tube conception, promiscuous sex, psychotropic drugs, virtual reality, and advertisements constantly blaring over the airwaves. Huxley's book was written as farce, but many of its world's attitudes and technologies seem uncomfortably close to our own (a trend Huxley himself discussed in his series of 1959 essays, "Brave New World Revisited").

More dystopian novels would follow, including George Orwell's "1984" (which Huxley's novel is inevitably compared to), Nevil Shute's novel of nuclear devastation "On The Beach", the 1966 novel *Colossus: The Forbin Project*, by D. F. Jones, about a gigantic computer created to defend the United States from nuclear attack which connects with its Soviet counterpart becoming sentient and deciding to take charge of the entire world, and Richard Matheson's "I Am Legend."

We are now in a period of time where it's important that we make intelligent choices about our future. The blindly optimistic (corporate and nationalistic) future visions seen at the World's Fairs of the past century now seem, at best, dangerously naïve; at worst a sure way to destroy the planet's resources and ourselves.

"Science fiction often portrays the future as being just like the past, except worse. In other words, you have worse wars, more deadly wars. You blow up a planet instead of blowing up a city. And the really human action of science and technology gets lost in the shuffle. All history shows that it is easy to make foolish use of technology. There's no law that says we have to be foolish. We can use technology wisely."

Isaac Asimov, interview with author Michael Korolenko, 1977

Chapter 1
A Tour of the History of the Future

"You may live to drive a plastic car powered by an atomic engine and reside in a completely air conditioned plastic house. Food will be cheap and abundant everywhere in the world... No one will need to work long hours. There will be much leisure and a network of large recreational areas will cover the country, if not the world."

Operation Atomic Vision, issued by the Atomic Energy Commission in 1948 for use in High Schools

The 1939 New York World's Fair is a central metaphor for this book. The fair was a place where people looked back at where they'd come from and sought to anticipate what technologies and changes lay ahead. Much of what that exhibition had to offer now appears quaint or naïve, especially since the World's Fair gates closed just at the beginning of the twentieth century's greatest crisis—the second World War. Five years later, World War II ended ominously with the detonation of atomic bombs over the Japanese cities of Hiroshima and Nagasaki. Technology brings great possibilities but also presents potentially disastrous results. As you read through this book, it should become progressively clearer that we need to look intelligently at the future based on our experiences in the past, anticipate the possible outcomes of new technologies, and make informed decisions about where we want to go on our journey to Tomorrowland.

Figure 1. Albert Robida's "Life in the XXth Century"—a family watches a war in the Middle East on their HDTV-sized "Telephonoscope" in Robida's 1883 illustration.

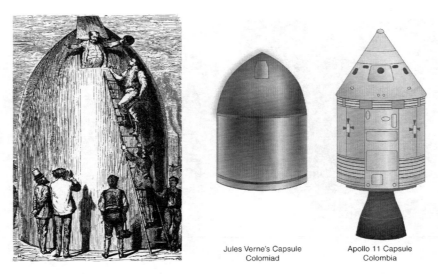

Jules Verne's Capsule
Colomiad

Apollo 11 Capsule
Colombia

Figure 2a and b. Jules Verne's original capsule (left and center) in *From the Earth to the Moon* compared with the 1969 Apollo 11 space module NASA.

I suppose we might lay the blame or the accolade for the creation of modern technology on French artist Albert Robida, who in the mid-1800s drew wonderfully baroque pictures of "Life in the XX Century" showing correspondents broadcasting news from some twentieth century war both audibly and visually into the comfortable homes of the very Victorian-looking populace via the *telephonoscope*. Or maybe we can lay it all on Gutenberg and the introduction of his printing press. It can be taken back hundreds or even thousands of years to those early cave artists who painted the news of the day on the walls of their dwellings.

Jules Verne, another technology visionary from Robida's era, wrote a book in 1865 called *From the Earth to the Moon* that describes a voyage from the coast of Florida to the moon. Many intriguing correspondences exist between Jules Verne's initial imagined flight to the moon in the nineteenth century and the actual first manned NASA moon mission that took place in July of 1969. Verne attempted to carry out approximate calculations regarding the amount of force necessary to launch a heavy stationary object into space. His calculations turned out to be surprisingly close to reality. However, Verne's space capsule had to be shot at the moon from a very large cannon, and the force of acceleration undoubtedly would have killed nineteenth century astronauts.

Other correspondences exist as well.

- Both space capsules had a similar, bullet-like appearance; they were approximately the same size.
- Both vehicles carried a crew of three.
- Both spacecraft were launched from the Florida peninsula in the United States.
- Verne's launch cannon was called the *Columbiad;* the Apollo 11 capsule was named the *Columbia.*
- Both capsules landed safely in the Pacific Ocean and were picked up by Navy vessels.

When Verne created his fictional trip to the moon, he wasn't shooting from the hip; he made imaginative projections into the future based on mathematical calculations and existing scientific theory and possible technologies. His inventions came from a solid understanding of what might be possible, given current trends of the mid-nineteenth century.

Some of his predictions regarding space travel weren't accurate. For example, although Verne correctly predicted that his Victorian astronauts would be weightless, he thought that weightlessness would only occur at a midway point between the Earth and the moon, where the gravitational fields of each of them would neutralize the effect of the other. Verne also correctly predicted the invention of submarines, helicopters, underwater diving suits, and televisions, but placed their appearance much further in the future than they actually occurred.

Figure 3. French stroller listens to his portable audio player. Albert Robida illustration from *The End of Books* (1894). Original Robida Caption: "Phonographic Literature for the Promenade".

Although some errors were made, Verne used real engineering analysis to arrive at the design of his cannon and manned moon projectile. As a result, at the time of the Apollo 8 and 11 missions it was noted that Verne had made a number of correct predictions about the actual missions.

Here's an excerpt from Verne's book a description that closely matches the actual NASA Apollo moon mission launches which took place in Florida 100 years later:

"Twelve o'clock struck! A gunshot suddenly pealed forth and shot its flame into the air. Twelve hundred melting-troughs were simultaneously opened and twelve hundred fiery serpents crept toward the central well, unrolling their incandescent curves. There, down they plunged with a terrific noise into a depth of 900 feet. It was an exciting and a magnificent spectacle. The ground trembled, while these molten waves, launching into the sky their wreaths of smoke, evaporated the moisture of the mould and hurled it upward through the vent-holes of the stone lining in the form of dense vapor-clouds. These artificial clouds unrolled their thick spirals to a height of 1,000 yards into the air. A savage, wandering somewhere beyond the limits of the horizon, might have believed that some new crater was forming in the bosom of Florida, although there was neither any eruption, nor typhoon, nor storm, nor struggle of the elements, nor any of those terrible phenomena which nature is capable of producing. No, it was man alone who had produced these reddish vapors, these gigantic flames worthy of a volcano itself, these tremendous vibrations resembling the shock of an earthquake, these reverberations rivaling those of hurricanes and storms; and it was his hand which precipitated into an abyss, dug by himself, a whole Niagara of molten metal!"[1]

Albert Robida's retro-futuristic views of the twentieth century from his art studio in 1870 were strikingly accurate, despite the obvious differences in style of dress, graphic styling, and architecture. He accurately portrayed the use of public telephones, the manufacture of a "microbe bomb" (biological weapon) for warfare, and the effects of industrial pollution from unregulated manufacturing. In 1894 he wrote an illustrated novel called *The End of Books* that showed people of the future using portable audio devices to listen to stories and news rather than read books. The illustration below shows a man carrying an audio device that plays into two wires that connect to his ears—an early precursor to the Sony Walkman and Apple iPod.

Another Forward-Looking Device from the Nineteenth Century: The Mechanical Computer

A common historical misconception is that the computer is a twentieth century invention, but in fact it was first created by a nineteenth century scientist and mathematician named Charles Babbage. Babbage was also an inventor who is credited with creating the first locomotive speedometer and "cowcatcher"—the metal grate at the front of nineteenth century trains designed to push wandering cattle away from the tracks. Babbage was a stickler for accuracy and was frustrated by the inaccuracies he found in published logarithmic tables that were used for various purposes, including navigation at sea. The math necessary to complete these tables was carried out by clerks, who were called *computers*. Many simple math mistakes were made by these flesh-and-blood calculators, and this led Babbage to come up with plans for a device he called the Difference Engine, which he thought would complete logarithmic math consistently and accurately.

In his memoirs, Babbage described the origin of this early automated calculating device:

"The earliest idea that I can trace in my own mind of calculating arithmetical tables by machinery rose in this manner: One evening I was sitting in the rooms of the Analytical society at Cambridge, my head leaning forward on the table in a kind of dreamy mood, with a Table of logarithms lying open before me. Another member, coming into the room, and seeing me half asleep, called out, 'Well, Babbage, what are you dreaming about?' To which I replied, 'I am thinking that all these Tables (pointing to the logarithms) might be calculated by machinery.'"[2]

Charles Babbage, *Passages from the Life of a Philosopher*

Babbage demonstrated a small working prototype of his calculating device to the Royal Astronomical Society in 1822. It was fully mechanical, consisting of interlocking metal gears and shafts. Based on this early success, Babbage was given a series of grants by the British government to finalize an advanced version of his new invention, which he called the Difference Engine.

After much experimentation and manufacturing delays, Babbage began to recognize the limitations of his Difference Engine, which was designed for a limited number of mathematical operations. Why not construct a more general-purpose calculating device that could handle a wider range of computational tasks? He then conceived of a more sophisticated calculator that he hoped would be powered by steam and delivered instructions by means of punched cards that, in turn, would control automated calculations. Based on these punch card instructions, the device could now handle a wider variety of mathematical procedures. He called this updated version of his automated calculator the Analytical Engine.

After seeing a demonstration of his early working model, a young, mathematically gifted woman offered her services to Babbage. Her name, which sounds like it was taken from a steampunk novel, was Ada Augusta Byron the Countess of Lovelace. She was the daughter of the famous English poet Lord Byron. Early on, she recognized the importance of Babbage's vision and worked out numerous strategies for delivering punch card instructions to the Analytical Engine. These instructions were, in fact, software to drive a hardware device, and Ada is recognized today as the world's first software engineer. Her description of this new craft was poetically described in her essay called *Observations on Mr. Babbage's Analytical Engine:*

"We may say most aptly that the Analytical Engine *weaves algebraical patterns* just as the Jacquard loom weaves flowers and leaves. . . ."[3]

Augusta Ada Byron

Contemporary computer programming concepts such as loops, branching, and conditional statements owe their origin to Ada Byron.

Unfortunately, Babbage was his own worst enemy. A visitor to Babbage's home later in his career saw several incomplete, nonworking versions of the Analytical Engine. A perfectionist by nature, Babbage kept changing and updating the design of his device, and consequently he was unable to finish it. Eventually the British government finally gave up financing his scheme, and Babbage spent most of his own considerable wealth trying to perfect the first computer. Ada Augusta Byron died at age thirty-nine. The precision that Babbage required was difficult to match based on the technology of the early Industrial Revolution. He was more than a century ahead of his time.

Interestingly, two Swedish engineers, George and Edward Schuetz, were able to construct Babbage's Difference Engine in 1834 based on his descriptions. A second version of the Difference Engine was built five years after Babbage's death by American inventor George Bernard Grant for the 1876 Philadelphia Centennial Fair. The mechanical calculator had more than 15,000 moving parts. Yet a third incarnation of Babbage's device was created from his designs by the Science Museum of London in 1991, commemorating Babbage's 200th birthday. Babbage went to his grave without the knowledge that his invention actually worked.

Charles Babbage and an illustrated section of the first computer—called the Analytical Engine. It was designed to include four primary functions that form the basis of modern computers: input, output, processing, and storage. Circa 1844.

It should be noted that Babbage made reference to steam, rather than electricity, as a means to power his new device. That's not surprising, because in Babbage's time the steam engine drove factories, locomotives, ships, and pumps. Harnessed steam was the *enabling technology* that supported and sustained the Industrial Revolution. As the nineteenth century unfolded, greater use was made of electricity rather than steam. By the late nineteenth and early twentieth centuries many innovations based on electricity, rather than steam, would lay the foundation for telecommunications technologies.

The 1876 Philadelphia Centennial Fair

The 1876 Philadelphia Centennial Fair was a seminal event in the "history of the future." The exposition was held to honor the 100th anniversary of the Declaration of Independence in Philadelphia and celebrated America's industrial prowess. Thirty thousand exhibitors displayed new technological marvels, including magic lanterns, printing presses, locomotives, sewing machines, typewriters, as well as Edison's light bulb and the new telegraph machine. Heinz Ketchup and Hires Root Beer made their first appearances. It was also the first major World's Fair to celebrate the contributions of women, and importantly, exhibit machines of the future. These included George Bernard Grant's Difference Engine, the first motion simulator (Edison's precursor to the motion picture projector), and Alexander Graham Bell's telephone. When the visiting Emperor Dom Pedro of Brazil heard a voice coming through Bell's telephone, he accidentally dropped the receiver, saying, "My God, it talks!"[4]

The exhibition marked a movement from steam power to devices powered by electricity and the internal combustion engine. It also established the United States as a preeminent technology innovator; it provided America with a reputation in the outside world as a country of engineers, inventors, and pioneers of the future. The stage had been set for this development by America's bloody Civil War (1861–1865), which also brought with it a string of technological precedents, including aerial reconnaissance by balloon, large scale railroad troop movement, photography, submarine warfare, ironclad warships, and telegraphy.

Before the Industrial Revolution, the future was always going to be the same as the past. People couldn't envision a future that was different from their own present until the seeds of the Industrial Revolution bore fruit. The 1876 Philadelphia Exposition marked a milestone year in the history of the future because for the first time people felt a sense of wonder about what progress and the future could bring. In 1876, progress for the first time meant new technology for the masses and looking forward to the future as something different—socially, politically, and economically. The term *Yankee ingenuity* didn't come into the lexicon until the 1870s. After the 1876 World's Fair, the inventions came fast and furious; early telecommunications technologies played a major role in this burgeoning era of invention.

Milestones in the Early History of Electronic Telecommunications

1844—Telegraph: Samuel Morse transmits the first official telegraph between Washington, DC, and Baltimore. The message read, "What hath God wrought?"

1876—The first fax machine: Elisha Gray's *telautograph* transmits facsimile writing and drawings via telegraph wires.

1884—German inventor Paul Nipkow creates the mechanical television: A wheel containing tiny holes was set in front of a picture, and as the wheel turned, each hole scanned one line of the picture.

1890s—Yellow journalism prevails in print media. William Randolph Hearst's "Journal" and Pulitzer's "World" duke it out in a circulation war. There are large, lurid headlines, comics, and sensational stories—the first tabloids.

1893—Nikola Tesla: First demonstration of radio communication; introduces alternating current, or AC.

1893—H.G. Wells writes *The Time Machine*.

Figure 4. The first telegraph receiver, used in the first long distance telegraph transmission between Washington, DC, and Baltimore. Courtesy of the Division of Rare and Manuscript Collections, Cornell University Library.

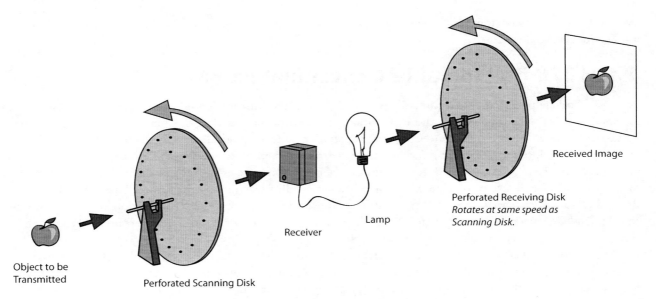

Figure 5. Paul Nikow's mechanical television (1884). Illustration by Kirsten Adams.

1895—H.G. Wells and film pioneer Robert Paul patent a "novel form of entertainment"—a Victorian multimedia presentation.

1896—The first motion photograph simulation. Thomas Edison: The Kinetoscope and motion picture camera. This has been called the poor man's virtual reality.

1897—Guglielmo Marconi goes wireless. He invents a device to transmit sound signals without a physical connection, the first wireless telegraph.

1904—John Fleming develops the vacuum tube, paving the way for actual voice transmission over Marconi's "wireless" or radio waves.

1905—Hugo Gernsback manufactures the first mass-produced home radio set: the Telimco Wireless.

1906—Reginald Fessender develops the idea of continuous sound broadcast on radio waves and broadcasts his own violin solo.

1912—The Radio Act of 1912 created after the sinking of the Titanic, requiring radio operators to have licenses and assigning specific wavelengths to transmitters.

1914—Radio corporations General Electric and Westinghouse emerge.

1920—Westinghouse applies for first broadcasting license and establishes the first radio station, KDKA.

1922—AT&T sells radio time, and the era of modern media advertising commences.

1926/1927—The large media corporations NBC Red Network and Columbia Broadcasting form.

1928—Felix the Cat becomes the first televised personality.

The History of Modern Media

For purposes of space and time, we'll start the history of modern media at the 1939 World's Fair. This event is culturally significant because before the premise of mass media, the 1939 World's Fair advertised the future. As Jerry Mander states in his book, *In The Absence of the Sacred:*

"... the paradigm as confirmed by the technological innovation was good, invariably good, and would be the principal means by which our society would solve its problems and produce a better world."[5]

What neither the purveyors of the World's Fair nor earlier inventors could foresee, let alone exhibit, was how these new technologies would affect how people viewed the world and "reality." Exhibits can show how you might have a "home theater" or "picturephone" in your house in thirty years, but they never touch on how our role models might be created in the future or what the economic, sociological, and political effects of new technology might be.

According to J.P. Telotte in his book *Replications,* the 1930s:

"... is almost bracketed by two world's fairs that traded on the promise of technological development. In 1933 Chicago hosted its 'Century of Progress Exposition,' and from 1939 to 1940 New York offered us 'The World of Tomorrow,' a vision of life in the America of 1960. Both fairs projected a broad interest in progress, in the future, in a truly scientific 'world of tomorrow,'" that reflected a general awareness of the technological changes then going on throughout our culture. And they offered images not only of the American landscape radically transformed, as General Motors' 1939-40 'Futurama' exhibit depicted, but also of a people who would be changed for the better, thanks to numerous labor-saving devices, new appliances (like television) that would alter how we lived our lives, and the development of figures like Westinghouse's Electro the 'Motoman.' This same attitude also surfaces in ... movements ... such as Howard Scott's Technocracy Crusade, the widespread fascination with streamline design and speed, and a renewed interest in utopian literature during the decade."[6]

The most significant medium of the 1930s was radio. This decade, called the Golden Age of Radio came about because of new technology and the times – cheap entertainment was necessary for the public during the years of the Depression.

First of all, microphones were made with greater fidelity, loudspeakers replaced the separate earphones, and the three-dial tuning system was replaced with the single-dial system.

Once the Depression hit, radio became the primary entertainment of American families because it was free. Shows such as *Amos & Andy* began to be syndicated, while particular corporations began to sponsor specific programs and target specific audiences. For example, soap manufacturers found they could reach the largest audience of housewives by sponsoring daytime dramas. In time, these dramas all became known as "soap operas."

Advertising agencies began to actually produce radio programs, and as early as 1932 more air time was spent on commercials than news, education, lectures, and religion combined.

The media of print and radio merged in 1932 when the Associated Press sold bulletins on the presidential elections to the network, and for the first time the interruption of programs by news flashes occurred. President Franklin Roosevelt was the first president to use radio to get public support and shape public opinion with his fireside chats.

An early media conglomerate, the Mutual Broadcasting Company, was formed in 1934, created by stations that decided to work together to obtain advertising. That same year, The Communications Act created the Federal Communications Commission, or the FCC, so that all regulations of communications would rest with one government body. This 1934 act still governs telecommunications and mass media today. Not long after it was created, the FCC prohibited one company from operating and owning more than one national radio network.

The power of this medium to affect mass audiences was powerfully illustrated on Halloween night, 1938, during Orson Welles' Mercury Theater presentation of H.G. Wells' revamped version of *War of the Worlds.* Wells updated the story to the late 1930s and moved the setting to New Jersey. Audiences already accustomed to hearing news updates about armies readying for war were now hearing someone who sounded like Franklin Roosevelt asking for calm as "news reporters" gave live coverage of Martian machines gassing downtown Manhattan. An estimated 1.2 million people succumbed to hysteria.

Although there were experimental television broadcasts as early as 1932, the first baby of radio took its first steps in public at the World's Fair of 1939. "Odd futuristic-looking sound trucks with poles sticking up on top like masts" were in fact RCA television trucks. Although reception was limited to 50 miles from the sending station, RCA and Westinghouse presented the medium of tomorrow as the world stood on the fragile cusp between the Depression and World War. President Roosevelt's opening of the World's Fair "to all mankind" was broadcast by cameras atop those futuristic trucks.

Unfortunately, television and other ideas put forward by the fair would have to wait until the end of World War II to crawl out of their infancy.

Germany, which had been broadcasting since the 1936 Olympics, continued to broadcast during the war. German TV was not used for family viewing, but as a group event. Mass viewing took place in specifically designed television sitting rooms. Nazi rallies were specifically tailored to become more effective for film, radio, and television. This is arguably one of the first uses of television as a medium for propaganda.

We've come a long way from wireless transmissions, the development of radio and film, and then the fusing of these two industries that gave way to television. Toward the end of the war, tape recorders were invented.

Early Computer Pioneers

In August 1945, Dr. Vannevar Bush, Director of The Office of Scientific Research and Development, published an article in the *Atlantic Monthly* titled "As We May Think." The article predicted the development of instant instant-developing microfilm, which would be accessed by a Memex desk machine. The Memex machine was a conceptual prototype for today's desktop computer. Bush described it as "a device in which an individual stores all his books, records, and communications, and which is mechanized so that it may be consulted with exceeding speed and flexibility."[7]

Over half a century later, we use a desktop, laptop, or handheld computer instead of Memex. We have the World Wide Web as our knowledge base and Google-like search engines as a means for finding what we want with *exceeding speed and flexibility.* In the same article, Bush had something to say about the future of computers; his prediction provides an extraordinarily accurate description of what eventually became reality:

> "The advanced arithmetical computation machines of the future will be electrical in nature and will perform at 100 times present speeds or more. Moreover, they will be far more versatile than present commercial machines, so that they may readily be adapted for a variety of operations . . . they will select their own data and manipulate it in accordance with the instructions . . . inserted, they will perform complex arithmetical computations and they will record results in such form as to be readily available for distribution or for later further manipulation."[8]

Also within "As We May Think," Bush predicted that paper would eventually become an inadequate medium for storing the large amount of information being generated and that the traditional hierarchical methods for organizing books and articles in a library were cumbersome and very user unfriendly. He proposed that human beings think in an associational fashion—in a weblike way, not a hierarchical one; technology would help reinforce this natural mode of thinking and remembering.

> "The human mind . . . operates by association. With one item in its grasp, it snaps instantly to the next that is suggested by the association of thoughts, in accordance with some intricate web of trails carried by the cells of the brain. It has other characteristics, of course; trails that are not frequently followed are prone to fade, items are not fully permanent, memory is transitory. Yet the speed of action, the intricacy of trails, the detail of mental pictures, is awe-inspiring beyond all else in nature."[9]

In the late 1940s and into the 1950s, MIT was an incubator of ideas regarding the use of computers to augment, amplify, and expand human intelligence along similar lines that Vannevar Bush described earlier. Although diverse in their approach and ideas, all shared the same long-range objective of using computational devices to bootstrap human thinking to new levels. Some of these early computer pioneers at MIT included:

Norbert Weiner—The scientist who first coined the term *cybernetics* and believed that intelligent machines should communicate on human terms, not the other way around.

JCR Licklider—A psychologist, not a computer scientist, who conceived of the first computer networks for sharing human knowledge.

Marvin Minsky—A leading theorist who popularized and extended approaches to artificial intelligence.

The Era of Television

By the 1950s, television was beginning to affect people's lives sometimes subtly, sometimes not-so-subtly.

Milestones in television broadcast history include the filming of *I Love Lucy* episodes instead of airing them live in 1951. Edward R. Murrow's *See It Now* new documentary series showed both the Atlantic and Pacific Oceans at the same time live.

The importance of television to the American political process became evident during the 1952 political nominating conventions were covered by the networks.

Television sets improved in size and quality, expanding beyond twelve VHF channels to seventy channels in the UHF, or ultra-high-frequency, band.

By this time, Senator Joseph McCarthy's witch hunts for communists had reached deep within the entertainment industry. The "Report of Communist Influence in Radio and Television" listed 151 people as communists.

In fact, the publication was put together by the owner of a grocery store chain, and in the fear ridden era of McCarthyism, the networks caved in.

Ironically, television broadcasting was to be instrumental in exposing the excess of the communist witch hunts. In live coverage of the Army-McCarthy hearings, the junior Senator from Wisconsin came across as a sweating bully, with his nervous giggle magnified into something that sounded downright maniacal.

Television production expanded in two critical areas during the 1950s with the acceptance by the FCC of a system for color television and the development of videotape.

Videotape revolutionized the medium of television. Laugh tracks could be added, mistakes could be edited, and scenes could be taped out of sequence and assembled in order later. With this technical innovation, the Golden Age of live television production ended.

Radio continued to prosper and grow, expanding from 950 wartime stations to more than 2,000 stations by 1950. As a result of an FCC ruling about the identification of recorded material each time it was played, the disc jockey became an integral part of radio communications.

One of the early DJs was Alan Freed, who began playing a new form of music that combined black rhythm and blues with country music and folk. Freed dubbed the music "rock & roll."

The social impact of this type of music began to chip away the old order of the big music giants: RCA, Columbia, and Decca. As David Halberstam notes in *The Fifties*: ". . . the bigger (the company) the more conservative. They watched the world of country-and-western and rhythm-and-blues with disdain bordering on disapproval. It was music that came from the wrong side of the tracks. Some companies even referred to black music as the 'sepia market.'"

Halberstam explains: "Recorded music, until the fifties bore the label of class. People from the upper middle class and upper class had the money for phonographs with which they listened to classical music, crooners and big bands. The people who liked country and black music listened to the radio. But the forces of change were far more powerful than anyone at the big companies realized. Technology was democratizing the business of music—phonographs and records alike were becoming cheaper. It was only a matter of time before the artists began to cross over on the traditionally segregated charts."

"You will see a procession of game shows, violence, audience participation shows, formula comedies about totally unbelievable families, blood, thunder, mayhem, violence, western badmen, western good men, private eyes, gangsters, more violence and cartoons. And endlessly, commercials—many screaming, cajoling, and offending . . . Is there one person in this room who claims that broadcasting can't do better?"

Newton Minow, Chairman of the FCC in 1961

For many television critics, not a lot has changed from this early address, in which Minow coined what has become a metaphor for television content, "a vast wasteland."

However, whatever doubts people had about the power of television to inform and unite the American people were shattered during the autumn of 1963 as television gave round the clock coverage of the assassination and burial of President Kennedy. From November 22 to November 25, 90% of the population sat, eyes glued to their television screens. Audiences also witnessed the first live murder committed on television when Jack Ruby shot Lee Harvey Oswald.

The 1960s brought the 1962 World's Fair to Seattle, Washington, once again showing the promise of future American media. A plexiglass-covered elevator, The Bubbleater, raised audiences into the next century, via pictures, films, and models that flashed in succession. On this ride through the future, the question was posed: "How will our descendants learn?" Images showed schools where television and "electronic teaching" machines assisted teachers, libraries whose books have "been digested" by computers and whose readers may order electronically sections from any author on a pertinent subject. According to the exhibits, business offices would use audio-visual communications systems in the next century and there would be home computers as well.

Tragedy on the Launch Pad

That technological race to the future, looked in considerable doubt just two months earlier, when the Apollo space program suffered a tragic birth, not long before the Summer of Love.

The AS/204 rocket due to have taken Col. Virgil Grissom, Col. Edward White, and Lt. Cmdr. Roger Chaffee on a two-week mission orbiting the Earth—as the first step toward the "one giant leap for mankind"—was destroyed by fire during a training simulation on January 27, 1967.

All three astronauts were killed in the accident, and AS/204 was renamed Apollo 1 in their honor. (Two more planned launches later in the year were scrubbed, and that's why the launch series skips from Apollo 1 to Apollo 4.)

The Apollo 1 capsule has never been displayed to the public. According to NASA, it remains in an environmentally controlled warehouse at the Langley Research Center in Hampton, Virginia.

As the quagmire of Vietnam, the social and political revolutions, and the growing violence in the streets played themselves out every night in American living rooms, another revolution was taking place. In its own way, this almost unnoticed revolution would have a more profound effect on our way of life than any of the manifestos being touted by either American college students or American politicians of the period. This was a revolution in computer and video technology, in essence the real revolution of the 1960s.

At the same time, computer scientists were quietly changing the future of communications, attempting to build a computer network that would enable researchers around the country to share ideas. By the 1990s the Internet would be a fact of life, used not only by researchers but also by students, librarians, lawyers, and computer users in general as media technology moved from the passive to the active.

In 1964 new ideas about the medium of television came from the typewriter of Marshall McLuhan. In his book *Understanding Media,* McLuhan coined the phrase "Global Village," stating that the new media were recording man's senses, weaning him from the age-old habit of collecting information "linearly" from the printed page. With television and the media of the future, an electronic culture would be created: an electronic tribal culture without bounds.

The mid-1960s saw a period when American audiences were seeing images night after night on their television screens of the civil rights movement and the grim reality of the Vietnam War. In 1965, NBC became the first television station to broadcast all new programming in color.

Commentator James Kilpatrick said that "[television] brought to the American people for the first time in the history of the country, the ugly reality of war, the whole head of war . . . and I think it contributed materially to the ultimate fed-upness of the public that finally led to Lyndon Johnson's retirement from office and the end of the war." The year 1968 has been called by many the most divisive year in America since the Civil War. It was a time of polarization and vivid violence, all played out in front of television cameras.

Was the media causing the violence or was it simply reflecting it? It was a question asked again and again. In 1968 it was answered by John A. Pastore, who became the chairman of the Senate subcommittee investigating violence and sex in the media. Suddenly, violence on television was being continually cut; not from the news shows, not the "real" violence, but the cartoon violence of Bugs Bunny and old Saturday serials. Numerous shows left the air, including (some say) *The Smothers Brothers,* which dared satirize Pastore, calling him and his committee "censors."

Although from where we stand today the leisure suits, music, and technology of the 1970s are thankfully passé, there were some important commentaries and predictions of technological advancements to come.

In the November 3, 1970, *Look Magazine,* John Kronenberger wrote a one page article titled "Push Button Movies: The Video-Cassette Revolution," where he projected that eight years into the future, consumers would be able to pop a "cartridge" containing a movie and watch it whenever they wanted to.[10]

Around that same time author Alvin Toffler coined the term "future shock." Serving as the title of Toffler's 1970s book, the idea behind *Future Shock* was that once upon a time, any obvious change took centuries to be observed. During the last 150 years, change had to be faced decade to decade. And now, according to Toffler, **change itself** was accelerating. One only had to look at the quickly changing technology to realize that there was much truth in Toffler's theory: We went from vacuum tubes to transistors to integrated circuit chips in a period of less than fifty years.

Serials of fictitious and historical dimensions played before us in the 1970s. The early 1970s saw the advent of the "mini-series" on American television and of course, the televised Watergate hearings when, as Linda Ellerbee stated, the "news media [became] perhaps a fourth part of the government."

The late 1970s was possibly the point when the three American television networks hit their peak of popularity even as television itself was about to begin what would be massive changes.

During the 1980s there was a restructuring of television and radio in this country resulting mainly from economic factors. This led to a series of mergers, acquisitions, and new start-up companies creating new networks, like FOX Television, Turner Broadcasting, Showtime, and MTV. In fact, the average share of the primetime viewership of the "big three" (NBC, CBS, and ABC) went from 85% in 1980 to 67% in 1989. Television was moving from being a medium geared toward mass appeal to being a much more fractionalized medium appealing to smaller and smaller audience groups. With the VCR and particularly with the remote control, audiences no longer felt compelled to stay switched to one channel for the evening.

In 1982, radio was deregulated and during the Reagan years the FCC would eliminate many of the regulations that had governed radio for years: Stations were no longer limited in the amount of commercial minutes they could program and were no longer required to program news and public affairs shows.

By 1984 deregulation began in earnest and with regulations lifted, television programming licenses were easier to obtain. A direct result of deregulation was the creation of the Home Shopping Network, a channel devoted entirely to advertisements of products people could purchase over their telephones.

With Ronald Reagan, a former film personality, Americans had their first matinee leader. Is it any wonder that the massive deregulation of the communications industries occurred under Ronald Reagan, known as "The Teflon President" administration?

As we reached the Orwellian year, Apple Computers aired an ad during the Super Bowl that asked why 1984 wasn't going to be the 1984 Orwell predicted. Orwell had thought that by 1984, television would become the controlling influence in our lives.

However, essayist Neil Postman disagreed. In his book *Amusing Ourselves to Death,* Postman pointed to Aldous Huxley's *Brave New World.* The novel, which was published in the early 1930s, created a world of the future filled with drugs to make you always feel good, with continually blaring advertisements, and with "feelie movies." As the title of his own book suggests, Postman felt that we were becoming an audience who could not tell fantasy from reality or entertainment from news and that our worst enemy wasn't an authoritarian Big Brother; it was ourselves and our craving for more and more entertainment. "In the Huxleyan prophecy, Big Brother does not watch us, by his choice. We watch him by ours."

The late 1980s and early 1990s saw more and more consumers using the term "digital." The analog system, the aim of which is to replicate sound or images via transmitted waves, had been around since 1887 when Edison captured and stored sound on tinfoil cylinders. With digital technology, signals or data are represented as a series of on/off impulses, with information being stored in "bits" rather than in a continuous wave. Sound and image quality is much better. To understand the difference between the two, think of an analog system as someone tracing an image with a piece of tracing paper—no matter how steady the artist's hand, the replica image still will not be exact. Now, compare this with say, a digital scan or photocopy of the original image. In this case, you couldn't tell the original from the copy.

Going digital brings an interactive future. The interactive future will be one where television goes online: a state where information is accessible electronically via computers, cable television, or telephone lines.

Dr. Thomas Furness, founder and director of the Human Interface Technology Laboratory at the University of Washington, is considered one of the fathers of virtual reality. Furness feels that the biggest boon for virtual reality will be how it fits into the merging of broadband telecommunications, computers, and the telephone. Furness states:

> "The interface for humans to that ubiquitous channel is going to be a virtual one. When you put [these different media] together, basically, what you get is the 'virtuphone,' a telephone that you wear. And basically now in your home, even through coax, you have the ability to disconnect your head from your body and go places—through what we used to have as television, only television wasn't interactive. Now [this new medium] is going to be completely interactive. You'll go to work with it, you'll play with it, you'll got to school with this new medium [which is] two generations beyond the print medium. We'll be taking ourselves—head and body, because we're going to feel as if we're present—to another place."[11]

On one level, the question then becomes, with the ability to interact with 500 or 1,000 channels, what happens to our shopping malls, not to mention the local video stores? It is conceivable that more and more shopping malls will become entertainment centers. But what happens to our transportation industry if people no longer have to travel by car, train, or plane to get to work? What happens to downtown urban areas where office buildings might presumably stand empty? And in the final analysis, will people want to spend even more time in front of their television sets than they do now? Corporations are betting millions that the answer is yes.

The prospect of this type of future also brings into question the impact it will have on social interaction and reality itself if you literally never have to leave your house.

It seems as if we're just beginning to understand the effects television has had on us since the late 1940s, let alone having more than an inkling of what effect the new media may have. Will there be a true "democratization" of media, where people can broadcast their own programming from their homes and receive instantaneous reactions?

Will McLuhan's "Global Village" come to pass? Or will the information highway be owned by corporations who will tout their own philosophies over the net, creating an electronic elite? "The Global Village" could, in fact, turn out to be more of an electronic metropolis or megalopolis, overseen by new corporate big brothers.

We are obviously in the midst of a media and technological revolution that will, like it or not, have a profound effect on us all. The digital media will certainly affect the way we interact with each other as well as the way we perceive ourselves. The hope is, as Issac Asimov said, that "we do not make foolish (or trivial use) of technology. That we use technology wisely."

It is our hope that we use the new media humanely. That the new worlds, virtual or otherwise, that we see and experience help us to understand not just ourselves, but the world around us. That, as Dr. Furness and others hope, we become sensitized to the basic ecological makeup of our planet, and that this sensitization leads us in new and more positive directions, assisting us as a species to, at long last, mature.

Endnotes

[1] Jules Verne, from the Earth to the Moon,(1865) WikiSource online reprinting, http://en.wikisource.org/wiki/From_the_Earth_to_the_Moon/Chapter_XV.

[2] Charles Babbage, *Passages from the Life of a Philosopher*, (Oxford University, Longman, Green, Longman, Roberts& Green, Oxford University, 1864), p. 42.

[3] Ada Augusta Byron as quoted by Howard Rheingold, Tools for Thought, 1985, http://www.rheingold.com/texts/tft/2.html.

[4] American Experience, More About Bell: A Family Affair, *The Telephone*, PBS, http://www.pbs.org/wgbh/amex/telephone/peopleevents/mabell.html.

[5] Jerry Mander, *In the Absence of the Sacred*, (1991, Sierra Club, San Francisco), p. 23.

[6] J.P. Telotte, *Replications*, (1995, University of Illionois Press), p. 93.

[7] Vannevar Bush, As We May Think, *The Atlantic Online*, July 1945, http://www.theatlantic.com/unbound/flashbks/computer/bushf.htm.

[8] Ibid.

[9] Ibid.

[10] John Kronenberger, Push Button Movies: The Videocassette Revolution, Look Magazine, New York, November 3, 1970 p. 94.

[11] Tom Furness interview with book author, Michael Korolenko, 1993.

Chapter 2
The Pavilion of American Culture

"The medium, or process, of our time—electric technology is reshaping and restructuring patterns of social interdependence and every aspect of our personal life. It is forcing us to reconsider and re-evaluate practically every thought, every action."

Marshall McLuhan

"Every technology is both a burden and a blessing; Not either-or, but this-and-that."

Neil Postman, *Technopoly*

Television is the focus of this chapter, because it provides an example of a leading telecommunication technology that has changed society on multiple levels—economically, politically, socially, and culturally. TV became a shared central information hub and metaphor for American society. The following *timeline of television* is as much an account of its social impact as it is a record of its technological advances. By understanding the profound influence of one chosen technology on society, we can identify ways to explore and discuss the consequences of other technical innovations, both existing and yet-to-be-actualized. It's also useful to think of technology changes in terms of *whole systems theory,* where one event engages a web of interrelated consequences, often in unpredictable ways.

Timeline of Television

1884—Paul Nipkow creates a mechanical scanning wheel. The wheel, containing tiny holes, is set in front of a picture, and as the wheel turns, each hole scans one line of the picture.

1909—Along with science fiction writers, mainstream writers also found the idea of new technology, particularly television, fascinating. As far back as 1909, E.M. Forster in his novella *The Machine Stops* wrote of a future where human beings live in a hive-like environment, completely isolated from each other and the outside world. Their only means of communication: interactive television.

The 1920s—Ernst Alexanderson, working for General Electric, utilizes the scanning system in a new way. Using the system, he creates a science fiction show of a missile attack on New York by scanning an aerial photo of the city that moves closer and closer and then disappears in an explosion. Audiences will watch the real thing seventy years later as missiles with tiny cameras attached rain down on Baghdad during Operation Desert Storm.

The researchers from General Electric, RCA, and Westinghouse, working together, solve a variety of problems the fledgling technology is experiencing: Lines of scanning were increased, along with definition, brightness, and image size.

1922 (summer)—At age fourteen, Philo Taylor Farnsworth, a farm boy from Rigby, Idaho, has the idea of electronic television.
1923—Farnsworth submits a patent for television.

1928—Felix the Cat becomes the first televised personality, his image sent from New York City to Kansas City, picked up by sixty-line experimental television sets.

It was necessary, in the early days of television, to carefully adjust the quality of the transmitted picture to get the best displayed result. Felix was an ideal actor for this, because he didn't mind working long hours under the intense heat from the intense, bright lights that were needed to make him visible to early electronic cameras. Felix was put on a record turntable and his image was broadcast from New York City to select stations. The received image was 2 inches tall.

1929—"Radio finds its eyes," announces the Saturday Evening Post, in a felicitous phrase.

This same year in Britain, John Logie Baird creates the *televisor*—the first commercial television for the British television market. His mechanical television is constructed of spinning parts that enable it to recompose images made up of small pulses of light that are scanned from a source object. The pulses of light are picked up by a photoelectric cell that in turn transmits electronic signals of varying intensities that are reconverted to pulses of transmitted light on a screen. The reconstructed moving images are of poor quality, but the televisor is well received in Baird's first public demonstration in a department store. The British Broadcasting Company (BBC) is reluctant to begin broadcasting, because of public concern that the new communications device could be damaging to public morals, and because of a perceived loss of privacy.

1932—Experimental broadcasts are transmitted from the Empire State Building.

1935—*Murder by Television,* a murky and altogether dreadful movie, in which Bela Lugosi plays a dual role.

David Sarnoff, president of RCA, announces that the company will invest millions of dollars to further develop television. "Television . . . will give new wings to the talents of creative and interpretive genius," Sarnoff announces.

1936—In Germany, television broadcasts the 1936 Olympics, and will continue to broadcast well into World War II. However, German television is used not for family viewing, but as a group event. Mass viewings take place in special television sitting rooms.

The Nazis were the first to really attempt to master this new electronic medium. They had television screening rooms where they broadcast the 1936 Olympics live, so the German "volk" could watch as young black American Jessie Owens took the gold medal, winning over the competing Aryans.

Nazi rallies are specifically tailored to be more effective for film, radio, and now television. This could be said to be the first use of television as a medium of propaganda.

1939—President Roosevelt opens The New York World's Fair, "The World of Tomorrow," "to all mankind" and is broadcast by television cameras atop "futuristic-looking sound trucks."

And so, RCA, along with Westinghouse (which had its own television studio in its pavilion), presented the medium of tomorrow as the world stood on the fragile cusp between the Depression and World War.

As Jerry Mander notes in his book *In the Absence of the Sacred,* before the advent of television, World's Fairs were the show places for American technology: new ideas, new philosophies, and most importantly, new products. Mander concentrates specifically on the 1939 New York World's Fair and its theme "The World of Tomorrow," where items such as nylon, television, picturephones, and superhighways were introduced to the public, who responded with a sense of awe and wonder.

1941—Stations go on the air, some 10,000 sets are sold, and the first commercial television time is bought by the Bulova Watch Company. However, by 1942, except for air raid warden training films broadcast by NBC, all broadcasting is halted for the duration of the war.

Figure 1. Franklin Roosevelt delivers the first presidential address on television in 1939 at the New York World's Fair.
David Sarnoff Library.

1945—With the end of World War II, more and more people begin to buy television sets, sitting enthralled in front of what were often small, flickering, ghostly images.

By the turn of the decade, television is beginning to affect people's lives, sometimes subtly, sometimes not-so-subtly. For example, on Tuesday nights, attendance at dining establishments, sports events, and most tellingly, motion picture theaters goes down to almost nil as millions tune in to watch *The Texaco Star Theater* (1948) starring Milton Berle.

As television technology improves and literally hundreds of new stations are licensed, there is an explosion of television purchases in the United States. At the end of 1949, there were 1 million sets in American homes. Three years later, there were sets in some 15 million American homes.

1947—The House Committee on Un-American Activities began an investigation of the film industry, and Senator Joseph R. McCarthy soon began to inveigh against what he claimed was communist infiltration of the government. Broadcasting, too, feels the impact of this growing national witch hunt. Three former members of the Federal Bureau of Investigation (FBI) publish "Counterattack: The Newsletter of Facts on Communism."

1949—Americans who lived within range of the growing number of television stations in the country could watch, for example, the children's program *Howdy Doody* (1947). They could also choose between two fifteen-minute newscasts, *CBS TV News* (1948) with Douglas Edwards and NBC's *Camel News Caravan* (1948) with John Cameron Swayze (who was required by the tobacco company sponsor to have a burning cigarette always visible when he was on camera).[1]

As television technology improves and literally hundreds of new stations are licensed, there is an explosion of television purchases in the United States. At the end of 1949, there were 1 million sets in American homes. Three years later, there were sets in some 15 million American homes.

1950—In partnership with the news producer Fred Friendly, Edward R. Murrow began *See It Now,* a television documentary series.[2] On June 22, *Red Channels: The Report of Communist Influence in Radio and Television,* an anti-communist tract (whose existence is denied by television executives) is published. Issued by the right-wing journal *Counterattack,* the pamphlet names 151 actors, writers, musicians, broadcast journalists, and others in the context of purported communist manipulation of the entertainment industry. Some of the 151 are already being denied employment because of their political beliefs, history, or mere association with suspected "subversives"; *Red Channels* effectively placed the rest on the industry blacklist. Political beliefs suddenly become grounds for getting fired. Most of the producers, writers, and actors who are accused of having had left-wing leanings find themselves blacklisted, unable to get work. CBS even institutes a loyalty oath for its employees.[3]

Red Channels would ruin countless lives (one example: veteran comedy movie actress Pert Kelton, who originated the role of Alice Kramden on *The Honeymooners*) as more names were added to the list and it would stay in effect until the early 1960s.

Figure 2. *Red Channels* identifies what it claims to be communist sympathizers in the entertainment industry at the height of the Red Scare in the early 1950s.

1951—CBS decides to launch the popular radio series *I Love Lucy* on the relatively new medium of TV. Lucy insists Desi be cast as her husband in the TV version, although the network executives say no one would believe the couple were married. Desi and Lucy perform before live audiences and film a pilot, convincing network executives that audiences responded well to their act. Not only does CBS cast Desi for the show, episodes are filmed so they can be shown again, helping to create some of the first *re-runs*. *I Love Lucy* will become one of the most popular TV situation comedies in history.

1952—Television news first covers the presidential nominating conventions of the two major parties. The term "anchorman" is used, probably for the first time, to describe Walter Cronkite's central role in CBS's convention coverage this year.[4]

One national figure is present during key moments in the unfolding relationship between television and politics: Richard Nixon. During the Eisenhower campaign, Nixon was accused of possessing illegal campaign funds. He went on television and gave what became known as "The Checkers Speech" where he used the new medium to communicate directly with the audience, creating a positive emotional reaction among viewers: "Pat doesn't have a mink coat," he said of his wife, "She has a respectable Republican cloth coat. And I always say, she looks good in anything." Nixon went on to talk about the little dog, Checkers, given to his daughters as a present by a supporter, and said he wouldn't give the dog back. The televised speech worked, and Eisenhower kept Nixon on as his vice president.

1952—The UNIVAC I is the world's first commercially available computer. Forty-six UNIVACs (Universal Automatic Computers) are sold in 1952. The machine is 25 feet by 50 feet in length, contains 5,600 tubes, 18,000 crystal diodes, and 300 relays. It utilizes serial circuitry, has a 2.25 MHz bit rate, and has an internal storage capacity of 1,000 words or 12,000 characters. The first UNIVAC I was delivered on June 14, 1951. From 1951 to 1958, a total of forty-six UNIVAC I computers are delivered and the system is used to accurately predict the 1952 election, although the results are not immediately reported by Walter Cronkite because they are not believed to be accurate. Democratic presidential candidate Adlai Stevenson was the front-runner in all the advance opinion polls, but by 8:30 p.m. on the east coast, well before polls are closed in the Western states, UNIVAC projects 100-to-1 odds that Dwight D. Eisenhower will win by a landslide, which is in fact what happens.

1954—On March 9, 1954, Edward R. Murrow narrates a report on McCarthy, exposing the senator's shoddy tactics. Of McCarthy, Murrow observes, "His mistake has been to confuse dissent with disloyalty." A nervous CBS refuses to promote Murrow and Friendly's program. Offered free time by CBS, McCarthy replies on April 6, calling Murrow "the leader and the cleverest of the jackal pack which is always found at the throat of anyone who dares to expose Communist traitors." In this TV appearance, McCarthy proves to be his own worst enemy, and it becomes apparent that Murrow has helped to break McCarthy's reign of fear. In 1954 the U.S. Senate censures McCarthy, and CBS's "security" office is closed down.[5]

Late 1950s—The transition from television's "Golden Age" of live drama, shot mostly in New York City, changes as the industry moves West—beginning the modern era of "Hollywood television" dominated by network-licensed film series.

1960—In the fall of 1960, the first televised debates (called "The Great Debates") in the history of politics take place. Watching Richard Nixon debate John F. Kennedy, it becomes clear that how the candidate looks is as important (or more important) than what he says. Those watching the debates on television feel Kennedy won handily, but radio listeners polled the same night feel Nixon has won. It should be noted that Nixon looked both pasty and shifty eyed and was getting over an illness while Kennedy, who usually was ill, looked healthy and robust. It was this debate in which style became more important than substance.

1961—Television has become a fact of life in most households. Newton Minow, appointed chairman of the FCC by President Kennedy, addresses the National Association of Broadcasters. It is in this address that Minow coins the term "vast wasteland." Minow goes on:

> "You will see a procession of game shows, violence, audience participation shows, formula comedies about totally unbelievable families, blood and thunder, mayhem, violence, western badmen, western good men, private eyes, gangsters, more violence and cartoons. And endlessly, commercials—many screaming, cajoling, and offending . . . Is there one person in this room who claims that broadcasting can't do better?"

Figure 3. The Telstar I communications satellite, launched in 1962, initiates an era of global television broadcasting. NASA.

Minow's term "vast wasteland" becomes a metaphor for American television programming. 1962—AT&T and NASA launch the Telstar I communications satellite. That same year, Richard Nixon loses to Pat Brown in a run for the governorship of California. Angry, Nixon tells the press that they "wouldn't have Nixon to kick around anymore." The remark is televised, and many feel Nixon's career is over. In fact, not long after, a news special airs titled *The Political Obituary of Richard Nixon.*

1963—New ideas about electronic media come from the typewriter of Marshall McLuhan. In his book *Understanding Media,* McLuhan coins the phrase "Global Village," stating that the new media were reordering man's senses, weaning him from the age-old habit of collecting information "linearly" from the printed page. With television and the media of the future, an electronic culture would be created: an electronic tribal culture without bounds.

During the same period, television begins to enter the classroom in earnest. In business and research, people refer more and more to "information retrieval." It seems to some as if our news, information, and history would soon be coming to us via television or computers.

There are numerous World's Fairs held during the 1960s, but only the smaller official Seattle Fair, which is more regional and less consumer oriented, and Montreal's Expo 1967, with its concentration on new modes of communication, are successful. New York's 1964 and 1965 World's Fair, held on the same site as the 1939 Fair, has as its theme "Peace Through Understanding." But the opening-day ceremonies are marred by civil rights demonstrations, and the anti-war movement is in full swing by the Fair's second year, pointing out the bitter irony of companies like Dow Chemical promoting "Better Living Through Chemistry" while aiding the government in the development of new weapons to be used in Vietnam. Also, many foreign exhibitors stay away because the fair is not officially recognized by the international World's Fair committee, and Robert Moses, the fair's president, turns to corporations to fill the sites that would have housed international pavilions. The irony is not lost on the American public, and the 1964-65 World's Fair is a financial disaster. By the late 1960s, the public begins to turn to television for previews of tomorrow's technologies.

1963—November 22, President John F. Kennedy is assassinated. CBS News is the first on air with a special report that shots were fired at the president's motorcade. A young Dan Rather calls in that the president has died (even though he himself is not completely sure of the information). For four days, the American public is glued to the television set. They also see the first live murder when Jack Ruby shoots suspect Lee Harvey Oswald. In a very horrible way, television has come of age.

1964—The mid-1960s sees the death of a myriad of newspapers and magazines. In *Newsweek,* Stewart Alsop, in writing of the demise of the *Saturday Evening Post,* states:

> "Television threatens to engulf the written word like a blob from outer space. The decay of the written word, of which the Saturday Evening Post's death is a symbol, is surely a tragedy, and maybe not a very small tragedy either."[6]

1966/1967—Color broadcasting had begun on primetime television by the late 1950s. The FCC initially approved a CBS color system, then swung in RCA's favor after Sarnoff swamped the marketplace with black-and-white sets compatible with RCA color[7] (the CBS color system was not compatible with black-and-white sets and would have required the purchase of new sets—it was also a better system). By 1966/1967, NBC becomes the first "full color" network. As *Huntley/Brinkley News* producer Shad Northshield says: "At the same time, the [Vietnam] War was heating up and, with color television, you get a higher degree of reality . . . it matters more."[8]

1967—A Carnegie Commission report recommends the creation of a fourth, noncommercial, public television network built around the educational nonprofit stations already in operation throughout the United States. Congress creates the Public Broadcasting System that year. Unlike commercial networks, which are centered in New York and Los Angeles, PBS's key stations, many of which produce programs that are shown throughout the network, are spread across the country.[9] Meanwhile, American television viewers, while enjoying shows like *Gomer Pyle* and *Bonanza,* watch the so-called Summer of Love unfold, race riots in Detroit, and the continuing war in Vietnam. The Beatles, meanwhile, sing "All You Need Is Love" on a telecast broadcast around the world via satellite.

1968—This was an incredibly important year, both socially and technologically. From January until November, the country is caught in a fever dream of horror, beginning with the Tet Offensive in Vietnam which belies the Johnson administration's line that there is "light at the end of the tunnel" in Vietnam. The huge North Vietnamese surge to the south is defeated, but on network news, Americans see dead Viet Cong lying on the steps of the U.S. Embassy in Saigon. Walter Cronkite gives his first editorial, condemning the war. In the White House, Lyndon Johnson watches and says, "If I've lost Walter Cronkite, I've lost America."[10] He soon announces he will not seek the renomination of his party for president. Robert Kennedy joins the race. In April, as his plane touches down in Indianapolis, he is told of the assassination of Martin Luther King. Kennedy is due to give a campaign speech in a poor black part of Indianapolis. He knows of the assassination, but in those pre-instant news days, the crowd doesn't. The sheriff's department tries to get Kennedy to cancel the speech, because it was too dangerous to address a crowd that night. He refuses. From the back of a flatbed truck, he abandons his campaign speech and tells the mostly black crowd the news, pleading for peace and understanding. There are riots in sixty American cities that night in outrage and grief at Dr. King's death. The one major city that sees no riots is Indianapolis, where Robert Kennedy has spoken.

Two months later, Robert Kennedy himself is assassinated after winning the Democratic California primary. A month earlier, college campuses across the United States exploded with protests and riots over the war. At Columbia University in New York, in a scene replayed on campuses throughout America, police attack student demonstrators with tear gas and night sticks. In Chicago, the scene of the Democratic Convention, students, hippies, and yippies (Youth International Party) join to protest the war (Yippie leader Abbie Hoffman later says, had Kennedy not been killed, there would have been no protests in Chicago[11]). What ensues is later called a "police riot" as Chicago police attack students, reporters, even delegates to the convention. News cameramen, now using more compact, easier to handle (and cheaper than film) video cameras, report on the event as it happens. In the meantime, Richard Nixon surprises everyone by making a huge comeback in 1968 as The New Nixon. He's packaged much like any commercial product would be. He holds televised town meetings with hand-picked audiences of supporters. He even appears on the highly rated television show *Rowan and Martin's Laugh-In* stating, "Sock it to me?" After the riots at the Democratic convention that summer, Nixon's support grows and he wins the presidency. Still convulsing from the horror that was 1968, America breathes a sigh of resignation and wonder as Apollo astronauts, orbiting the moon, broadcast live images back to the earth on Christmas Eve as they read from the Book of Genesis. The worst and most divisive year in American history since the Civil War is over, and television was there to bring it all into our living rooms.

1970—The November 3, 1970, issue of *LOOK* magazine publishes a special issue on "The Now Hollywood," with the accent on "Now." John Kronenberger writes a one-page article titled "Push Button Movies: The Video-Cassette Revolution," where he projects that eight years into the future consumers will be able to pop a "cartridge" containing the movie *Butch Cassidy and The Sundance Kid* on video and watch it whenever they want to. He mentions what is already available: expensive and "crude" video cassette machines and tapes with only fifty minutes of black and white or twenty-five minutes of color material on them. Kronenberg also mentions the problem of compatibility of different "VTR" systems (a problem that would come to a head in the early 1980s, when Sony's higher quality betamax system lost out to the more compatible VHS system). But Kronenberg, and others, knew that another revolution was on the way:

> "As the costs come down, as the range of items available grows, the video-cassette revolution seems inevitable. And somebody will have to be providing the content for it. Will it be what is still called Hollywood?"

Mid-1970s—With the Watergate Hearings, television helps our democratic society by just showing the hearings without doing anything else. Some feel it is the weakness of television's own agenda that makes it dangerous. By the 1980s, Nixon, forced to resign the presidency in part because of the televised hearings, is back in the public eye, flying to Egypt for President Sadat's funeral and appearing in numerous television interviews. When a docudrama about him airs, Nixon cancels his phone service, AT&T, which sponsors the two-part television movie. Today, in the Nixon library, an interactive museum allows people to ask Nixon about anything, and get his version of the truth.

Late 1970s—Possibly the point when the three American television networks hit their peak of popularity even as television itself is about to begin what will be massive changes.

1980s—There is a restructuring of television and radio in this country resulting mainly from economic factors. This leads to a series of mergers, acquisitions, and new start-up companies appearing, creating, among other networks, FOX Television, Turner Broadcasting, Showtime, and MTV. In fact, the average share of the primetime viewership of the "big three" (NBC, CBS, and ABC) goes from 85% in 1980 to 67% in 1989.

Television is moving from being a medium geared toward mass appeal to being a much more fractionalized medium appealing to smaller and smaller audience groups. With the VCR and, particularly, with the remote control, audiences no longer feel compelled to stay switched to one channel for the evening. In fact, the act of using the remote control to zip through a variety of channels leads to a new term: "channel surfing" (originally known as "grazing").

1984—Orwell had thought that, by 1984, television would become the controlling influence in our lives. Essayist Neil Postman disagreed. In his book *Amusing Ourselves to Death,* Postman points to Aldous Huxley's *Brave New World.* The novel, which was published in the early 1930s, created a world of the future filled with drugs to make you always feel good, with continually blaring advertisements, and with "feelie movies." As the title of his own book suggests, Postman feels that we were becoming an audience who could not tell fantasy from reality or entertainment from news and that our worst enemy wasn't an authoritarian Big Brother; it was ourselves and our own craving for more and more entertainment.

> "What Huxley teaches is that in the age of advanced technology, spiritual devastation is more likely to come from an enemy with a smiling face than from one whose countenance exudes suspicion and hate. In the Huxleyan prophecy, Big Brother does not watch us, by his choice. We watch him, by ours."[12]

By the mid-1980s, it seems as if Huxley's future (which had, it should be noted, originally been considered sharp satire) has all but come true. Deregulation begins in earnest in 1984 and with restrictions lifted, television programming licenses are easier to obtain. A direct result of deregulation is the creation of the Home Shopping Network, a channel devoted entirely to advertisements of products people can purchase over their telephones. Thus, "Interactive Television" is born (although some might point to a much earlier form of interactive TV: the old *Winkie Dink & You* show whereby children put a special screen over the TV set and drew items to help Winkie out with his problems—and how many of you out there got yelled at by irate parents when you didn't have that special screen and just began to draw on the television screen itself?).

1990s—In his book *Life After Television,* George Gilder writes about what he sees as the future of interactive technology and the "telecomputer":

> "a new system that can transform the possibilities of all human society."

> "Tired of watching TV? With artful programming of telecomputers, you could spend a day interacting on the screen with Henry Kissinger, Kim Bassinger, or Billy Graham. Celebrities could produce and sell their own software or make themselves available for two-way personal video communication [this has already begun in a sense with a number of current rock stars communicating with their fans during certain specified times on the Internet—ed.]. You could take a fully interactive course in physics or computer science with the world's most exciting professors, who respond to your questions and let you move at your own learning speed. You could have a fully interactive workday without commuting to the office or run a global corporation without ever getting on a plane." George Gilder

> "Television is the *soma* of Aldous Huxley's *Brave New World.*"
>
> Robert MacNeil

"The problem does not reside in *what* we watch—it is in *that* we watch—the solution must be found in *how* we watch . . . For no medium is excessively dangerous if its users understand what its dangers are."

Neil Postman

TV, Los Angeles, New Myths

"Television production in Los Angeles is an engineered reality. We're selling a product, essentially." Richard Albarino, VP of comedy development, VIACOM

In the late 1950s, with the end of the "Golden Age" of live television in New York City, American television production moved to Los Angeles, California where the climate was better and movie studio sets already existed. In fact, the motion picture industry had already been selling a version of reality to America and the world for over half a century. Movies like The Andy Hardy series showed a world where everything was bright, everyone but the "help" was white, and everything could be solved by putting on a show. Late 1950s and early 1960s television series continued to perpetuate the myth. Network television soon merged with the Los Angeles lifestyle and sensibility and "held out a promise, not of a radiant future, but of a radiant present."

"Modern media, television, promises to explore any subject, but only a tiny minority get to carry out this promise, and they all come from Los Angeles. The people who produce television are at any given moment about two hundred people. They have the same culture in common: this culture of culturelessness."

Todd Gitlin

Most television shows had some kind of resolution—stories were usually structured so all problems are overcome by people of good will. And yet, certain shows, like Bill Cosby's comedy series, allowed many Americans to see a black family in an extremely positive way and thus had a positive effect on American viewers. The visual media have always been extremely powerful in communicating emotions; people often define their emotions and relationships by television, and the characters in television shows become metaphors for our own emotions and relationships.

With the coming of cable television and new networks like FOX and shows produced by people like Steve Bochco who constantly push the envelope of what is allowed on network television (*Hill Street Blues, NYPD Blue,* and, lest we forget, *Cop Rock*), television began to grudgingly open up to new attitudes and emotions. This was all primarily because of competition with cable, VCRs, and pay-per-view.

By the early 21st Century, "reality television" had become a mainstay of network and cable broadcasts. "Reality television", a genre that dates back at least to 1948's *Candid Camera*, supposedly presents unscripted actual events, and features non-actors in these events or situations. The term "reality television" is a misnomer, since most of the shows are, at best manipulative and, at worst, tightly scripted and directed.

Interestingly, "reality television" was a staple of science fiction since the invention of television. Orwell's *1984* presented what might be called the ultimate reality television, with Big Brother and the other leaders of society being the audience and the rest of humanity the actors. Robert Sheckley's 1958 short story, *The Prize of Peril* concerned a live television show in which volunteers were hunted by trained assassins and received a large cash prize if they managed to survive. This was echoed in Stephen King's *The Running Man*. Motion pictures like *Edtv* and *The Truman Show* have also tackled this phenomenon that continues to be popular despite the fact that most audience members realize the shows bear little resemblance to reality.

With the coming of interactive media and equipment that was affordable, allowing the average American to make his or her own statements about life, the age of the television may be over. One thing is certain: We have long moved out of the age of the printed word and into the age of the electronic and now, the digital image.

The Medium Is the Metaphor: *1984* or *Brave New World?*

Niel Postman has noted that the images of our culture have become the basis of our daily decisions, our expectations, and the way we view the world and how we think we should operate in it. In a way, our sense about the way things should be done and how life should be lived are managed by the images of modern society. These images create the patterns of what our behavior is going to be and also create the content of our culture. Look at it this way: If the book or newspaper can be seen as a metaphor for nineteenth and early twentieth century America, then certainly television became a metaphor for mid-twentieth century America. In the early 1980s, *USA Today* began publication: a newspaper made to look like a television screen.

In 1992, *Wired* magazine appeared on the scene: a magazine made to look like a computer screen, which is certainly the metaphor for America in the 1990s and beyond. With digital technology, it becomes even easier to manipulate the images we see. Television, video games, computers: all have been moving our culture inexorably away from the printed word, in effect, training us for the future that corporations continually advertise.

"In introducing the personal computer to the classroom, we shall be breaking a four-hundred-year-old truce between the gregariousness and openness fostered by orality and the introspection and isolation fostered by the printed word. Orality stresses group learning, cooperation, and a sense of social responsibility. Print stresses individualized learning, competition, and personal autonomy. Now comes the computer, carrying anew the banner of private learning and individual problem-solving. Will the widespread use of computers in the classroom defeat once and for all the claims of communal speech? Will the computer raise egocentrism to the status of a virtue? It is not possible to contain the effects of a new technology to a limited sphere of human activity."

Neil Postman, *Technopoly*

In his book *Amusing Ourselves to Death,* Postman points to two different visions of the future and communication technology's role in it. On the one hand, there is George Orwell's dystopia *1984,* where the ever present eye of Big Brother watches a grim and depressed public through television. On the other hand, there is Aldous Huxley's *Brave New World.* Written originally as a farce in the early 1930s, Huxley's book details a society where people use pills to go to sleep and stay awake, conception is by test tube, people can enjoy "feelie" movies (a version of virtual reality), and advertisements continually blare over sound systems. Postman feels that Huxley's vision (already on its way to becoming a reality in 1960 when he published his essay "Brave New World Revisited") really shows what we have become. That, in fact, we are living in a science fiction world and we need not be watched by the omnipotent eye of television. Instead, we watch television of our own volition. That we live in a consumer culture where people crave instant gratification and where even the "talk" shows on television (which were once sophisticated and urbane in the days of Jack Parr and even the early days of Carson) have bowed to the lowest common denominator, where the idiocies of Leno have replaced the wit of Parr and Carson. In other words, the final result of all this new technology is that we as a people no longer want to think, we want to be entertained.

George Orwell wrote in his book *1984* of a society where culture has become a prison.

Aldous Huxley wrote of a society in his book *Brave New World* where culture has become burlesque. This, according to Neil Postman, is the profound difference in the philosophy of the two books. It is Postman's belief that, today, we watch "Big Brother" by choice. Postman feels it is Huxley's vision that has come true:

"George Orwell would have been stymied by this situation; there is nothing 'Orwellian' about it. The President does not have the press under his thumb . . . there is no Newspeak here. Lies have not been defined as truth nor truth as lies. All that has happened is that the public has adjusted to incoherence and been amused into indifference. Which is why Aldous Huxley would not in the least be surprised . . . he prophesied its coming. He believed that the Western democracies will dance and dream themselves into oblivion rather than march into it, single filed and manacled. Huxley grasped, as Orwell did not, that it is not necessary to conceal anything from a public insensible to contradiction and narcoticized by technological diversions . . . In the age of advanced technology, spiritual devastation is more likely to come from an enemy with a smiling face than one which exudes suspicion and hate."

Neil Postman

Still, Postman makes certain that the reader understands he believes Huxley's vision to be "an ideology nonetheless, for it imposes a way of life, a set of relations among people and ideas, about which there is no consensus, no discussion, and no opposition."

According to Postman, technology **is** an ideology!

Whenever you introduce a technological innovation, be it an alphabet, a printing press, or speed of light transmission of images, you are creating a cultural revolution. From the World's Fairs of the first half of the century, to the slogans of the second half (one example: Dupont's "Better living through chemistry"), we have been trained to believe in the inevitability of progress and that change is good and that change is, in essence, technology.

It is estimated that 100% of American households have television sets. DVD players and TiVo have, in many cases, replaced video recorders, and the number of households with computers has risen exponentially. Today, almost every high school has some sort of computer classes, and some have said that without computer skills, anyone going into law, moviemaking, accounting, or medicine is functionally illiterate. We have moved from a print culture into a culture of electronic and digital language. Although many people do not "bother" to read books today, books still endure. And they have endured for a reason.

Forty years ago the early proponents of computer technology argued that computers would bring a more efficient, paperless workforce, and that the printed word, newspapers, and books would eventually become obsolete.

Let's imagine that books and computers were invented and released into the marketplace at the same time. How would the two technologies compare? Ten years ago, Richard C. Hsu and William E. Mitchell wrote an article for *The New York Times* imagining just such a "what if" scenario. Their conclusions?

- **Ergonomics**—Books are less strenuous to use. It takes more physical dexterity and more toll on the body to operate a computer. Today, this just isn't as true, particularly with the introduction of palm pilots and other handheld devices. Is there still something more soothing about reading off the printed page rather than off a computer screen? Hsu and Mitchell certainly thought so.

- **Contrast, Luminance, Resolution, Viewing Angle**—The printed page is easier to read. Print resolution is greater than pixel density. You can't read a computer screen if bright light is reflecting off the screen. Again, this is not as true today, and one could argue that you still need, at the very least, a laptop computer screen to look at if you're going to do work (or play or watch something) on an airplane for five to eight hours. iPod and iPhone screens are certainly amazing in their clarity, but looking at the screen for hours on end will still cause eyestrain.

- **Durability, Life Expectancy**—This is true—computers seem to have the life expectancy of a mosquito. Even a paperback book can last years. A good hardbound edition can last decades. And you don't have to worry about a book breaking if you drop it or if it's mishandled by the guy in luggage.

- **Power Consumption**—Does anything even need to be added here? Obviously, books don't need batteries, chargers, or electrical outlets.

- **Editorial Quality**—In print, space is limited, forcing careful attention to length and content (one would hope).

- **Intangibles**—The information stored in books is permanent and measureable. Electronic data are susceptible to disappearance, changes, and continuation. This has become true even of movies; with the availability of DVDs and digital editing, you can now watch three alternative endings or even five alternative versions of the same movie.

- **Search Capability**—Here finally computers come out on top. Try looking through the index of a book, then try the same search via a computer. And books aren't connected to Google.

Consequences of Television

In 1884, when the German inventor Paul Nipkow first demonstrated the ability to electronically transmit moving images, he had little idea how influential and transformative this idea would become. Although Nipkow's electro-mechanical approach was replaced by more sophisticated designs, his early concept carried long-term consequences. By 1962, beginning with the launch of the Telstar communications satellite, the era of instant global news and live real-time visual coverage of events was born. When President John F. Kennedy was assassinated the following year in Dallas, Texas, members of the American Ballet Company, who were performing in Moscow, were able to watch live news from the event on the other side of the world.

This chapter details numerous historic milestones that mark how early television affected economics, institutions, interpersonal relationships, and personal lives. Because many of these changes took place gradually, they were eventually taken in stride and integrated into everyday life. This was not the case with the Dene Indians of Northern Canada, as described by Jerry Mander in his book, *In the Absence of the Sacred.*

Television had not been introduced to the Dene society until the early 1980s, when the Canadian government provided broadcast access to American and Canadian programming. Up until this time, the indigenous Dene lived much like they had traditionally for 20,000 years—hunting and fishing in small self-sufficient communities spread across thousands of square miles of arctic tundra in northern Canada. In 1983, Mander was invited by the Native Women's Association of the Northern Territories to consult with them about what they felt was a negative impact on their way of life.

Cindy Gilday, one of the members of the Native Women's Association, provided Mander with this assessment of TV's influence on her native tribe, the Dene:

> "The effect has been to glamorize behaviors and values that are poisonous to life up here. Our traditions have a lot to do with survival. Cooperation, sharing, and nonmaterialism are the only ways that people can live here. TV always seems to present values opposite to these.
>
> I used to be a schoolteacher, and when TV came to the villages I saw an immediate change. People lost interest in the native stories, legends, and languages, which are really important because they teach people how to live. And it's hurting the relationships between men and women too, and between young and old. We used to honor our old people and listen to them, but that's changing fast. TV makes it seem like the young people are all that's important and the old have nothing to say."

> Jerry Mander, *In the Absence of the Sacred*

One of the groups that have been most notable in questioning the acceptance of new technology have been the Old Order Amish, who in the year 2000 had thriving communities in twenty-one states. For centuries, they've resisted changes taking place in the outside world to maintain their traditional way of life. Howard Rheingold, a San Francisco–based author who writes about media and technology issues, interviewed an Amish farmer in 1998 who had made some reluctant concessions to modern farm equipment by using diesel-powered engines. He told Rheingold: "We don't stop with asking what a tool does. We ask about what kind of people we become when we use it."

A broader question arises: just how dependent have we become on our electronic communications gadgets? Mara Adelman, a professor of communications at Seattle University, conducts an informal experiment with her graduate students to find out what happens if they have to spend four days without the use of any form of electronic-mediated communication, including radio, television, telephone, music player, computer, iPod, videogame, and so on. The results of one of this "media disengagement" in spring 2007 was reported in local and national news. A video interview of Dr. Adelman, where she describes her assignment in greater detail, can be found as a video link on the course website in Chapter 9. In this interview, she describes the importance of establishing a healthy relationship with new, ubiquitous communications gadgets, where time to be alone and self-reflective is becoming c. Here is a portion of that interview.

Could You Make It Without Media for 4 Days?

An interview with Mara Adelman, professor of communications at Seattle University about her class on media disengagement.[13]

This was an upper level course on restorative solitude. The technological part of the course was interesting because I had them spend a week logging their media activity, whether it was television, email, Internet, anything that had to do with the computer, radio, telephones, and so forth. And keeping a log of what was going on before, during, and after this period of time. And then we came back and debriefed it. Of course one of major insights that students had was that they were just dumbfounded by the amount of time that they engaged.

I asked them if they could have seven days of media deprivation or media diet. And we had a class discussion about this—and it turned out that seven days was just not possible, so we negotiated. And collectively we agreed that four days, they could do it. . . they were to be on. . . a media diet, or liberation!

What they found was very interesting. It wasn't easy for them. It wasn't just because of their personal obsession, addictions, or need for perpetual contact. It was also the external demands that they be connected 24/7. Family and friends wanted to have access to them, parents wanted access-I had one parent call me who was irate because their child wasn't going to be in contact with them on a daily basis. So there were a lot of social and normative demands to be in contact.

(Students) are going to be entering fields and professions where organizations are going to expect 24/7 access to them - and this is actually an ethical as well as a personal decision that many of them are going to have to make. The question is that if they haven't made it in their own personal life-how are we going to have them make it in their profession life. In other words, if this 24/7 access is just a cultural wash, if people assume that we're available because the media makes us available-that's problematic!

One of the things that students discovered during this exercise is the lack of human agency. Many of them felt they didn't have a right to turn off the computer, or not answer the emails-there was a sense of being compelled; the compulsion of the call, or to answer the phone call-they feel this with text messaging, they feel this with email. . . If they have no sense of agency, if they have no sense of themselves being able to turn it off - then I don't know where they can establish boundaries in their personal lives. We're creating an infrastructure, organizational, professional, and personal-that you are available to people 24/7.

Endnotes

[1]Mitchell Stephens, www.nyu.edu/classes/stephens/History%20of%20Television%20page.htm.

[2]Ibid.

[3]Ibid.

[4]Ibid.

[5]Ibid.

[6]*This Fabulous Century, Volume VI 1960-1970* (New York: Time Life Books, 1970), p. 130.

[7]Mitchell Stephens, www.nyu.edu/classes/stephens/History%20of%20Television%20page.htm.

[8]Interview with Shad Northshield by the author Michael Korolenko for film "Since '45," 1978.

[9]Mitchell Stephens, www.nyu.edu/classes/stephens/History%20of%20Television%20page.htm.

[10]http://www.pbs.org/wnet/americanmasters/database/cronkite_w_interview.html.

[11]Interview with author Michael Korolenko, 1981.

[12]Neil Postman, *Amusing Ourselves to Death*.

[13]Mara Adelman, interview with author Bruce Wolcott, August 2008.

Chapter 3
The Hall of Personal Communication

"The telephone's such a *convenient* thing; it just sits there and *demands* you call someone who doesn't want to be called. Friends were always calling, calling, calling me. Hell, I hadn't any time of my own.... What is it about these conveniences that make them so temptingly convenient? ... Convenient for my office, so when I'm in the field with my radio car there's no moment when I'm not in touch. In *touch! There's* a slimy phrase. Touch, hell. *Gripped!* Pawed, rather. Mauled and massaged and pounded by FM voices."

Ray Bradbury, *The Murderer*
From Golden Apples of the Sun, (HarperCollins, 1990), 51–52.

"... communication is the way we weave together a personality, a family, a business, a nation, and a world. The telecosm—the world enabled and defined by new communications technology—will make human communication universal, instantaneous, unlimited in capacity, and at the margins free."

George Gilder, *Telecosm*
(New York: The Free Press—A Division of Simon & Schuster, 2000).

In the long history of interpersonal human communications technologies, the primary challenge has always been the same. How do you transmit a message beyond the normal range of the human voice and physical expressions? As you visit this chapter, the *Hall of Personal Communication*, you'll experience a quick tour of this communications history and how people have exchanged messages over long distances using a variety of methods. The chapter ends with the introduction and use of two world altering electronic inventions—the telegraph and the telephone, in its many incarnations.

This history of personal communications is divided into five major sections:

The Spoken Word—*primary orality;* voice, gesture, and facial expressions
The Written Word—*chirography* or handwritten language and pictographs
The Printed Word—*typography* or mass production of written ideas via moveable type
The Electronic Word—communication based on signals modulated and transmitted by electricity
The Digital Word—communication using electronically modulated binary signals or 0s and 1s.

From Arched Brows to Semaphores—A Quick Tour of Early Communications Technologies

Table 1. The Spoken Word

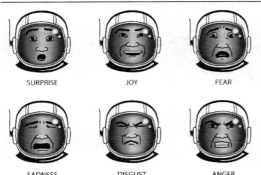

SURPRISE   JOY   FEAR

SADNESS   DISGUST   ANGER

Figure 1. Six universal facial expressions: Surprise, joy, fear, sadness, disgust, anger. Illustration by Kirsten Adams.

Our most archaic communications "technology" is our voice and the many varieties of gestures and human facial expressions. Some linguists, like Noam Chomsky, have theorized that we are "hard wired" for language, and that children are genetically predisposed to learn words, grammar, and syntax.[1]

It also appears that there are at least six universal facial expressions that communicate the same emotional messages across cultural boundaries, namely disgust, sadness, happiness, fear, anger, and surprise.[2] These may indicate built-in, genetically based communications signals rather than socially conditioned ones.

The Oral Tradition

Figure 2. © Alexander Shebanov | Dreamstime.com.

In preliterate societies, spoken recitation, gesture, song, and human memory provided the media for representing human experience. Before the alphabet, or the visual representation of language as symbols, epic poems, folk tales, and parables were the primary containers for transmitted histories. Bards and storytellers specialized in memorizing and retelling accounts that preserved the shared values of a culture's worldview. These stories can be religious, provide moral teaching, and give instructions for adapting to social norms. They are the glue that binds together a shared view of the universe. Orally transmitted epics of the Babylonian *Gilgamesh,* the Greek *Iliad* and the *Odyssey,* and the Celtic *Beowulf* all served to bring individuals within a society into a relationship with a common history and purpose. Early epic stories were often crafted in a rhythmic framework so they could be efficiently memorized and accurately retold from generation to generation.

The "Talking Drum"

Figure 3. Illustration by Kirsten Adams.

No complete history of the use of drumming for long-distance communication is available, but numerous African societies to this day make use of "talking drums" to convey messages across long distances. This form of communication may have been used for thousands of years and now continues among ethnic groups such as the Yoruba (Nigeria), Bulu (West Africa), and Dagomba (Ghana). Drums may be heard 3 to 4 miles away by day, and 10 to 15 miles away at night.[3]

---

650 BC - Babylonian Couriers

Babylonian kings use couriers to relay messages along major highways. Guard stations along these routes also make use of fire beacons to transmit signals from one to the other. The Greek adventurer Xenophon provided an early record of this messaging system.

"We have observed still another device of Cyrus' [King of Persia, circa 530 BC] for coping with the magnitude of his

Figure 4. Illustration by Kirsten Adams.

empire; by means of this institution he would speedily discover the condition of affairs, no matter how far distant they might be from him: he experimented to find out how great a distance a horse could cover in a day when ridden hard, but not so hard as to break down, and then he erected post-stations at just such distances and equipped them with horses, and men to take care of them; at each one of the stations he had the proper official appointed to receive the horses and riders and send on fresh ones."
Xenophon in *Cryopaedia* (559–529 BC)[4]

490 BC—Phidippides	Phidippides, probably the most well-remembered messenger in history, runs from Marathon to Athens to warn Athenians that the Persian army is approaching. A modern day long-distance track event, the marathon, commemorates this event. Phidippides is said to have died from exhaustion after delivering his warning.
AD 14—Cursus Publicus	The Roman Empire makes use of a runner messenger service to convey news and information along its many well built roads. Messages sent by way of this early communication network, the *Cursus Publicus,* traveled approximately 50 miles per day.

Table 2. The Written Word

Figure 5. 30,000 BC—Time Factoring. Illustration by Kirsten Adams.

Alexander Marshack in his book *The Roots of Civilization* describes the earliest known instances of human beings recording events in a process he calls "time factoring." Marshack claims our early ancestors recorded cyclical natural events such as lunar cycles through carving notches in animal bones. Marshack states:

> "Apparently as far back as 30,000 BC the Ice Age hunter of western Europe was using a system of notation that was already evolved, complex, and sophisticated, a tradition that would seem to have been thousands of years old by this point."[5]

The "system of notation" in this case refers to the process of recording an event using an animal bone for storage and presentation of information.

17,000 BC—Cave of Lascaux	In 1940, two brothers discovered a cave near Lascaux, France, that contained visually expressive paintings on its stone walls. They're considered one of the world's best examples of prehistoric art, because they date back to approximately 17,000 BC. The caves contain anatomically sophisticated drawings of horses, ibexes, bison, stags, oxen, mammoths, a human hand, and various figures. No one can accurately guess the purpose of this artwork after so many centuries, but they certainly represent conditions of daily life at that time. Some archeologists have stated that the layout of these caves suggests the location of a place for religious rituals or reenactments of the hunt—stories told as paintings.[6]

Figure 6. 3300 BC—Egyptian hieroglyphics. © Waiheng | Dreamstime.com.

Hieroglyphics emerged from preliterate early artistic traditions in ancient Egypt, and over time changed from pictorial representations and stories to more abstract signs and figures associated with vocal sounds—a precursor to the modern alphabet. The earliest hieroglyphics were found represented as friezes within burial tombs or engraved on stone monuments. Later, the lightweight and portable papyrus (made from the Nile River papyrus plant) was used as a recording medium. It was also subsequently used extensively by the Greek and Roman empires. Its name provides the origin for the word *paper.*

Jean-Francois Champollion, the French scholar who first was able to decipher the ancient hieroglyphic script in 1820, described this early written communications form as follows: "It is a complex system, writing figurative, symbolic, and phonetic all at once. . ."[7]

3100 BC—Cuneiform

Figure 7. © Jakub Cejpek | Dreamstime.com.

An early form of written communication took place in an area between the Tigris and Euphrates Rivers (in present-day Iraq). It's called *cuneiform,* taken from a Latin word meaning "wedge-shaped." Some of the first examples of cuneiform appeared in the ancient city of Uruk in Sumer.

A stiff reed was used by early scribes as a writing utensil to make marks into wet clay tablets. These tablets were then baked so that the inscribed marks became a permanent record. Remarkably, many of these baked clay tablets survived intact for many centuries after they were created.

The cuneiform tablets, many of them palm-sized for easy portability, were used for business records and legal documents.

750 BC—Greece: Introduction of the Alphabet

The Western alphabet as we know it today, a written representation of vocal sounds, arrived in ancient Greece about 2,750 years ago. It was derived from an earlier Phoenician version. It provided little punctuation and was read alternately from left to right on one line followed by a movement from right to left on the subsequent line, in a zigzag fashion from the top to the bottom of a page.

One of the earliest critics of this new technology was the Greek philosopher Socrates, as portrayed by Plato in *Phaedrus.* In this dialog, Socrates believes that the written word will deprive its users of a cultivated memory, because a written record will take its place:

> "for this discovery of yours will create forgetfulness in the learners' souls, because they will not use their memories; they will trust to the external written characters and not remember of themselves. The specific which you have discovered is an aid not to memory, but to reminiscence, and you give your disciples not truth, but only the semblance of truth; they will be hearers of many things and will have learned nothing; they will appear to be omniscient and will generally know nothing; they will be tiresome company, having the show of wisdom without the reality."[8]

"You would imagine that they had intelligence, but if you want to know anything and put a question to one of them, the speaker always gives one unvarying answer. And when they have been once written down they are tumbled about anywhere among those who may or may not understand them, and know not to whom they should reply, to whom not: and, if they are maltreated or abused, they have no parent to protect them; and they cannot protect or defend themselves."[9]

Socrates was concerned that the new invention of writing would have a negative impact on learning and discussion based on the oral tradition. Some have written that this particular passage might well be history's first critique concerning the negative impact of a communications technology on society.

Carrier Pigeons

Figure 8. Illustration by Kirsten Adams.

Carrier pigeons are birds that have remarkable homing instincts that allow them to find their home nests even when they're hundreds of miles away. Over the centuries, this homing instinct has been bred more strongly into these birds, which makes them fast and reliable message carriers. Pigeons can fly up to 58 miles per hour, and may have been used as early as 2900 BC in Egypt, where they were used to announce the arrival of dignitaries by ship before they came into port.

In 776 BC the results of the Olympic games were delivered by carrier pigeons.

In 1918, the British Air Force made use of 20,000 homing pigeons cared for by 380 pigeon keepers for their World War I operations.

As recently as 1981, courier pigeons were used to deliver film negatives of drawings by a group of Lockheed engineers from Sunnyvale, California, to a test station 25 miles away. Jon Bentley describes the benefits of working with homing pigeons:

"The pigeon took just half the time and less than one percent of the dollar amount of the car. Over a 16-month period the pigeons transmitted hundreds of rolls of film and lost only two."[10]

Horseback Delivery

The Mongol ruler Kublai Khan (1215–1294) had a system of horses and messengers to relay messages across vast distances. The Italian explorer Marco Polo described the speed of this operation in terms that would have been considered hard to believe in his time:

"When the need arises for the Great Khan to receive immediate tidings by mounted messenger, as of the rebellion of a subject country or of one of his barons or any matter that may concern him deeply, I assure you that the messengers ride 200 miles in a day, sometimes even 250."

A more contemporary version of this thirteenth century horse-based delivery system was the Pony Express, which was in operation in the United States from April 1860 to October 1861. Each Pony Express rider covered approximately 90 miles per day and changed horses every 9 miles. Records show that the Pony Express delivered mail between Missouri and California in ten days, a distance of about 1,900 miles, using seventy-five ponies.

Table 3. The Printed Word

AD 105—Paper and Printing in China

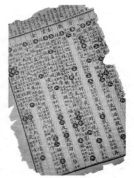

Figure 9. **Section of early printed Chinese.** © Feng Yu | Dreamstime.com.

A key event in the development of the printed word was the discovery of paper in China around AD 105 made from processed cloth or silk rags and various plant fibers. The Chinese also developed a block printing process, whereby engraved letters and figures in wood were inked and pressed onto paper. Paper money, playing cards, calendars, and simple illustrations were reproduced using this method. It is thought that the large number of characters in the early Chinese alphabet made it impractical to use block printing as an approach to large scale print publishing.[11]

1455—Gutenberg's Printing Press

Quod factū est in ipo vita erat: ꝛ vita Quod
bris lu erat lux hominū: et lux in tenebris lu
cet· ꝛ tenebre eā nō cōphenderūt. Fu cet· ꝛ te
a deo: cui nomē erat io it hānes nullus a deo: n
ut testi hānes. Hic venit ī testimoniū ut testi
mine: ut omēs crederent p illū. Nō erat ille lux: sed ut crederet
ibere de lumine. Erat testimoniū phiberet d
: que illuminat omnē homi lux vera: que
mundū. In mūdo erat ꝛ mūdus p ipm factus est: et

Figure 10. © Yury Khristich | Dreamstime.com.

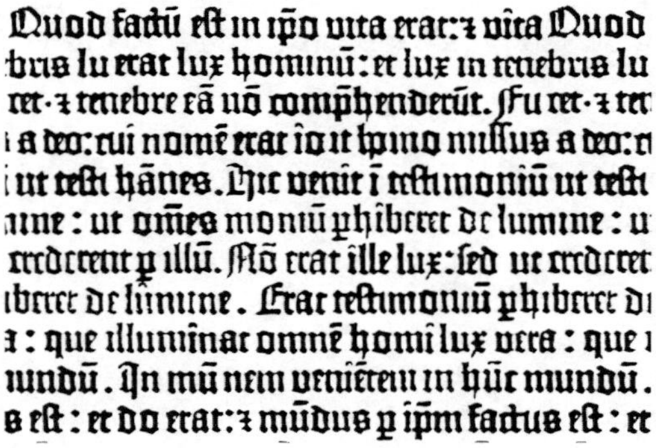

Johannes Gutenberg was a businessman and goldsmith from the city of Mainz in southern Germany. During the early 1450s, he saw a growing demand for the rapid production of low-cost written documents. Up until this time, scribes were hired to manufacture or reproduce documents using pen and ink. One interesting area of demand was for indulgences, which the Roman Catholic Church sold to raise money for military campaigns and new building projects. These small written contracts officially absolved the purchaser from sins.

Gutenberg recognized the need to mass-produce written documents. His answer was the printing press, a device that joined together several technologies:

1) Paper, which was becoming cheap and plentiful in Gutenberg's time.
2) The wine press, which was a screw-mounted platen used to compress grapes on a flat surface.
3) Ink, which would not smear or fade over time.
4) Moveable metal type, which provided the key to quickly assembling printed words. Gutenberg's background as a goldsmith allowed him to fashion small square bases of lead that had the reverse image of letters engraved on them. These embossed squares were organized into words and sentences on a flat grid, which in turn was inked and pressed to sheets of paper. One of these metal print templates could mass-produce thousands of paper copies.

In 1455, he published the Gutenberg Bible, which was the first book ever printed in Europe. He published around 300

Figure 11. Early Printing Press—1568.

Gutenberg Bibles, which cost thirty florins—approximately three years of income for an average worker at the time.

After Gutenberg set up his printing operation, hundreds of print shops sprung up all over Europe. Neither Gutenberg nor anyone else could have predicted the long-term social consequences of his new technology.

Up until that time, the Bible was available only in hand-produced, limited editions and was written in Latin. The printing press could produce many copies at lower cost and in the local vernacular. Now people could read the Bible in their own language and make their own interpretations of scripture. These new interpretations, in turn, could be printed and publicly distributed. The centuries-old information monopoly put in effect by the monasteries and the Roman Catholic hierarchy began to erode. The Church could no longer be considered the ultimate authority and sole arbiter between God and the man on the street.[12]

The printing press also set the stage for the emergence of early science, because experiments could be published and reviewed by peers for validation or criticism.

Because of its speed and convenience, the mass-produced printed page became the most powerful and influential communications medium for several centuries following Gutenberg's invention.

Neil Postman in his book *Amusing Ourselves to Death* describes the all-pervasive influence of the printed word during these centuries in the following way:

> *"The influence of the printed word in every area of public discourse was insistent and powerful not merely because of the quantity of printed matter but because of its monopoly . . . There were no movies to see, radio to hear, photographic displays to look at, records to play. There was no television. Public business was channeled into and expressed through print, which became the model, the metaphor and the measure of all discourse."*[13]

1794—The Optical Telegraph Using Semaphores

Figure 12. Claude Frappe's Optical Telegraph, 1795.

A *semaphore* is a signal flag often used at sea to send messages between ships. Often two semaphores are used by signalers using a variety of arm positions to indicate letters and numbers.

In the late eighteenth century, the Frenchman Claude Chappe devised a system of towers spaced within visible range of one another to relay messages quickly across long distances, using a semaphore-based language. He called his new invention the *optical telegraph*. Alexander Dumas in his classic novel *The Count of Monte Cristo* provides a good description of how the early signaling system worked:

"A telegraph?" repeated Madame de Villefort.

"Yes, a telegraph. I had often seen one placed at the end of a road on a hillock, and in the light of the sun its black arms, bending in every direction, always reminded me of the claws

Figure 13. Semaphore routes in France, early 1800s. Illustration by Kirsten Adams.

of an immense beetle, and I assure you it was never without emotion that I gazed on it, for I could not help thinking how wonderful it was that these various signs should be made to cleave the air with such precision as to convey to the distance of three hundred leagues the ideas and wishes of a man sitting at a table at one end of the line to another man similarly placed at the opposite extremity . . . I began to think of genii, sylphs, gnomes, in short, of all the ministers of the occult sciences, until I laughed aloud at the freaks of my own imagination. Now, it never occurred to me to wish for a nearer inspection of these large insects, with their long black claws, for I always feared to find under their stone wings some little human genius fagged to death with cabals, factions, and government intrigues. But one fine day I learned that the mover of this telegraph was only a poor wretch, hired for twelve hundred francs a year. . ."[14]

Inside each telegraph tower, an operator would read an incoming message from another tower through a telescope. The operator would recreate that received message through the use of pulleys that controlled the positions of mechanical semaphores, which transmitted the message to the next tower.

France adopted this system of long-distance communications, and it proved to be useful until the mid-nineteenth century, when it was replaced by the electronic telegraphic system. With skilled operators, the optical telegraph was capable of sending a message 150 miles in two minutes. The optical telegraph system was used mostly for official government communications and was not available for general use.

Harold Innis in his book *Empire and Communications* talks about the differences between traditional communications media that emphasize time and those that emphasize space.

"Media that emphasize time are those that are durable in character, such as parchment, clay, and stone. The heavy materials are suited to the development of architecture and sculpture. Media that emphasize space are apt to be less durable and light in character, such as papyrus and paper. The latter are suited to wide areas in administration and trade."[15]

Innis points to the fact that geographically extended civilizations, such as the Roman Empire, required lightweight and transportable media such as paper to record and disseminate information about business transactions, inventories, and daily activities. A stream of recorded and transmitted information became an important part of the ongoing maintenance of cities, government, and military operations spread across thousands of miles. Lightweight documents are less permanent than their more durable stone and clay counterparts, but they can be more easily transported for longer distances.

Up until the mid-nineteenth century, all nonspoken human communications required the recording and/or transmission of messages by way of a physical medium like stone, clay, or lightweight (and mobile) papyrus, velum, or paper, as Innis describes. The communications system in France based on Chappe's optical telegraph (described previously) was expensive to maintain, slow, and available only to a limited number of users. Many teams of operators were required, and messages couldn't be transmitted at night or in bad weather. Telegraph towers had to be built away from rivers or lakes because of problems with fog and mist. The discovery of a new property of nature, namely electromagnetism, was about to change all of that and usher in the era of the Electronic Word.

The Electronic Word

In April 1746, the abbé Jean-Antoine Nollet, a well-known scientist, carried out an early experiment with electricity. Nollet assembled approximately 200 monks in a long line. Each of them held two 25-foot wires that connected them to monks standing to their left and right. Nollet connected the wire from a monk at one end of the line to a primitive battery and turned it on. All of the monks standing in the mile-long human electrical circuit received a shock and appeared to physically react to this jolt of electricity at the same time. Nollet incorrectly concluded that electricity covered the entire length of the wire instantly. Certainly, it was the fastest transmission of a long-distance signal that anyone had seen up until that time. The electrical signal was also capable of moving around corners, and at night, without the benefit of a visual line-of-sight. [16]

During the early nineteenth century, many attempts were made to harness this newly discovered electricity (whose properties weren't completely understood) for the purposes of communicating messages over long distances.

The Telegraph

Samuel Morse was an American inventor born in 1791. Early in his career, he came up with numerous inventions, none of which brought him fame or wealth. In 1832, Morse was studying painting in Europe and working on a scheme to recreate thirty-eight miniatures of the most famous classic paintings in the Louvre Museum onto one large canvas, which he called the *Treasures of the Louvre*. The idea was to take this canvas of miniature reproductions on tour and charge a fee. On a six-week Atlantic Ocean voyage back to the United States, Morse ran into a man who would profoundly change his career. Dr. Charles Jackson was an early expert in electromagnetism, and he provided Morse with a demonstration and explanation of how it worked. Like the French scientist Nollet, Jackson believed that electricity was present instantaneously along every point on a wired circuit. Afterward, Morse is claimed to have said, "If the presence of electricity can be made visible in any desired part of the circuit, I can see no reason why intelligence might not be instantaneously transmitted by electricity to any distance."

With this idea in mind and while still aboard the ship, Morse came up with an idea of using keystrokes to tap out streams of electricity, an electronic code to carry messages long distances across wire. To implement this, he devised a signaling system that was made up short and long bursts of electric current, what he termed a "bi-signal" scheme. This approach to translating letters and numbers into a universal code of electronically modulated dashes and dots became the basis of Morse code - the fundamental language of telegraph transmissions. [17]

Morse teamed up with Leonard Gale, a chemistry professor at New York University, and Alfred Vail, an independent investor, to complete his work on the telegraph. By 1838, Morse had a working telegraph prototype that he demonstrated both in Europe and to the United States Congress, but with little success at first. Morse's early telegraph was made up of long and short metal bars that represented a Morse code version of the alphabet and number values. The telegraph operator moved a pointer, which was wired to a battery across these bars, and corresponding long and short signals were automatically transmitted over the line. On the receiving end, a magnet-driven

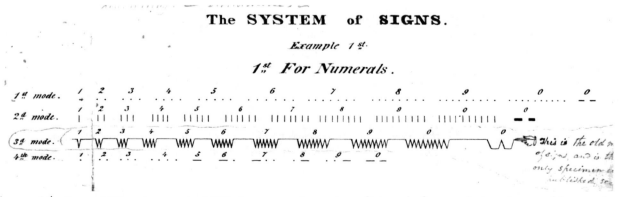

Figure 14. Samuel Morse's notes in 1839 show an early section of his code for translating short and long pulses of electricity into numbers. Library of Congress, Prints and Photographs, 12001/0154d.

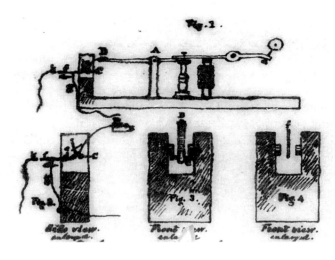

Figure 15. Samuel Morse hand-drawn diagram of an early telegraph. Library of Congress, Prints and Photographs, 3c10409v.

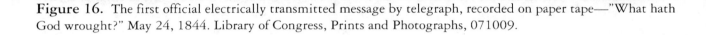

Figure 16. The first official electrically transmitted message by telegraph, recorded on paper tape—"What hath God wrought?" May 24, 1844. Library of Congress, Prints and Photographs, 071009.

stylus on a moving arm made etch marks on a strip of paper tape that the telegraph operator translated into numbers and letters. Morse obtained a patent for his new invention in 1840. Meanwhile, in England, Charles Wheatstone and William Cook had simultaneously and independently devised their own version of the telegraph.

In 1842, Morse returned to Washington, DC, and gave a demonstration; this time was given $30,000 to set up a test line to further develop his invention. The money was awarded by Congress by an eighty-seven to eighty-three vote, with seventy congressmen abstaining—they refused to support a newfangled technology they didn't understand.

Morse was determined now to prove the worth of his invention. First he set up a telegraph connection between Washington, DC, and Baltimore—a distance of approximately 40 miles. He made arrangements with the Baltimore & Ohio Railroad company to run a telegraph line alongside their tracks. On May 24, 1844, Morse officially sent the first telegram from the Supreme Court building in Washington, DC, to Baltimore that said, *"What hath God wrought?"*

Surprisingly, the telegraph wasn't immediately accepted or taken seriously; several early business ventures making use of the new technology failed within their first few weeks of operation. But that situation was soon to change. Two years after Morse sent his first message from Washington, DC, to Baltimore, there were 2,000 miles of installed telegraph wire in the United States, and by 1850, that number jumped to 12,000 miles. Two years later, there were 23,000 miles of installed telegraph lines, with 10,000 more under construction.[18]

By 1851 Morse's invention was adopted as the standard for telegraph messaging in Europe. In 1866 a telegraph cable connecting the United States with Europe was completed. One hundred thousand miles of undersea cables were in place by 1880. In this same year, Western Union was delivering more than 80% of all telegraph communications in the United States and making a huge profit. American businesses had become so dependent on the telegraph for their daily transactions that Western Union president William Orton said the following: "The fact is, the telegraph lives upon commerce. It is the nervous system of the commercial system. If you will sit down with me at my office for twenty minutes, I will show you what the condition of business is at any given time in any locality in the United States."[19]

By the mid-1850s the use of telegrams was common. Messenger boys were hired to deliver messages to and from telegraph offices. During the Civil War (1861–1865), the telegraph was used extensively by both the Union and Confederate forces to communicate and relay military intelligence.

Electricity Connects the World

The introduction of the telegraph meant for the first time in history that communication was no longer dependent on physical transportation by foot, wheel, or water. The Battle of Lexington at the beginning of the American Revolution took place on April 19, 1775, between American militiamen and British regulars. News of the battle in Lexington, Massachusetts reached New York on April 24, Virginia by April 26, and finally arrived in England almost six weeks later, on May 28.[20]

Almost a century later, when President Abraham Lincoln was assassinated at the end of the Civil War in 1865, news of his death took twelve days to reach England. The information was first telegraphed over land from New York to the eastern tip of New Foundland in Canada. A steamship picked up the message and delivered it to Ireland, where it was again transmitted by telegraph to England.[21]

After several mishaps, business entrepreneur Cyrus Field was finally able to successfully lay a transatlantic telegraph cable between England and the United States in July 1866. Europe and North America were finally successfully wired together. Referring to Field's accomplishment, the *Atlantic Monthly* predicted that the telegraph would encourage ". . . unity, peace, and good-will among men."

THE LAYING OF THE CABLE—JOHN AND JONATHAN JOINING HANDS.

Figure 17. A political cartoon from 1856 shows the United States shaking hands with Great Britain (John Bull) in recognition of the first transatlantic telegraph cable. Library of Congress. A portion of John Bull's cartoon word balloon reads: **"May the feeling of friendship . . . be like the electric current which now unites our lands, and links our destiny with yours!"** Library of Congress, Prints and Photographs, LC-USZ62-5309.

Morse the Photographer

Samuel Morse began his career as a visual artist, not a scientist. While he was working on his invention of the telegraph, Morse developed an avid interest in early photography. In 1839, he traveled to Paris to meet with Louis Daguerre, inventor of the first photograph, which was called the *daguerreotype.* Morse returned to the United States, where he published the first description of this new photographic process. He also opened a daguerreotype portrait studio in New York, where he later trained several apprentice photographers, including Matthew Brady, who went on to become the leading documentary photographer of the Civil War.

Figure 18. Samuel Morse with his photographic gear. Library of Congress, Prints and Photographs, LC-USZ62-12900.

In 1871 Morse was honored at a banquet where a statue of the inventor was unveiled, built from donations that came in from telegraph operators in the United States and Canada. A telegraph key was set up that was connected to all of the major cities in North America. A telegraph operator named Sadie Cornwell sent out the following message, "Greetings and thanks to the telegraph fraternity throughout the world. Glory to God in the highest, on earth peace. Good will to men." Samuel Morse then took his place at the telegraph and keyed in his signature, "S.F.B. Morse."[22]

The Telephone

It could be argued that no communications technology in history has transformed the lives of everyday people more than the telephone. The early telephone's basic operation can be simply described: It converts sound waves into electrical signals, transmits these signals along a wire, and reconverts the electrical pulses back into sound waves when it arrives at its destination. Early in the nineteenth century, however, the properties of electricity were not clearly understood, and it took a number of key scientific discoveries to clear the way for the invention of the first telephone. Probably the most important of these was a discovery by the English scientist Michael Faraday, who in 1831 demonstrated that vibrating metal could be converted into electrical signals.

The telegraph had demonstrated how electricity could be used to pulse dots and dashes along a metal wire, but transmitting the complex range of vibrations produced by a human voice seemed to be too daunting a task. Telegraph devices had numerous limitations. A well-trained telegraph operator could only transmit about thirty words per minute. Two human operators were needed for each message: one to send and the other to receive. Customers had to physically go to a telegraph office to receive messages or hire delivery boys to pick them up. Telegrams were priced by the number of words in a message and lacked the natural give and take of human speech. Finally, only one message could be sent at a time along a telegraph wire, and Western Union was looking for a system that could handle multiple messages simultaneously.

It was this problem that attracted Alexander Graham Bell, a young Scottish immigrant living in Boston. Bell had an idea for creating a "harmonic telegraph" that would carry up to eight messages simultaneously on a telegraph wire. In much the same way that a piano key causes harmonic vibrations in other strings, Bell thought he could use harmonic frequencies to carry multiple electrical telegraph signals. Bell's idea caught the attention of a wealthy patent attorney named Gardiner Hubbard and another investor, Thomas Sanders. They began to fund the young inventor's work.

Bell's work with the harmonic telegraph led him to believe that he'd be able to eventually transmit a human voice, a device he called the *audiotelegraph.* On March 10, 1876, Bell was working on an improved version of the telephone transmitter in his lab. His assistant, Thomas Watson, was listening in another room when he heard Bell's voice shouting through the experimental phone receiver, "Mr. Watson, come here, I want you!" Watson later added, ". . . I rushed down the hall into his room and found he had upset the acid of a battery over his clothes. He [Bell] forgot the accident in his joy over the success of the new transmitter."[23]

Surprisingly, Bell was dragging his heels in getting his new invention registered with the U.S. patent office. His investor, Gardiner Hubbard, grew impatient and decided to apply for the patent himself. In one of the most

Figure 19. Alexander Graham Bell in 1876. Courtesy of AT&T Archives and History Center.

Figure 20. Thomas Watson— Bell's Assistant. Courtesy of AT&T Archives and History Center.

Figure 21. The first telephone, 1876. Courtesy of AT&T Archives and History Center.

unusual coincidences in history, Hubbard applied for the telephone patent a mere *two hours* before another inventor, Elijah Gray, submitted his own patent for the telephone later the same day. Bell's patent prevailed, despite many legal battles later on, and Gray's contribution to the development of the telephone was largely forgotten.

Although Gray continued a successful career as a professor at Oberlin College in Ohio, he never overcame his bitterness over losing his patent rights to the telephone. After he died, a note was found among his personal papers that read: "The history of the telephone will never be fully written . . . It is partly hidden in 20 or 30 thousand pages of testimony and partly lying on the hearts and consciences of a few whose lips are sealed—some in death and others by a golden clasp whose grip is even tighter."[24]

It should also be noted that numerous other inventors in Europe and the United States contributed to the development of the telephone, including Thomas Edison. It was Bell who was best positioned to promote and build on his early success, however. Early on, Bell recognized the significance of the telephone. On the day, he successfully demonstrated his telephone with Watson, Bell wrote: "This is a great day with me and I feel I have at last struck the solution of a great problem and the day is coming when telephone wires will be laid on to houses, just like water or gas, and friends will converse without leaving home."[25]

Like its predecessor, the telegraph, forty years earlier, the telephone met with early resistance. Gardiner Hubbard tried to sell patent rights of the telephone to the Western Union Telegraph company. Its president, William Orten, dismissed Hubbard by saying, "What use would this office make of an electrical toy?"

Orten had what seemed to be good reasons for rejecting the telephone. By 1876, there were 214,000 miles of installed telegraph wire and 8,500 Western Union offices. Businesses, stock brokers, police departments, fire stations, and government agencies all used their own specialized forms of the telegraph. Telegrams provided a permanent record for a message in paper form—they were legal documents. Telephones were also too pricey for the ordinary user, and service was limited to local calls. Telegrams meant serious business; telephones were an expensive novelty.[26]

During the spring of 1876, Bell and Watson gave public demonstrations of their new device for several scientific groups in Boston. Although these presentations were successful, word of their new invention didn't spread beyond the Boston area. Bell decided to take his invention to the Centennial Exhibition in Philadelphia. Sunday, June 26, 1876, is the date that General George Custer was defeated at the battle of Little Big Horn River. This was the same day that Bell received a big break in his promotional campaign for the telephone. Dom Pedro, emperor of Brazil, was visiting the Philadelphia Centennial, followed by a group of journalists. He happened to come by Bell's display booth. With Dom Pedro sitting in a gallery across the exhibit floor with his ear to a receiver, Bell began to recite Hamlet's famous speech into the phone transmitter: "To be, or not to be . . ." Dom Pedro stood up from his chair and exclaimed, "I hear! I hear!" Another celebrity, the eminent British scientist Sir William Kelvin, tried Bell's telephone and later wrote, "I need hardly say I was astonished and delighted . . . This, perhaps the greatest marvel hitherto achieved by the electric telegraph . . ."[27]

After the first two years of promoting the telephone, Bell and Watson had managed to attract a small but growing number of users. By the end of the first year, more than 600 phones had been installed in New England. These first phones had their own dedicated lines connecting them to manually operated telephone exchanges. By 1878, although most major cities in the United States had exchanges in place, it was only the wealthy or technologically curious who could afford to own a telephone. It was still largely considered to be an expensive luxury. At the time, telephones sold for around $10 each. Wealthy bankers and physicians could have telephones installed and operational for about $40 a year, which was a large sum of money in the nineteenth century.

That attitude began to change overnight when a train filled with passengers returning from a revival meeting fell into the Farmington River from a collapsing bridge just outside of Tariffville, Connecticut, in January 1878. A local drugstore had a telephone and was able to directly contact over a dozen doctors, who arrived quickly to help injured passengers. A local livery was called, and immediately sent a wagon loaded with medical supplies to the scene of the accident. The benefits of telephones and the exchanges were immediately apparent. It was a milestone event for bringing public attention to Bell's invention.

People began to realize that unlike the telegraph, the telephone allowed you to instantaneously hold a conversation with someone who was miles away. You no longer had to wait for a message to be encoded, decoded, and printed to paper. It was interactive, with two people enjoying the natural conversational rhythm of talking, listening, and interacting in real time. However, telegraph continued to be the best way to send a message over longer distances because the voice signal weakened the further it traveled along a phone line.

Figure 22. AT&T advertisement, 1890s. Courtesy of AT&T Archives and History Center.

Figure 23. AT&T President Theodore Vail, who built the company into a telecommunications giant. Courtesy of AT&T Archives and History Center.

An AT&T advertisement from the 1890s extols the benefits of a telephone compared with mail or the telegraph: *"The mail is quick. Telegraph is quicker; but long distance telephone is instantaneous and you don't have to wait for an answer."*

In 1877, Graham Bell, Gardiner Hubbard, and Thomas Sanders created the Bell Telephone Company. It licensed its telephone technology to privately owned exchanges. Over time, most of these licensed exchanges were bought up and owned by the Bell Company and eventually became known as the Bell System. To handle long-distance phone calls, a subsidiary company was set up in 1885 called American Telephone and Telegraph, or AT&T. AT&T and the Bell System became a monopoly over time and came under legal regulation by the U.S. Federal government. In 1907, AT&T president Theodore Vail wrote the company's annual report that government oversight "provided it is independent, intelligent, considerate, thorough and just . . ." would serve the public well.[28] He conceded the inevitable.

Alexander Bell is best known for his invention of the telephone. However, his interests led him to pursue a variety of inventions, including an airplane, a hydrofoil boat that could travel over 70 miles per hour, an artificial respiration machine that was an early version of the iron long, methods for removing salt from seawater, and a device called the *photophone,* which he used to transmit sound on beams of light for a distance exceeding 200 yards. He called this idea ". . . the greatest invention I have ever made; greater than the telephone."[29] Modern fiber optics are based on this concept. In 1881, Bell hastily created an electromagnetic metal detector to unsuccessfully locate an assassin's bullet lodged in President Garfield as he lay dying from his wounds. Notably, Bell was a devoted teacher and advocate for the deaf and became a mentor and friend of Helen Keller, the well-known disabilities activist.

Alexander Bell, much like Samuel Morse, set an early example for entrepreneurs and their new inventions. He accurately understood the importance of the telephone as it laid a foundation for electronic telecommunications in the twentieth century.

". . . the telephone would be a new factor in the new urbanization, without the telephone the 20th century metropolis would have been stunted by congestion and slowed to the primordial pace of messengers and postmen. And the modern industrial age would have been born with cerebral palsy."[30]

Table 4. The Telephone Revisited

Bell's original drawing of the telephone in 1876 demonstrates how his invention works.

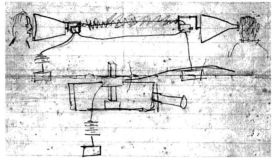

Figure 24. Bell's original drawing of the telephone, 1876. Library of Congress, Alexander Graham Bell Family Papers, Manuscript Division.

In early telephone exchanges, operators connect one caller to the next by manually patching their phone lines together. Boys are initially hired to do this job, as seen in this photograph of a central telephone office in 1879. Later, women are hired as operators because they are considered more dependable. Many women find careers outside the home for the first time working for the phone company.

Figure 25. Boys working as operators at a central exchange, 1879. Courtesy of AT&T Archives and History Center.

With one dedicated phone line assigned for each telephone, urban skyscapes become cluttered with wires, as seen in this photograph in New York City after the blizzard of 1888. As a result of this snowstorm, phone service is closed down from the months of March through May.

Figure 26. New York City, Snow Storm of 1888. Courtesy of AT&T Archives and History Center.

1880—The Blake Transmitter
Inventor Francis Blake greatly improves the quality of telephone transmissions through the use of carbon inserts.

Figure 27. The Blake Transmitter—1880. Courtesy of AT&T Archives and History Center.

1897—The Desk Set
One of the first phones for use on a desk is developed just before the turn of the century.

Figure 28. The Desk Set—1897. Courtesy of AT&T Archives and History Center.

1892—Alexander Graham Bell inaugurates the first long-distance telephone line between New York and Chicago.

Figure 29. Bell calls long distance from New York to Chicago, 1892. Alexander Graham Bell Family Papers. Library of Congress, Gilbert H. Grosvenor Collection, Prints and Photographs Division, LC-G9-Z228-608B.

Almon Strowger, an undertaker from Kansas City, invents the first automated phone exchange in 1891, which can automatically connect up to ninety-nine telephones, bypassing a human operator. His company later goes on to patent the first rotary dial phone in 1896, called the Strowger Automatic.

Figure 30. The Strowger Automatic telephone—circa 1905. Courtesy of AT&T Archives and History Center.

1919—A desk phone with a built-in rotary dialer, called the "Dial Candlestick." The transmitter and receiver are separate units.

Figure 31. Dial Candlestick phone—circa 1919. Courtesy of AT&T Archives and History Center.

1930—Desk set with a rotary dial known as the "French phone," where the receiver and transmitter were built into the same handset.

Figure 32. Desk phone with rotary dial—circa 1930. Courtesy of AT&T Archives and History Center.

1930—AT&T opens up transatlantic telephone connections via radio between New York and London. Only one call can be made at a time. The cost is exorbitant for 1930: $75 for the first three minutes. The first transpacific telephone service is opened in 1934, connecting the continental United States and Japan.

Figure 33. Transatlantic switchboard—1930. Courtesy of AT&T Archives and History Center.

1940—The six button multiple line rotary phone allows multiple phone connections to be accessed from one location.

Figure 34. Desk phone with rotary dial—circa 1940. Courtesy of AT&T Archives and History Center.

A radio-based mobile telephone is created by the Bell Telephone Company and first used in New York City police cars in 1924. Later, in 1946, commercial mobile telephone service is introduced in St. Louis, Missouri. This technology is the precursor to cell phones. In the adjacent photograph, a mobile radio phone user makes a call in Chicago.

Figure 35. Commercial mobile phone user, 1946. Courtesy of AT&T Archives and History Center.

1956—AT&T's first transatlantic telephone service via its new TAT-1 undersea cable begins on September 26, 1956. On the first day of commercial service, 600 calls were made between England and the United States. Sound quality is improved over wireless connections. Calls cost $12 for the first three minutes.

1964—Eight years later, the first undersea telephone cable is laid across the Pacific Ocean, linking the United States with Japan via Hawaii.

Figure 36. Installing the first transpacific telephone cable off the coast of Hawaii, 1964. Courtesy of AT&T Archives and History Center.

1962—AT&T and NASA launch *Telstar,* the first telecommunications satellite. As a result, in November 1963 the killing of Lee Harvey Oswald is broadcast to the world as it happens live in Dallas, Texas. In April 1965 the satellite *Early Bird* is launched, providing commercial telephone communication over the North Atlantic via satellite for the first time.

Figure 37. NASA and AT&T launch the first telecommunications satellite. Courtesy of AT&T Archives and History Center.

1968—Trimline twelve button Touch-Tone Telephone. The first AT&T Touch-Tone phone was released in 1963. In 1968, the # and * keys were added to access advanced services.

Figure 38. Trimline twelve button Touch-Tone phone—circa 1968. Courtesy of AT&T Archives and History Center.

During the twentieth century, communities around the world became connected by the telephone. As the century came to a close, telephones began to change from talking devices connected by wires to multipurpose handheld computers that communicate with each other over the airwaves using the binary language of 0s and 1s.

Entering the Wireless Era of Telephones

Wireless communication is not new. The Italian Inventor Gugliemo Marconi was able to demonstrate in the early 1900s that radio waves could transmit information over long distances without the use of wires if the transmitter and receiver were tuned to the same frequency. As early as 1901, Marconi sent radiotelegraph messages across the Atlantic Ocean. In 1912, the sinking passenger ship *Titanic* transmitted wireless distress signals in Morse code that were picked up in New York City, and the first live news reports of a major disaster at sea were communicated. Canadian-born inventor Reginald Fessenden successfully demonstrated the wireless broadcast of a human voice in 1900 and was able to set up the first two-way radio transatlantic voice communication in 1906.

A mobile radio-based telephone was invented by the Bell Telephone Company, where it was used in 1924 by the New York City Police Department for its squad cars. Wireless radio became standard for air traffic and marine communication. During World War II, portable two-way "walkie-talkie" radios were used effectively on the battlefield. The first commercial mobile telephone service was introduced in St. Louis in 1946.

Table 5. Wireless Communications—Key Concepts

1) **Electromagnetic waves** surround us every day, coming from many different sources. Some are visible, such as the light we see from the sun and light bulbs. Most of these waves aren't visible to the human eye, such as radio and television signals or cosmic rays from outer space. Electromagnetic waves travel at 186,000 miles a second.

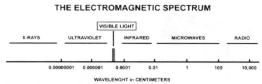

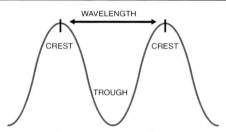

Figure 39. Illustration of the electromagnetic spectrum showing the visible range and the range outside of human perception, ultraviolet and infrared. Illustration by Kirsten Adams.

2) **Wavelength** is the distance between the peak of one wave to the peak of an adjacent wave. Radio waves are those wavelengths that are capable of transmitting information.

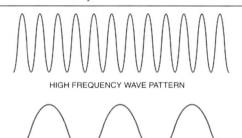

Figure 40. Illustration of an electromagnetic wave, showing measurement ticks between the peaks of two adjacent waves. Illustration by Kirsten Adams.

3) **Frequency** is the number of times per second that wave cycles repeat. Each cycle is described as a Hertz; multiple cycles are described as kHz (kilohertz or 1,000 Hertz), MHz (megahertz or 1 million Hertz), GHz (gigahertz or 1 billion Hertz), etc.

HIGH FREQUENCY WAVE PATTERN

LOW FREQUENCY WAVE PATTERN

Figure 41. Illustration of two wave patterns— one of higher and one of lower frequency. Illustration by Kirsten Adams.

4) **Tuning** occurs when a radio receiver is adjusted to accept the same signal frequency as a transmitter.

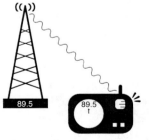

Figure 42. Illustration of a transmitter sending a frequency and a radio adjusted to receive that signal. Illustration by Kirsten Adams.

Figure 43. AT&T researcher Morgan Sparks views an early transistor from Bell Labs, a technology that later made possible personal computing and cell phones. Courtesy of AT&T Archives and History Center.

Table 6. Cell Phone Technology

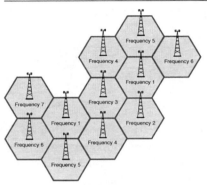

Figure 44. Cells are limited geographical areas containing towers that transmit and receive signals within a limited range of frequencies. Radio frequencies within one cell can be reused in other cells if they are out of each others' transmission range and don't overlap. Illustration by Kirsten Adams.

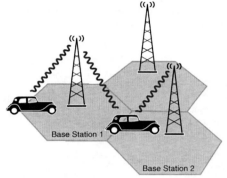

Figure 45. As a mobile phone user moves from one cell to the next, the original cell tower hands off the signal to the next one while changing the calling frequency. The phone signal may also be passed on to ground-based wired connections and switching stations. Illustration by Kirsten Adams.

In the late 1940s, two inventions came out of the Bell Research Labs that were destined to change telephones forever. One invention was the transistor, created by Bell Lab scientists John Bardeen, Walter Brattain, and William Shockley. The transistor was a small electronic device that eventually replaced the bulky and energy-inefficient radio tube. It later formed the fundamental electronic switching unit of the integrated chip, which made possible portable computing and digital cell phones. (See Chapter 6 for more information on integrated chips, microprocessors, and computing.)

The second idea came in December 1947, when Bell Laboratory scientist D.H. Ring and W.R. Young demonstrated a system of wireless telephone communication where geographical areas called "cells" enable callers on portable radio phones to connect to local transmitting and receiving towers. This idea became the basis for the later development of cell phones. The concept worked like this: A wireless telephone call takes place in a moving car as it moves between two geographical calling areas; the transmission towers *hand off* the connection from one cell's transmission tower to next. Each cell supports its own assigned frequencies within a limited range of coverage. As the mobile call moves from one cell transmission area to the next, it picks up a frequency supported by the new cell territory. This means that more phone calls can be handled within a wireless calling region, because frequencies can be reused as the mobile phone user moves to cells located further away from the original connection.

This approach had been considered for a time before the first implementation by Bell Labs in 1947, and was summarized by Federal Communications Commission (FCC) commissioner E.K. Jett in the *Saturday Evening Post* magazine in its July 28, 1945, issue: *"Thanks to this extremely limited reach, the same wave lengths may be employed simultaneously in thousands of zones in this country. Citizens in two towns only fifteen miles apart—or even less if the terrain is especially flat—will be able to send messages on the same lanes at the same time without getting in one another's way."*[31]

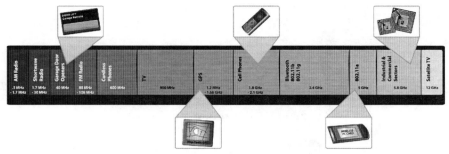

Figure 46. Chart showing the distribution of electromagnetic transmission frequencies. Illustration by Kirsten Adams.

When AT&T first proposed its cell phone idea to the FCC and asked for radio frequencies to support the device, it was turned down. The FCC considered the cell phone to be more of a walkie-talkie than a telephone and decided that the large number of callers using radio waves would be too difficult to regulate. There were also other commercial interests that didn't want to share the radio spectrum. They allowed only twenty-three call frequencies for each geographical area. Almost twenty years later, in 1966, the FCC finally agreed to open up a larger portion of the broadcast spectrum (airwaves) dedicated to cell phone use.

Surprisingly, the first working cell phone was developed by Motorola, not AT&T, and the man credited with inventing it was the General Manager of Systems, Dr. Martin Cooper. On April 3, 1973, Cooper's first phone call on Motorola's newly completed cell phone prototype was to his leading scientific competitor, Joel Engel, who was in charge of research at AT&T's Bell Labs. Cooper was walking on the streets of New York City amid a crowd of curious reporters when he made his call.

Cooper claims that it was an episode of *Star Trek* on TV that inspired him to move forward with the cell phone idea: "Suddenly there was Captain Kirk talking on his communicator. Talking! With no wires! . . . To the rest of the world it was a fantasy. To me it was an objective."[32] Ironically, in 2007 William Shatner, who played Captain Kirk in the first *Star Trek* television series, said of a later generation of cell phones supporting wireless video, "I think that this phone exceeds the imagination of *Star Trek* . . . This fact exceeds the fiction."[33]

By 1977, A&T had built the first operating prototype cell phone network and later initiated a trial with 2,000 early customers. Japanese commercial cell phone operations began in Tokyo in 1979, developed by the telecommunications company NTT. Motorola had a radio-based cell phone network in place by 1981. In 1983 the FCC approved the first mobile phone, The Motorola Dyna-Tac, which weighed 2.5 pounds. The earliest cell phones were installed in automobiles; they were heavy, awkward to handle, and cost around $3,000.

To get a big picture of how wireless cell phones and other portable devices operate, it's important to know about the role of the FCC in regulating how various electromagnetic frequencies are used. Without this regulation, every wireless electronic signal could potentially interfere with signals coming from other devices. After all, wireless technologies are used in garage door openers, radios, radio-controlled toys, televisions, traffic lights, kitchen appliances, DVD/VCR remote controllers, cardiac pacemakers, global positioning satellites, and countless other devices. To make sure that these wireless gadgets operate within their own domains of use, the FCC assigns specific electromagnetic frequencies to commercial and noncommercial interests. The airwaves legally belong to the citizens of the United States and are rented for broadcasting and communication purposes through an auction process.

The following diagram shows how the radio frequency spectrum is broken down. Much like rental properties in different neighborhoods, specific ranges of electromagnetic frequencies are assigned to work with a wide variety of wireless technologies.

A more detailed visual chart of the Federal Communication Commission's electromagnetic spectrum allocations can be found at http://www.ntia.doc.gov/osmhome/allochrt.pdf.

Another important change that took place in cell phone technology was the conversion from *analog* to *digital* messaging. Both Samuel Morse and Alexander Graham Bell made use of pulsed electrical waves travelling through metal wires. Bell's telephone was able to capture the wider range of frequencies generated by the human voice— vibrations of air were translated into electrical waves and then retranslated into audible sounds by a receiver. This kind of transmitted information is referred to as an *analog* signal. The output signal is closely married to the input

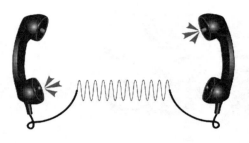

Figure 47. Illustration showing a traditional telephone translating speech into electronic waves and reconverting it to speech by a receiver. Illustration by Kirsten Adams.

Figure 48. Illustration showing the digital conversion of human speech by a cell phone into streams of binary 1s and 0s.

signal, such as film emulsion responding to the color and intensity of light, audio tape copying music onto a magnetically sensitive surface, mercury rising in a thermometer as the temperature increases. Analog is generally a *continuous representation of information.*

Digital is different. All forms of information input, whether music, video, photographs, text, graphics, or human speech, are translated into streams of digital bits, or 0s and 1s, so they can be used by a computer, handheld device, or telephone. In a digital cell phone, the human voice is converted to digital information by a modulator, which converts vibrating currents of air into 1s and 0s. These *bits* are transmitted over wireless or wired connections to a receiving phone, where a demodulator reconverts the digital information into spoken words. A digital signal is not continuous but consists of many discrete "samples" of the original voice sounds. Since all of the information is represented as 0s and 1s, the message can easily be stored, copied, or modified. Unlike analog, digital information can be copied many times without a loss of the original signal quality.

Digital Convergence and the Future of Cell Phones

On April 16, 2002, AT&T advertised the release of a new product, based on their earlier digital cell phone technology. They called it the *mMode.*

> *Suddenly you can do much more with a wireless phone than make or take a call. Thanks to mMode service, you can now us it to manage your life, entertain yourself, and connect in new ways to the people, information, and things you care about. Games, music, web sites, stock quotes, email, and much more.*[34]

The mMode looked just like a cell phone, but it could do much more than handle phone conversations. The cell telephone had morphed into a multimedia device, designed to provide real-time stock quotes, calendar entries, music, images, radar-based weather reports, text chat, email, Internet access, and other personalized services. This "telephone" now carried many of the features that up until then were associated with a computer. What made this possible?

First of all, the electronic components were much smaller than those in earlier computers and could be fit into a hand-sized console. The mMode had more processing power than the early mainframe computers of the 1950s and took up one tiny fraction of the space. Second, as mentioned earlier, the mMode was a *digital* device, capable of translating media of any type (visual, sound, text, or graphic) into a digital stream of 1s and 0s. In the analog era, each type of message, whether recorded on paper, video tape, audio tape, or film, required a separate method of recording and playback. Not so with digital information—all media types could be represented by the same binary language. The telephone had entered the era of digital convergence—*the delivery of text, graphics, video, voice, images, and data communication through a single media device, by means of a digital network.* Cell phones that demonstrate these advanced features are called *smartphones.*

Table 7. Cell Phone Terminology

Cell (as in cell phone)	A **cell** is a geographical area that makes use of a limited number of available frequencies to manage and distribute electronic messages. Because each connection requires its own frequency, only about 1,000 connections can be supported simultaneously by each cell. Two separate cells can make use of the same frequency as long as their transmission boundaries don't overlap.
Wi-Fi (Wireless Fidelity)	**Wi-Fi** is a generic trade name given to a family of wireless technologies used by home/commercial networks, computers, digital cameras, video game consoles, personal digital assistants (PDAs), cell phones, and other technologies. These devices operate within range of a "hotspot" or wireless transmitter/receiver that can cover a range as small as a single room; these access points provide connections to the Internet. Wi-Fi networks are used by families to interconnect personal computers, laptops, and entertainment devices, and Wi-Fi networks can be found in coffee shops, malls, banks, hotel lobbies, and schools. Generally these networks have a broadcast range of less than 150 feet. Wi-Fi is a universal wireless networking standard; currently, several varieties of Wi-Fi technology are in use: 802.11a—introduced in 1999. 802.11b—introduced in 1999. 802.11g—introduced in 2003. 802.11n—this protocol is the most recent, but is incomplete. It provides the fastest signal, widest coverage, and is the least vulnerable to interference from other frequencies. 802.16—introduces standards that will include wireless multimedia applications.
PCS (Personal Communications Service)	**PCS** is a Federal Communications Commission (FCC) description applied to wireless communications that (1) are all digital, (2) operate within the 800 MHz and 1900 MHz frequency range, (3) can be used internationally, and (4) contain functions that go beyond voice communication (text messaging, paging, etc.). PCS permits greater mobility for users.
Bluetooth	Bluetooth is a technology standard developed by Toshiba, Intel, Nokia, Ericsson, and IBM to allow short-range wireless connections between mobile phones, computers, and other devices to "talk" to each other when they come into close proximity.
GPS (Global Positioning Satellite)	**GPS** is a navigation system that allows electronic communications users to determine their exact position on land, sea, or air. There are twenty-four Global Positioning Satellites that are in stationary orbits 10,600 miles above the Earth. They pinpoint the location of a transmitted signal from the Earth and provide exact coordinates for that position. GPS capabilities are now being included as a feature of cell phone service and allow users to locate their own position within 100 meters.

One of the best examples of digital convergence on a smartphone arrived with the announcement of the iPhone by Apple Corporation on June 11, 2007. The iPhone pioneered a new touch screen interface that allows users to select menus, browse images, play videos, listen to music, connect to websites on the Internet, type emails with a visual keyboard display, access maps, and have phone conversations with one or more people simultaneously. The iPhone can share data with Apple and Windows-based computers. Steve Jobs, CEO of Apple, describes one of the most innovative characteristics of this modern "telephone" by saying, "The iPhone is bringing the Internet to a mobile device for the first time. For the first time you really do have the Internet in your pocket."[35]

On January 6, 2008, Bill Gates, CEO of Microsoft Corporation, addressed the Consumer Electronics Show in Las Vegas, Nevada. He described the transformation of computing and communications that began in the mid-1990s.[36]

"My first keynote was in 1994, a long time ago. That was a time when Windows 95 was just coming together, the Internet was just getting started, and it was within a few years of that that we entered the start of what we call the first digital decade. During that decade, the PC install base grew to over one billion machines. Broadband went from almost nothing to over 250 million users. Mobile phones achieved a penetration of over 40 percent of the people in the world. Digital photos moved from being a film-based activity to being something that's done through the power of software. And music went through that same transformation where today your ability to organize, and select, and communicate is driven fully by the power of software. *The trend here is clear, all media and entertainment will be software driven . . .*"

"The second digital decade will be more focused on connecting people. It will be more focused on being user-centric. Microsoft will deliver platforms that will let people build applications. Those applications will run not only on the PC, they'll run up in the Internet, or in the cloud, as we say, on the phone, in the car, in the TV . . . In fact, if you just pick up the device and authenticate who you are, then you'll connect up to your information. So when you get a new phone, or want to borrow a device it will be a very, very simple thing to be up and running in a strong way . . . The devices will know your context, they'll know your location."

The message is clear—from Microsoft's point of view, the Internet, telephone, computer, television, music (MP3) player, and video game console (Xbox 360) will all operate seamlessly with one another, delivering a wide variety of multimedia experiences. Each user will draw from a "cloud" of available information appearing on a number of delivery platforms and from the wireless Internet. The telephone is no longer just a specialized device for voice communications but is now integrated into a larger personalized digital communications network. The cell phone, that tiny descendant of Alexander Graham Bell's "grand machine," has become a flexible, all purpose information resource manager, personal entertainment device, and networking hub. Voice communication is now just one part of a wider mix of digital services and features, wrapped into the same container.

Endnotes

[1] John Maynard Smith, Eörs Szathmáry, *The Origins of Life: From the Birth of Life to the Origin of Language* (Oxford University Press, 1999), p. 149.

[2] Paul Ekman, Paul Ekman Publishing Abstracts, http://mambo.ucsc.edu/psl/ekman.html.

[3] Drum Telegraphy, *Time Magazine,* September 21, 1942, http://www.time.com/time/magazine/article/0,9171,773609,00.html

[4] World Adam J. Silverstein, *Postal Systems in the Pre-Islamic World* (Cambridge University Press, 1983), Introduction.

[5] Alexander Marshack, *The Roots of Civilization: The Cognitive Beginnings of Man's First Art, Symbol and Notation* (London: Moyer Bell Ltd., 1991).

[6] Joseph Campbell, *Way of the Animal Powers* (New York: Harper and Row, 1983). pp. 61–66.

[7] Jean-François Champollion, Letter to M. Dacier, September 27, 1822.

[8] *Phaedrus by Plato,* Translated by Benjamin Jowett, http://classics.mit.edu/Plato/phaedrus.html.

[9] Ibid.

[10] Jon Bentley, *Programming Pearls,* second edition (Boston: Addison-Wesley Professional, 1999), pp. 47–48.

[11] Team Mainz Gutenberg, *Gutenberg's unknown brothers: Early Chinese Painting,* Gutenberg.de, http://www.gutenberg.de/english/erfindu2.htm.

[12] W.E.H. Lecky, *History of the Rise and Influence of the Spirit of Nationalism in Europe* (London, 1913), p. 259. Originally found in Empire and Communications by Harold Innis, p. 145.

[13] Neil Postman, *Amusing Ourselves to Death*, Penguin Group (USA), Non-classics: 2005), p. 41.

[14] Alexandre Dumas, *The Count of Monte Christo,* Chapter 60: The Telegraph. Translated version available at http://www.literature.org/authors/dumas-alexandre/the-count-of-monte-cristo/chapter-60.html.

[15] Harold Innis, *Empire and Communications*, Victoria, Press Porcepic, 1986), p. 5.

[16] Tom Standage, *The Victorian Internet* (New York: Berkley Books, 1998), p. 1.

[17] Ibid, pp. 26–29.

[18] Ibid, p. 58.

[19] Ibid, pp. 170–171.

[20] John Steele Gordon, excerpted from an interview in *The Great Transatlantic Cable,* PBS website, http://www.pbs.org/wgbh/amex/cable/sfeature/sf_excerpts.html.

[21]Ibid, Gillian Cookson.

[22]Lewis Coe, *The Telegraph: A History of Morse's Invention and Its Predecessors in the United States,* (Jefferson, North Carolina, McFarland, 2003), pp. 37–38.

[23]John Brooks, *Telephone: The First Hundred Years* (New York: Harper and Row Publishers, 1975), p. 49.

[24]John Bray, *Innovations and Communications Revolution: From the Victorian Pioneers to Broadband Internet* (Tanzania, IET, 2002), p. 47.

[25]Ibid, p. 47.

[26]Bruce Sterling, *The Hacker Crackdown: Law and Disorder on the Electronic Frontier,* http://www.chriswaltrip.com/sterling/crack1b.html.

[27]Brooks, p. 51.

[28]*History of AT&T,* 2008, AT&T website, http://www.att.com/history/index.html.

[29]Mary Bellis, *Alexander Graham Bell—Biography,* 2008, http://inventors.about.com/library/inventors/bltelephone2.htm.

[30]Bray, p. 47.

[31]Tom Farley, *Mobile Telephone History,* http://www.privateline.com/PCS/history5.htm.

[32]Lance Laytner, *Star Trek Tech,* Edit International, 2007, http://www.calgarysun.com/cgi-bin/publish.cgi?p=177924&s=showbiz&x=articles

[33]Steve Tilley, VideoPhone Has Kirk Beamin', *The Calgary Sun,* April 3, 2007, http://www.calgarysun.com/cgi-bin/publish.cgi?p=177924&s=showbiz&x=articles.

[34]AT&T, mMode advertisement copy, *The Seattle Times,* April 16, 2002, p. A6.

[35]Steve Jobs, Apple Town Hall, Cupertino, CA. March 6, 2008. QuickTime video available at http://www.apple.com/quicktime/qtv/iphoneroadmap/.

[36]Bill Gates, keynote address at the Consumer Electronics Show, January 6, 2008, Las Vegas, http://www.cesweb.org/docs/01062008_CES_Bill_Gates-transcript.doc.

Chapter 4
The Labyrinth: A Nostalgic Look at the Future

"In the darkest days of the Depression, they dreamed of orderly hygienic cities and houses. . . .
They looked ahead to safe, fast travel on luxurious streamlined aircraft, trains, buses, ships, and automobiles. Unlike modern architects, whose utopias rarely develop beyond the drawing stage, the first American industrial designers were able to build their model city, the 1939 New York World's Fair."[1]

Donald J. Bush, *The Streamlined Decade*

"You notice the indoor swimming pool and garden, the private heliport, the way your home of tomorrow rotates to take advantage of the sun. You marvel at the slip-proof bathroom, wall to wall television and flick-of-the switch windows . . .
"We'll work shorter hours," your mysterious guide continues. "We'll have more time for art, sports and hobbies. Some of us will fly; some drive our air cars. But most of us will use rapid transit jet-propelled monorail systems . . . Executives of the next century will earn a minimum of twelve thousand dollars a year for a twenty-four hour work week," you are told.[2]

From Official Souvenir Program, Seattle 1962 World's Fair

"Does it have a radar controlled supersonic, neutronic fission freezer?"

From Official Souvenir Program, Seattle 1962 World's Fair

The point of this chapter is to show how World's Fairs have always been the gathering point for societies to imagine their futures and dream about how their lives will change based on present possibilities. As you'll see, early on many of these visions were created and controlled by corporations, such as General Motors' Futurama exhibit in both 1939 and 1964, which largely saw a future with freeways and an abundance of cars, taking us wherever we want to go. That previsioning largely came true!

"What's good for the country is good for General Motors, and vice versa," is supposedly a statement made by Charles E. Wilson when he was president of GM (Wilson later became secretary of the federal Department of Defense).[3] In other words, the future the corporations presented was probably very close to the future we were going to get. And technology was seen as a very positive tool in which to arrive at this one-to-many future. First World's Fairs and later television (in the form of shows like *Disneyland*) touted the idea of what our future would be. There were, of course, others who had ideas about the future—science fiction writers and those who would later be called "futurists." But books could never reach as many people as the newsreels about World's Fairs or Disney's television shows about the future of space travel. Now, with the Internet, this has changed dramatically. Our views on the future may no longer be the utopian visions of Hugo Gernsback or of General Motors. But they may just be more realistic and, perhaps, more environmentally and people friendly.

World's *Fair?*

Long before the advent of interactive media and the World Wide Web, World's Fairs and Expositions were created to be showplaces for marvels of the new Industrial Age. The fairs held in the United States and abroad in the nineteenth and twentieth centuries celebrated the past while introducing visions of the future. Both the past and the

51

future were highly idealized, almost utopian. The World's Columbian Exposition held in Chicago in 1893 presented what Catholic World proclaimed was a "city of realized dreams."

The World's Columbian Exposition of 1893 exhibited the marvels of the next century for all to see. Presumably a celebration of the 400th anniversary of Columbus' landing in the New World, this White City of the future was really a showpiece for American ingenuity and invention—the apex of the era that Twain had named "The Gilded Age." It was perhaps the first time that the technology that would eventually evolve into multimedia was shown to vast audiences in one particular location.

From demonstrations of long-distance telephone calls to Thomas Edison's Kinetoscopes heralding the birth of motion pictures and live orchestra music transmitted over wires from New York City, the public could view all the marvels the coming century had to offer, including Elisha Gray's wondrous *teleautograph*, a device that transmitted facsimile writing and drawings, the first fax machine.[4]

Not long before the Fair opened, in the spring of 1893, the inventor Nikola Tesla, long an unsung hero of our electronic century, made the first public demonstration of radio communication in St. Louis. Invited personally by George Westinghouse, it was Tesla who presided over exhibits in the Palace of Electricity at the Chicago Fair.[5]

What neither the purveyors of the Fair nor the inventors could foresee, let alone exhibit, was how these new technologies would affect people's views not only of the world, but also of "reality." Exhibits can show you how you might have a "home projected kinetoscope" in your house in thirty years, present teleautographs or "picturephones," but they never touch on what the economic, sociological, and political effects of new technology might be. The problem with the World's Fairs of the late nineteenth and early twentieth centuries was that their future predictions usually took the morals and etiquette of the "present," be it 1893 or 1939, and propelled them into 1900 or 1960. Few realized that new technology would not only change etiquette but would, by its very nature, make it necessary to invent new etiquette.

Beginning with the 1893 Exposition, the World's Fairs "promoted globalization, world trade, and a national identity that supported overseas expansion."[6] The fairs contrasted the "progress" and "civilization" the United States had created with peoples who were considered savage or primitive, whether from other continents or on the Indian reservations the government provided to those indigenous people conquered during the nineteenth century, the Native Americans. These people and their "quaint" villages, dances, and culture were displayed at the fairs, often in the midway or amusement park areas.

Discussing the 1893 Exposition, Frederick Douglass stated that "the spirit of American caste made itself conspicuously felt against the educated American Negro, and to this extent, the Exposition was made simply an American Exposition and that is one of America's most illiberal features."[7]

That the 1893 Fair's utopian façade was called "The White City" is an irony probably all but lost on the people who created the fair. For a while, the visage of "The White City" would appear often, in the drawing of Winsor McKay and the great dream cities of his Little Nemo, to the very gates of neoclassical Emerald City as imagined by illustrators W.W. Denslow and John R. Neill.

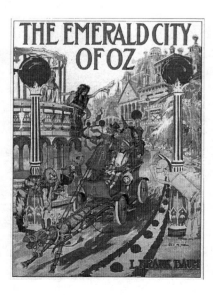

Figure 1. *Emerald City of Oz*. Frank Baum, book cover.

Figure 2. White City, Chicago Exposition, 1893. Library of Congress, Prints and Photographs, LC-USZ62-116999.

Another example of the unfairness of these "fairs" involves the famous African American ragtime pianist, Scott Joplin. His music publisher begged officials of the 1904 Louisiana Purchase Exposition in St. Louis ("Meet Me In St. Louis, Louis; Meet Me At the Fair," the song went) to let Joplin perform. Finally, Joplin was given a tiny stage to perform on—right next to the large stage upon which John Philip Sousa and his orchestra blared their loud compositions, all but drowning out Joplin's piano.

At this same Exposition, the Philippines exhibit was the largest and most popular midway attraction. Decorated with American flags, it celebrated the newly consolidated empire, displaying, in the words of a contemporary review, "savages made by American methods into civilized workers."[8]

"The Fair had also plundered the sculpture and art work of numerous 'primitive peoples,' from the Apache to various indigenous peoples of the Philippines and Puerto Rico to be shown to the more 'civilized' whites attending the exhibition."[9]

As late as 1939, at the New York World's Fair, "colored" jitterbuggers were put on display for the amusement of white crowds. Although these fairs pointed to the future, they also said a great deal about the "present" and the past of Manifest Destiny.

But the 1939 New York World's Fair was the first major exposition whose very theme was "The World of Tomorrow."

"The eyes of the Fair are on the future—not in the sense of peering toward the unknown nor attempting to foretell the events of tomorrow and the shape of things to come, but in the sense of presenting a new and clearer view of today in preparation for tomorrow; a view of the forces and ideas that prevail as well as the machines.

"To its visitors the Fair will say: 'Here are the materials, ideas, and forces at work in our world. These are the tools with which the World of Tomorrow must be made. They are all interesting and much effort has been expended to lay them before you in an interesting way. Familiarity with today is the best preparation for the future.'"

Official New York World's Fair pamphlet

Exhibits included the Westinghouse Time Capsule (not to be opened for 5,000 years), futuristic teardrop-shaped cars, nylon fabric, streamlined devices from pencil sharpeners to hair dryers, and a group of television sets in the RCA Exhibit. In fact, the fair was the first exposition to be shot by huge television cameras when President Franklin Roosevelt declared it "open to all mankind."

One of the most talked about exhibits was General Motors' Futurama. A ride designed by industrial designer Norman Bel Geddes, the Futurama attempted to show the landscape of America in that far off future of 1960.

Figure 3. Futurama Pavilion: 1939, Harry Ransom Humanities Research Center, The University of Texas at Austin and © Estate of Margaret Bourke-White/Licensed by VAGA, New York, NY.

Figure 4. Westinghouse ad of the *Middletons.* Courtesy of Westinghouse Electric Corporation.

Although highways were automated and cars radio controlled in the '39 Futurama, the exhibit did get the clover-leafed, six-lane superhighways correct as well as the suburbs.

Interestingly, "Futurama had green spaces and amusement parks but no churches, something the pious noted immediately. By the time the fair closed in 1940, hundreds of steeples had sprung from the glittering cities and tree-shaded countryside."[10]

Leaving the Futurama, people were handed a button that said "I Have Seen The Future." In some ways, they had.

In the Westinghouse Pavilion, according to a publicity film made by the company, the Middleton family spent their entire time at the fair, it seems, gazing in wonder at a time capsule to be buried for 5,000 years (the planners of the pavilion were nothing if not optimistic), futuristic kitchens with dish washers, Elektro the Motoman and his dog Sparko, and of course, television.

The idea of a device, a radio with images, that could allow millions of Americans to see dramas, comedies, and distant places, was something many Americans eyed with wonder. The television was seen as a device that could educate as well as entertain. Some rather wealthy New Yorkers did purchase television sets, but they would remain silent, their screens blank, until World War II ended.

In the meantime, visitors to the Fair could shoot home movies with 16 mm Kodak color film. By the time of the next New York fair, in 1964, most had 8 mm home movie cameras. Home video cameras were, of course, another twenty years away.

Disneyland

"Disneyland will never be completed, as long as there is imagination left in the world." Walt Disney, July 18, 1955, at the opening of Disneyland.

What has been called the capstone to Walt Disney's career, Disneyland, opened on a sweltering day in July of 1955. Many of the rides were unfinished, and it was so hot that some of the streets of Main Street and other parts of the park had literally begun to melt. In the meantime, once water was pumped into the various "streams," "rivers," and other bodies of water in the park, they almost immediately ran dry and had to be rebottomed with clay to hold the moisture.[11]

But Disneyland became a huge success—*the* place to go for children around the nation—helped in no small measure by the television show *Disneyland* that had premiered in the fall of 1954. Disneyland was truly the vision of one individual, at least at first. As Richard Schickel wrote in his 1968 book *The Disney Version:*

"If not quite an extension of man, in the McLuhanesque sense of the term, then surely an extension of *a* man in the way that the pleasant grounds of Versailles were an extension of the Sun King. It [had] none of the discreet impersonality of, say, Rockefeller Center [or the 1939 New York World's Fair, for that matter—mk]. It was . . . a statement containing, in general and in particular, conscious expressions of everything that was important to Disney, unconscious expressions of everything that had shaped his personality and of a good many things that had, for good and ill, shaped all of us who are Americans born of [the twentieth century]."[12]

The opening of the park was televised and the park itself continued to be promoted by the successful television show *Disneyland* (which divided its telecasts into the same areas as the park: Frontier Land, Adventure Land, Fantasy Land, and Tomorrowland).

For our purposes, we'd like to take a look at Tomorrowland—or at least the Tomorrowland of the early days of Disneyland, as well as some of the technology the Disney "Imagineers" (as they were called) used to bring people and creatures of all types to life.

"Tomorrow can be a wonderful age. Our scientists today are opening the doors of the Space Age to achievements that will benefit our children and generations to come. The Tomorrowland attractions have been designed to give you an opportunity to participate in adventures that are a living blueprint of our future."

Walt Disney's opening dedication to Tomorrowland, 1955

Like the World's Fairs that preceded it, Tomorrowland showed a somewhat corporate future, planned and watched over by the benign Disney himself and, er, um, Wernher von Braun. Yes, that's right. The brilliant scientist who led a team of Nazis to create the V-2 rocket that would rain death on Great Britain (and be the prototype of the Saturn V that would take Americans to the moon) became one of Disney's main Imagineers. It had been the science fiction novels of Jules Verne that had initially inspired von Braun. Even while designing the V-2 rocket, von Braun "also dreamed of developing vehicles that would propel artificial satellites and men into outer space. In fact, his interest in developing rockets for space exploration, rather than for defense, angered the Gestapo and led to two weeks in a German prison."[13]

Disney became aware of von Braun's visions for the future when the scientist wrote a series of articles for *Collier's* magazine about space travel being accomplished in the near future. Aided by the vivid and beautifully realistic artwork of Chesley Bonestell, an illustrator and painter for both science fact and science fiction books and magazines, the articles excited *Collier's* 4 million readers.

"Even so, there were already more than 15 million television sets in America by 1952 and von Braun recognized that this change in American culture had the potential to fundamentally reshape American past perceptions."[14] So did Walter Elias Disney, who had used film as a powerful medium to entertain and inform Americans since the 1940s. "Neither Walt Disney nor Dr. von Braun were ever backward in making maximum use of new media for advancing their ideas: Now was the age of television," said one observer.[15]

According to Mike Wright in his article "The Disney-Von Braun Collaboration and Its Influence on Space Exploration," "Von Braun served as technical advisor on three space-related television films that Disney produced in the 1950s. Together, von Braun (the engineer) and Disney (the artist) used the new medium of television to illustrate how high man might fly on the strength of technology and the spirit of human imagination . . . The *Collier's* series had appeared about the time that Disney decided to use television to promote Disneyland in California . . . Disney producers would incorporate ideas from Disney fantasy films like *Snow White, Pinocchio,* and others to promote the first area of the park. The second and third areas would be built around *Davy Crockett* and other adventure films. Tomorrowland, however, represented a real challenge. In response, [Ward Kimball at Disney] contacted von Braun who, according to Smith, 'pounced on the opportunity' . . . [von Bruan] later called the [television episode "Man Into Space" on *Disneyland*] 'science factual.' The show[s] represented something new in [their] approach to science. But [they] also relied on Disney's trademark animation techniques."[16]

These episodes of "Disneyland" also advertised Disneyland the park, particularly Tomorrowland and its various space rides.

In fact, the same men who served as technical advisors to the Tomorrowland episodes on the show, including Wernher von Braun, Willy Ley, and Heinz Haber, also served as consultants on the original design of the park's Tomorrowland.[17] Thus, one of the first attractions to open at the park was the Rocket to the Moon ride. The ride was sponsored by TWA.

> "Peace and unity are no small goal for a theme park, but Walt was never one for thinking small. Tomorrowland was his kingdom's attempt to predict which unbelievable technologies would make our lives better. Back in 1955, that looked like freeways and monorails and plastic houses and men on Mars—a vision that was played out over the years through rides like the PeopleMover (a snail-like tram), the Flying Saucers ride (essentially, bumper cars held up by air), multiple Autopia rides (even kids can drive a car!) and a ceaseless stream of 360-degree CircleVision movies that took you to the Moon, into atoms, out to Mars."[18]

Then there was the Monsanto House of the Future, "an oddly shaped house in which everything was made of synthetic materials. The plastic was so strong that workers had to use hacksaws to break it down when it was retired in 1967"[19]—the same year that Dustin Hoffman in *The Graduate* was told that the future lay, in one word, "plastics."[20] Some say that the house was so strong that the wrecking ball hit it and bounced off. 1967 became the year for the "New Tomorrowland". This part of Disneyland was again remodeled in 1998 when its focus actually changed to a "retro-future" theme park that reminded many of the illustrations of Albert Robida.

Still in "retro" mode, Finding Nemo Submarine Voyage opened on June 11, 2007. It resurrected the original Nemo Submarine Voyage, which closed in 1998.

Back in 1997, Seth Schiesel in his *New York Times* article "Once Visionary, Disney Calls Future a Thing of the Past" wrote:

> "There is a place here where the future looks old. It is called Tomorrowland, and it is part of Walt Disney World, the most popular tourist destination on Earth.

> "When the Walt Disney Company decided to give Tomorrowland a makeover in 1995, it went retro."

Visitors to Tomorrowland's main drag, the Avenue of Planets, stroll not through some asphalt version of the information superhighway, but through a green, gray and purple canyon of neon, oversized bolts and swooping arches of anodized steel—an antique remake of *The Jetsons*.

"The new Tomorrowland begins with Jules Verne and ends with Buck Rogers," said Beth Dunlop, a Florida architecture critic who recently released a company-approved book on Disney architecture.

"Tomorrowland is hardly alone. The future is growing old all over Disney's magic kingdom. From the film lot to the Epcot theme park to the real-life town that the company calls Celebration, Disney has largely given up on imagining a new future. When a story line or ride design calls for a touch of times to come, it is usually, as posters for the new Tomorrowland boast, 'the future that never was.'"[21]

Disneyland during its first fifteen or so years of operation was always immaculate with staff that was always pleasant and, for lack of better terms, incredibly white and incredibly Christian. In fact, the way the staff is described by Schickel in his 1968 book sounds like they could have stepped straight out of Gibson's "Gernsback Continuum":

> "The staff is as well scrubbed as the grounds and is so polite and well mannered that, by the end of the day a visitor's face muscles begin to ache from the effort of returning so many smiles and murmuring so many return pleasantries . . . The girls are generally blonde, blue-eyed and self-effacing, all looking as if they stepped out of an ad for California sportswear and are heading for suburban motherhood. The boys, who pilot vehicles and help you on and off rides, are outdoorsy, All-American types, the kind of vacuously pleasant lad your mother was always telling you to imitate."[22]

Schickel goes on to write, "The aim of the staff is to keep everyone in a spending mood without ever once overtly suggesting that Disneyland is, in the last analysis, hardly a charitable enterprise. The trick is not to harass the visitor into spending but rather to relax him to the point where the inner guardians of his frugality are lulled into semiconsciousness."[23]

Throughout the late 1960s, the park had a policy of not allowing "long-hairs" in (high school and college aged males would tuck their hair into baseball caps or tie their hair in pony tails and attempt to hide it in the back of their shirts).[24]

Again, the "fruitiness" that Gibson writes about in his short story was almost palpable.

In her article "Who Stole Tomorrowland's Soul?" Janelle Brown writes, "The new Tomorrowland attractions certainly seem nostalgic for the old Tomorrowland. The new Redd Rockett's Pizza Port restaurant—a pizza joint designed to look like an intergalactic diner—displays a series of old Tomorrowland posters, and the giant white-and-red rocket that stands in the middle of Tomorrowland's plaza is a more modern replica of the original rocket that stood over Tomorrowland in 1955 (today, it serves up Coca-Cola). The entrance to the flashy roller coaster Rocket Rods, which zooms you in open cars over the main Tomorrowland plaza, is the old CircleVision theater, which once played dioramic movies about America. Now, it shows an old black-and-white movie of Walt Disney talking about freeways, intercut with spaceship animations."[25]

Brown goes on to write, "Several old Tomorrowland rides have been echoed as well. The new 3-D movie *Honey, I Shrunk the Audience,* which inflicts viewers with animal sneezes and eye-popping effects based on the irritating movie series, is simply a snazzier version of a '50s classic and past Disneyland feature, the 3-D movie. The gold and green and purple Astro Orbitor ride, which looms over the entrance to Tomorrowland and lets kids ride personal 'rockets' attached to arms that rotate around a pole, is a rehash of an old Tomorrowland classic—the Rocket Jets.

"Even pieces of old rides have been recycled: an old PeopleMover tram and an outdated Monorail car have been repainted in blue and fluorescent pink and stuck under a black light in the Rocket Rod entrance.

"Martin Sklar, one of the original Imagineers, sums up the difficulties with transforming Tomorrowland: 'Disneyland is hard to change because there's a continuity here that doesn't exist in our everyday lives,' he says. 'This place means a lot to a lot of people. When we find things to anchor to, we don't like them to change.'"[26]

During the first five or six years of its opening, Disneyland was advertised not only on the *Disneyland* television program or at travel agencies, but also anywhere the American consumer might find himself or herself, particularly at Christmas time.

I remember being perhaps five years old and being taken with my older brother by our mother to Best and Company, a large department store in New York City (eventually torn down and replaced by the Trump Tower). Best had a section of the store that had been made into a "mini-Disneyland." Most importantly, it was essentially a mini Fantasyland and mini Tomorrowland. There was a smaller version of the Rocket To The Moon where I was seated next to my brother in the interior of a space ship bathed in green light. A narrator told us to strap ourselves in, and we blasted off (the rocket moved—a precursor of VR rides of the 1990s) and in front of us was a large view screen. My memory may be playing tricks, but I seem to remember passing the moon and actually seeing Saturn. Mainly, I remember my brother's profile bathed in that eerie light. The ride couldn't have lasted more than a few minutes, but I was filled with what I would later come to know as the "sense of wonder" all great science fiction and science fantasy aspires to create.

After leaving the space ship, my brother and I were put aboard a miniature train with Mickey Mouse as the engineer. Well, not Mickey himself, but a girl (which I found out to my chagrin when Mickey's giant head turned and a sweet feminine voice came from inside asking us not to lean out of the train cars). The train rode in a circle, passing through a tunnel filled with—color television sets! That's right. RCA color televisions were displayed, swirling colors on most of their screens, although on a few I could make out what seemed to be a battle from one of the *Davey Crocket* episodes.

When we left, my mother purchased a Captain Hook sword for my brother (Captain Hook, not the wussy Peter Pan, was his hero), two Disney character hand puppets (with feet, I remember—very odd), and miniature Disney characters called "Disneykins." They must be worth a fortune now. I wish we still had them. And the main point wasn't lost on us—we both begged our parents to fly us, not to California, but to "Disneyland" (alas, my family honestly didn't have the money, and I first saw the "Magic Kingdom" on a drizzly February day in 1979—and, I hate to admit it, I loved every minute of it).

Welcome to the 1962 Seattle World's Fair

Spread across the fair's site is a glittering world of the future, an animated jewel mined from the intellect and creativity of scientists, artists and men of vision. Visitors of all ages and interests will find something to amuse and entertain, to stimulate and challenge them in this panorama of tomorrow dedicated to man in the space age. Rising six hundred feet above the grounds is the Space Needle, symbolizing the fair's thrust into the new frontier of space.

The world of Science is embodied in the United States Science Pavilion, a complex of buildings at the south end of the grounds, and in the nearby National Aeronautics and Space Administration Pavilion. The visitor passes through five areas in the Science Pavilion, including the House of Science, the Development of Science, the Spacearium, in which he takes a simulated rocket ride through space, the Methods of Science, and the Horizons of Science, which dramatizes the role of science in the world of tomorrow.

The World of Century 21 awaits in the Washington State Coliseum, at the west entrance to the grounds. The building encloses the state's theme show, a dramatic concept of the 21st century man's environment presented in a unique cube structure rising above the Coliseum floor. On the floor level are industrial and government exhibits, all contributing to the image of the future. These are but the foundations of the exposition. On them rises the most stimulating world's fair ever staged, dedicated to the future and designed to provide insight to tomorrow.[27]

Official Souvenir Program, Seattle 1962 World's Fair

In 1962, however, another American World's Fair once again held out the promise of American media in the future. Seattle's Twenty-first Century Exposition featured the Bubblelator, a plexiglass-covered elevator in the Washington State Pavilion that raised audiences into the next century, via pictures, films, and models that flashed on in succession:

"And how will our descendants learn? The artists' images show schools where television and electronic teaching machines assist human instructors; libraries whose books have been digested by computers and whose readers may order, electronically, sections from any author on a pertinent subject."[28]

According to the exhibits, business offices would use audio-visual communications systems in the next century and there would be home computers as well. There would also be electric sinks, which frankly sounded really dangerous.

"Suddenly, through the soft blue light of springtime, you see a circle shaped city of Century 21. Beams from the city's jetport searchlights probe the skyline's slender fingers. Then comes a burst of yellow-golden summer sunlight and a home unlike any other you have seen appears. You notice the indoor swimming pool and garden, the private heliport, the way your home of tomorrow rotates to take advantage of the sun. You marvel at the slip-proof bathroom, wall to wall television and flick-of-the switch windows."

"Does it have a radar controlled supersonic, neutronic fission freezer?" It is a woman's voice.

"I'm not wise enough to predict all the inventions of tomorrow," comes the answer.

"But certainly you'll have undreamed of conveniences. Your kitchen will be a miracle of push-button efficiency. Your telephone will be cordless. You'll see who you are talking to. You'll change the interior colors of your home to suit your mood."

Instantly, the lighting of the home before you changes to create a new, equally attractive decor. Now you are in a rust-red world of autumn. A commuter's gyrocopter comes into view, its motor emitting hardly more than a purr. You gaze, fascinated, at cars with engines the size of a typewriter, planes that fly to any spot in the world in an hour's time, rocket belts that enable a man to stride thirty feet.

"We'll work shorter hours," your mysterious guide continues. "We'll have more time for art, sports and hobbies. Some of us will fly; some drive our air cars. But most of us will use rapid transit jet-propelled monorail systems."

The scene changes to reveal an office of tomorrow, its computers producing a metallic cacophony of sound. Automatic door openers, self-correcting office machines and TV telephones are as commonplace as today's typewriter.

"Executives of the next century will earn a minimum of twelve thousand dollars a year for a twenty-four hour work week," you are told.[29]

Official Souvenir Program, Seattle 1962 World's Fair

It sounded very much like futuristic cartoon family, *The Jetsons,* whose television show premiered September 23, 1962.

The U.S. Science Pavilion boasted two major media exhibits, both using motion picture technology. The first was the Boeing Spacearium, which projected thirty-five millimeter film images onto a dome-surface screen.

The second exhibit was designed by Charles Eames and dealt with the history of science. He mechanically synchronized seven 35 mm projectors together so that they ran simultaneously, creating one of the first multi-image theater installations.[30]

Some of the fantastic communications services which may be yours in the 21st century can be seen at the Bell System exhibit at Seattle World's Fair. In the main rotunda, visitors will thrill to a demonstration of communications by satellites in orbit around the earth.

Other exhibits dramatically depict present and future communications for business, industry and the home. For example, you'll see machines "talking" to machines and future design telephones such as the picture phone, which one day may make it possible to display books, clothing, groceries and even art treasures in your home.

The next forty years will see astonishing advances over those made by the communications industry in the last eighty-five. But plans for tomorrow, "far out" as they may sound, are inextricably tied to the fantastic network of circuits and switches which now guide your voice wherever you wish to send it.[31]

Official Souvenir Program, Seattle 1962 World's Fair

The fair closed on October 21, 1962, in the middle of the Cuban Missile Crisis.

The same year as the Seattle fair, AT&T and NASA launched the Telstar I communications satellite. Arthur C. Clarke had predicted communications satellites in detail back in 1945; now his prediction had come true.

As already noted in Chapter 2, Marshall McLuhan's 1963 book *Understanding Media* touted, new ideas about electronic media In *Understanding Media,* McLuhan coined the phrase "Global Village," stating that the new media were reordering man's senses, weaning him from the age-old habit of collecting information "linearly" from the printed page. With television and the media of the future, an electronic culture would be created: an electronic tribal culture without bounds.**

During the same period, television began to enter the classroom in earnest as a teaching tool to augment lectures and rote learning. In business and research, people referred more and more to "information retrieval." It seemed to some as if our news, information, and history would soon be coming to us via television or computers. It was not just coincidence that the mid-1960s saw the death of a myriad of newspapers and magazines (see Chapter 2 Timeline).

And yet, in November of 1963, television was able to bring the American people together in a way no one could have predicted at any of the past World's Fairs. With the assassination of President Kennedy, Americans learned, for the first time instantaneously, of a calamitous event. For four days, Americans watched as the accused assassin was caught, the president's body was brought back to Washington, DC, from Dallas, and the funeral took place. ABC news also broadcast a first that horrible weekend: the live murder of accused assassin Lee Harvey Oswald by Jack Ruby. America, and television, would never be the same.

The year 1964 was the first year of New York's second World's Fair of the century. The theme of the Fair was "Peace Through Understanding," and its symbol, the Universe, a great steel globe that showed three satellites hurtling around it, had been constructed by US Steel. It stood on the same spot as 1939's Trylon and Perisphere (both taken down for the steel needed during World War II). More a showplace for products and corporations than international understanding, the fair did give glimpses into both new technology and new communications media and how they might eventually affect us. The Johnson Wax Pavilion used three screens to show the film *To Be Alive,* an eighteen-minute piece depicting, as the fair catalog put it, "the joys of living shared by all people."[32] Scenes of children at play in Africa, North and South America, and a variety of other regions were shown at the same time

---

** Jerry Mander, in his book In The Absence of the Sacred, noted eloquently that McLuhan was, in effect, saying that the mere existence of new media, of television "causes society to be organized in new ways. As information is moved through different channels its character and its content change; political relationships, concepts, and styles change as well. Even the human spirit and body change." 40

via split-screen effects. (Such imagery would be used thirty years later by Watts-Silverstein and Associates for their CD ROM highlighting families and cultures from around the world.)[33] Across the Avenue of Commerce, The IBM building housed a 500-seat "people wall" that rose into an egg shaped theater housing fifteen screens that showed "how computers and the human mind solve problems in much the same way."[34]

Interestingly, the Fair was not even an "official" World's Fair. The Seattle World's Fair of 1962 held that title (the next official Fair would be in Montreal, Canada). Without the official seal of the World's Fair commission, Robert Moses, president of the fair, took it upon himself to make the fair in his image. Although built on the site of the glorious 1939-40 World's Fair (the last prewar fair), the 1964 World's Fair showcased American Corporations over foreign nations and American technology over the idea of people of the world working together toward a common goal.

The opening of the fair itself was marred by protests. Civil rights leaders, angered at the fair's seeming ignorance of major social problems, organized protestors who attempted to tie up traffic into the fair ground.

Still, the exhibits at the World's Fair did showcase new technological frontiers: the Space Age, the Information Age of computers and communication, the Consumer Age of new materials and products for everyday life, and the Atomic Age of electricity "too cheap to meter." New "multimedia" presentations by companies such as IBM and Johnson Wax used entertainment technology in new ways. "The message was of optimism with little thought to environmental or sociological consequences. The purpose was to educate the public, particularly children of school age, who were thought to be far behind the Russians in mathematical and scientific skills. It was the age of Sputnik and Americans seemed to be just catching up."[35]

It was a time in America's history that the country was at the very crest of its postwar (World War II) technological and economic prowess. Americans were infatuated by the space program's goal of landing a man on the moon, intrigued by the promise of a computer and the information era and pursuing a nuclear power program to provide electricity "too cheap to meter."[36]

It was an era of giant mainframe computers sorting through punch cards containing information. At the Fair, computers were exhibited in abundance: from the National Cash Register Pavilion (where, for example, I chose my birth date and received a list of events that happened on that day—none were of particular interest to me) to Clairol's "hair color and style" computer, to the Parker Pen exhibited where a computer matched you up with a foreign pen pal (I met a nine year old girl from France—we stayed in touch for two years—a lifetime when you're young).

> **Mother:** "Today our whole downtown is completely enclosed. Whatever the weather is outside, it's always dry and comfortable inside."
> **Father:** "General Electric calls it a climate-controlled environment. But Mother calls it. . ."
> **Mother:** "A sparkling jewel. Now far off to your right, we have a welcome neighbor. . ."
> **Father:** "Our GE nuclear power plant, dear."
> **General Electric's "Carousel of Progress," presented by the Walt Disney Company**

As someone once said: "The future isn't what it used to be." The theme song of the General Electric pavilion was "There's a great big beautiful tomorrow / shining at the end of every day."

Figure 5. Unisphere and Rocket Thrower. Copyright New York World's Fair 1964/1965 Corporation.

Figure 6. Bell Telephone Picturephone. Courtesy of AT&T Archives and History Center.

The IBM Pavilion attempted to show that computers were not bent on world domination. Electronic puppet theaters showed Sherlock Holmes solve a problem only to reveal that he himself was a computer (the Watson puppet seemed less than thrilled).

The main presentation at IBM was its "People Wall" that moved people 500 viewers upwards into a great egg-shaped theater (that looked, not coincidentally, like the ball on the new IBM electric typewriters). In the theater a fifteen minute multimedia extravaganza by Charles Eames was shown, using 14 synchronized projectors and 9 screens which used the human brain as a metaphor to show how a computer obtains and processes information.

There was the ubiquitous Bell Telephone Picturephone as well as the Vocoder, a speech analyzer and synthesizer that had actually been around since the 1930s. The one true technology of the future was the touch tone phone. In fact, to officially mark the breaking of ground at the fair site, President Kennedy had used a touch-tone phone and the buttons 1-9-6-4. There was also a ride called "From Drumbeat to Telstar," which used one man in a series of short films acting as a guide to different communications devices.

By this time, television was a technology everyone either knew about or owned (they might even own two or three). So, at the RCA pavilion, the exhibit was of a color television studio. Within the next few years, the major television networks would broadcast all their new shows in color, which would have an enormous effect on the public's perception of the first televised war in Vietnam.

It seemed that the exhibitors at the Fair believed, along with McLuhan, that the globalization of instantaneous communications would truly make us one world (or the great Global Village McLuhan discussed) while computers and robotics (or, as it was called at the Fair, automation) would bring the prices of goods down and create a lot more leisure time (one question many Pavilions at the Fair asked: how were we going to deal with only a three day work week?).

Obviously, the Space Age was a big part of the 1964-65 Fair. There were a variety of Cinerama and multimedia exhibits on the future of space flight. Even Ford's popular "Magic Skyway" ride, which mainly exhibited a prehistoric past as presented by the Disney Corporation (including cute baby dinosaurs) ended with a glimpse of man's future in space. But the big news at the fair was the future of what we now commonly call consumerism.

Dupont's *Wonderful World of Chemistry* (a musical including numbers like "The Happy Plastic Family") would later be mocked by antiwar groups who accused the chemical company of helping develop Agent Orange along with other chemical weapons used in Vietnam. The company did develop chemicals to kill off insects and help in the growing of fruits and vegetables, but many of those chemicals were found to be toxic, and people living near Dupont Chemical plants argued that the toxicity around the plant could cause cancer.

The corporate pavilions at the fair also pointed to the future of atomic power. There were even images of atomic-powered cars of the future such as the concept car The Ford Nucleon. First introduced as a car of the future in 1958, The Nucleon was to be powered by a nuclear reactor that would be behind and under the driver and passengers. I don't know about you, but nothing would make me feel more secure than sitting in front of and behind a small nuclear reactor while I was driving to work.

There was also a machine that visitors could put a dime into and have it come back irradiated. The irradiated dimes were given a blue plastic carrier with an atomic logo on it to hold them in place.

I carried one of those dimes with me for years as a good luck charm in my right pocket. Another comforting thought.

Figure 7. Irradiated dime from the 1964 World's Fair. Michael Korolenko.

The General Electric Pavilion had its "Wonders of Atomic Energy." After visitors exited Disney's Carousel of Progress, a moving Time Tube brought them to the "Skydome Spectacular" to experience electricity's future: Fusion On Earth. According to the Official Guide to the Fair:

> "In the first demonstration of controlled thermonuclear fusion to be witnessed by a large general audience, a magnetic field squeezes a plasma of deuterium gas for a few millionths of a second at a temperature of 20 million degrees Fahrenheit. There is a vivid flash and a loud report as atoms collide, creating free energy (evidenced on instruments)."[37]

There certainly was a loud report! It scared the heck out of me. I don't remember seeing instruments showing powerful free energy, but I thought it "neat" that man could now produce the very energy of the sun. The future was definitely going to be cool. I later heard that Robert Moses, the Fair's president, had wanted the U.S. Atomic Energy Commission to build an operating nuclear fission plant at the Fair. Now *that* would have been really neat (though probably very dangerous).

Figure 8. Futurama Exhibit 1964/65 World's Fair. Copyright 2008 GM Corporation. Used with permission, GM Media Archive.

The fair was also big on great cities of soaring, plasticine like buildings. As in fairs and predictions past, the cities were gigantic, with impossibly tall buildings connected by skyways and sleek glass covered bridges. The streets were filled, not with people, but with cars and monorails. Whatever people happened to be shown in dioramas, moving models, or paintings, were all white, blond, and no-doubt blue eyed.

The Gernsback Continuum, indeed.

The 1939 New York World's Fair had its Futurama, and the 1964-65 Fair had its Futurama II. Instead of highlighting just one city of the future as the 1939 exhibit did, the 1964 Futurama II covered the entire world and beyond. Under the sea would be great resorts, deserts would be turned into gardens, and a gigantic atom-powered vehicle would use great lasers to cut through the jungles of the Amazon, building a gigantic multilevel, multilane highway (and we think what's actually being done to the rain forests is bad!). And, of course, there would be American lunar colonies on the moon.

Once again, Futurama's city of the future showed gigantic skyscraper cities with 12 lane superhighways carrying people directly into the heart of the city. Robert Moses, the fair's president, also ordered that churches be added to the exhibit. There had been complaints in 1939 when no houses of worship were seen in Futurama I's city of 1960.

After the ride into the future, visitors were treated to abstract dioramas of futuristic, gleaming, and streamlined automobile shapes while, from hidden speakers all around, voices chanted in unison, almost like some weird mantra, "Faster, faster! Drive it faster!"

Multiscreen films would again prove popular at the Montreal World's Fair, Expo '67. In La Ronde, the Expo's amusement area, people could experience the Laterna Magika, combining simultaneous movie and transparency projection, sound recording, and live action. The technique was pioneered in Europe and was one of the first well-known "multimedia" extravaganzas.

A number of exhibits promoted new modes of communication and media. The Czechoslovakian exhibit made use of hundreds of slide projectors in gigantic screen matrixes that were synchronized with sound. Then there was The Labyrinth. In this exhibit, people experienced firsthand a core archetypal symbol from the collective unconscious: the labyrinth, which makes its appearance in cultures and stories from all over the world. Visitors underwent a journey through a maze of corridors that at one point opened up onto a gallery where one could see huge movies projected on three gigantic screens. It depicted old age, birth, the work world—every person's life magnified.

Then people were led into a darkened corridor that was actually lined with mirrors so that when they turned on these tiny lights, it looked like they were standing in the midst of an infinity of stars. The finale had visitors enter a darkened theater that showed an African native on a terrifying nighttime hunt for a crocodile.

"This experience was so bizarre and wonderful I'm not sure whether it really happened or if I am just remembering some kind of delirium I had once when I was sick with the flu."[38]

There was also an "interactive-movie" where the audience, via a split screen and two projectors that responded to buttons on the seats of the theater, could interact with an onscreen murder mystery: deciding who is the victim, the murderer, and so on.

Although people marveled at new entertainment forms at the fair, on the other side of the continent, the counterculture was in full bloom. During the so-called Summer of Love, a number of "Be-Ins" and "Happenings" took place in and around San Francisco. Luria Castell of The Family Dog described what was taking place to writer Ralph Gleason:

"We want to bring in the artistic underground, use light machines, boxes projecting a light pulse from the tonal qualities of the music . . . I think that rock 'n' roll people are just starting to know how to use their instruments. They're doing new things in electronics, the generation brought up in the insanity . . . young people today are torn between the insanity and the advances of the electronic age."[39]

One event in particular would influence numerous "hippie" artists who would one day be on the frontlines of digital communication: The Trips Festival, a three-day event held in January of 1967 at the Longshoreman's Hall, which boasted a multimedia light show that Ralph J. Gleason immortalized in his book *The Jefferson Airplane and The San Francisco Sound:*

"There were five movie screens up on the wall and projectors for the flicks and other light mixes spread around the balcony. A huge platform in the middle of the room housed the engineers who directed the sound and the lights. Loudspeakers ringed the hall and were set up under the balcony and in the entrance . . . Stroboscopic lights set at vantage points beamed down into the crowd and lissome maidens danced under them for hours, whirling jewelry. . ."[40]

As the quagmire of Vietnam, the social and political revolutions, and the growing violence in the streets played themselves out every night in American living rooms, another revolution was taking place. In its own way, this quiet, almost unnoticed revolution would have a more profound effect on our way of life than any of the manifestos being touted by either American college students or American politicians of the period. This was a revolution in computer and video technology, in effect the real revolution of the 1960s. Spurred on in part by the space race, technicians raced to develop video cameras small enough to be handled by astronauts on the moon as well as more compact and faster computers. At universities and colleges around the country, researchers worked on the development of interactive computer-based multimedia. At the same time, computer scientists were quietly changing the future of communications, attempting to build a computer network that would enable researchers around the country to share ideas.[41] By the 1990s, the Internet would be a fact of life, used not only by researchers but also by students, librarians, lawyers, and computer users in general as media technology moved from the passive to the active. By the early twenty-first century, the web had supplanted television in many households as the main source of both entertainment and communication.

The November 3, 1970, issue of *LOOK* magazine was a special issue on "The Now Hollywood," with the accent on "Now." All the articles on new movie ratings, the new faces of Hollywood, the new moguls, the "new sex styles," today read like exactly what they are: pieces written twenty-five years ago, separated by the way we are today as if by light years. But hidden between glossy photographs of the newest starlets and Paul Mazursky directing the "Now" movie *Alex In Wonderland* are pieces that gave the reader of 1970 a glimpse into the near future.

We mentioned in chapter 2 John Kronenberger's one-page article titled "Push Button Movies: The Video-Cassette Revolution," where he projected that eight years into the future consumers would be able to pop a "cartridge" containing the movie *Butch Cassidy and The Sundance Kid* on video and watch it whenever they wanted to. He mentioned what was already available: expensive and "crude" video cassette machines and tapes with only fifty minutes of black and white or twenty-five minutes of color material on them. Kronenberger also mentioned the problem of compatibility of different "VTR" systems (a problem that would come to a head in the early 1980s when Sony's higher quality betamax system lost out to the more compatible VHS system). But Kronenberger, and others, knew that another revolution was on the way:

Around the same time the special issue of *LOOK* appeared on news stands, author Alvin Toffler coined the term "future shock" which became the title of his 1970 book. The idea behind *Future Shock* was that, once upon a time, any obvious change took centuries to be observed. During the last hundred and fifty years, change had to be faced decade to decade. And now, according to Toffler, change itself was accelerating. One only had to look at the quickly changing technology to realize that there was much in Toffler's theory: we went from vacuum tubes to transistors to integrated circuit chips in a period of less than fifty years.

In 1981, the New York firm Ramirez and Woods, working with MIT, put together one of the first truly interactive exhibits using what was then the cutting edge of laser and computer technology. The exhibit was designed for the U.S. Pavilion at the 1982 Knoxville World's Fairs—not one of the more well-known expositions to say the least. Yet this interactive exhibit offering different views on the energy crisis (the fair was a hold-over from the Carter years and the theme was "Energy Turns The World") provided a jumping off point for writers, filmmakers, videographers, and technicians and scientists at MIT's Media Lab.

In 1982, three years after I finally got to see the original Disneyland, Epcot opened in Florida. Much more of a corporate fair than the official Knoxville World's Fair of the same year, Epcot was Walt Disney's last hurrah as far as showing how technology could make the future a better place to live. The opening was televised live on major television channels where it was proudly announced that Epcot was the largest private construction project in American history, costing a billion dollars to complete.

Walt Disney's idea had originally been to create an Experimental Prototype Community of Tomorrow. Part of Epcot would be an actual community, a kind of living futurama where people would live and bring up their families. Disney, a fan of 20th Century World's Fairs (it's been said that Walt's father actually worked on the 1893 Columbia Exposition's White City), also hoped that Epcot could be a World's Fair that never closed but continually changed. He wanted Epcot to be different than the one or two year "official" World's Fairs that he'd visited (and contributed to). Disney had hoped to use Flushing Meadows, site of the 1939 and 1964 New York

World's Fairs, as the location for his East Coast Disneyland and future community, but Robert Moses had other ideas.[1]

The costs for Epcot were so enormous that corporate sponsors were called in to defray the costs, much like Robert Moses called in corporate sponsors for the 1964/65 World's Fair, "Future World", the part of Epcot that Disney had hoped would be his innovative World's Fair became, like the New York 64/65 Fair, an advertisement for huge corporations. Walt Disney's original idea of a technological utopia is still evident, though citizenship has been completely replaced by consumerism and, by the mid 1990s, Epcot was fast beginning to look dated, something Disney had never wanted to happen.

As we reached the Orwellian year, Apple Computers aired an ad during the Super Bowl that asked why 1984 wasn't going to be the 1984 Orwell predicted (still, we did have MX missiles called "peacekeepers"—not that far removed from the Orwellian phrase "War Is Peace"). With the introduction of a graphical interface on the Macintosh in 1984, computers became more "user-friendly."

George Orwell had believed that, by 1984, television would become the controlling influence in our lives. Essayist Neil Postman disagreed. In his book *Amusing Ourselves to Death,* Postman pointed to Aldous Huxley's *Brave New World*. The novel, which was published in the early 1930s, created a world of the future filled with drugs to make you always feel good, with continually blaring advertisements, and with "feelie movies." As the title of his own book suggests, Postman felt that we were becoming an audience who could not tell fantasy from reality or entertainment from news. Our worst enemy wasn't an authoritarian Big Brother; it was ourselves and our own craving for more and more entertainment.

"What Huxley teaches is that in the age of advanced technology, spiritual devastation is more likely to come from an enemy with a smiling face than from one whose countenance exudes suspicion and hate. In the Huxleyan prophecy, Big Brother does not watch us, by his choice. We watch him, by ours."[42]

By the mid-1980s, it seemed as if Huxley's future (which had, it should be noted, originally been considered sharp satire) had all but come true. Deregulation began in earnest in 1984, and with restrictions lifted, television programming licenses were easier to obtain. A direct result of deregulation was the creation of the Home Shopping Network, a channel devoted entirely to advertisements of products people could purchase over their telephones. Thus, "Interactive Television" was born (although some might point to a much earlier form of interactive TV: the old *Winkie Dink & You* show whereby children put a special screen over the TV set and drew items to help Winkie out with his problems—and how many of you out there got yelled at by irate parents when you didn't have that special screen and just began to draw on the television screen itself?).

In the meantime, spurred on by the popularity of graphical user interfaces on the 1984 Macintosh, Microsoft Windows was introduced in 1986 and users began to see applications that could work with and display both text and graphics simultaneously: a major component of multimedia.

However, there still were show places and international fairs taking place. In 1986, The World Exposition on Transportation and Communication, or simply Expo '86, was held in Vancouver, British Columbia, Canada. The fair's theme was "Transportation and Communication: World in Motion—World in Touch." Interestingly, there was little that was "futuristic" at this fair. Despite its official name, most of the exhibits at this fair centered on history rather than the future. In fact, General Motor's exhibit at this fair, rather than being another in a line of futuramas, was about the Native people of British Columbia. Called "Spirit Lodge," it was a live show augmented with holographic and other special effects. It was produced by Bob Rogers and created with the assistance of the Kwagulth Native reserve in Alert Bay (British Columbia).[43] It was, in all seriousness, a moving and powerful experience. If only the creators of the fairs of the first half of the twentieth century could have been there.

---

[1]Like the 1939 Fair, the 1964 Fair was destroyed after it closed in the autumn of 1965 – a few of the buildings of the Fair remained and Moses hoped to make the site a community area and park, but it had all but fallen into disrepair by the late 1960s and early 1970s – the one real point of interest on the site is what used to be the New York City Pavilion at both fairs (and served as the place where the United Nations met before the UN building was completed) and is now The Queens Museum—a terrific museum which includes much in the way of Fair memorabilia.

During the 1980s, there was a restructuring of television and radio in this country mainly resulting from economic factors. This led to a series of mergers, acquisitions, and new start-up companies creating, among other networks, FOX Television, Turner Broadcasting, Showtime, and MTV. In fact, the average share of the primetime viewership of the "big three" (NBC, CBS, and ABC) went from 85% in 1980 to 67% in 1989.[44]

Television was also moving from being a medium geared toward mass appeal to being a much more fractionalized medium appealing to smaller and smaller audience groups. With the VCR and particularly with the remote control, audiences no longer felt compelled to stay switched to one channel for the evening. In fact, the act of using the remote control to zip through a variety of channels led to a new term: "channel surfing" (originally called "grazing"—you have to admit, "surfing" does sound much more athletic).

In the meantime, the marketplace for personal computers continued to grow. With graphics getting better and user interfaces getting more user-friendly each year, there was less of a reason to make a pilgrimage to a World's Fair when the entire world, including the most modern technology available, was right at your fingertips.

By 1992, "most of the largest players in personal computing and consumer electronics—Apple, IBM, Microsoft, SONY, Tandy, Dell, Sega, Nintendo—began spending large budgets to advertise and market multimedia products and equipment."[45] This was true particularly in the area of interactive gaming, which within ten years would begin to replace television as the main source of young peoples' entertainment.

In many ways, Marshall McLuhan's Global Village began to come true during the 1990s in the form of the Internet.

In 1996 there was another World's Fair. It wasn't held in any particular city or country—it took place on the Internet. It was called "The Internet 1996 World Exposition: A World's Fair for the Information Age." This fair wasn't so much about the future as it was about the technological present. In a word, this fair *was* the future!

> "As we leave the industrial age and enter a new age of information, it is time for a new kind of world's fair. This one will continue throughout 1996. This is the first world's fair where anybody can open a pavilion, where anybody can participate."[46]

In his foreword to the book on the exposition, *A World's Fair For The Global Village,* the Dalai Lama wrote how the combination of new communications media had created a revolution not only in communications, but in the attainment and use of knowledge and information. For the Dalai Lama, the Internet held the seeds for true democratic communications and knowledge sharing since no one owns it and no single group can control it. His hope was that the Internet would give the poor, the disenfranchised, and all marginalized groups in the world a new voice to express their hopes and dreams.

In other words, this was a true World's Fair for the late twentieth century and beyond. Such "fairs" continue—not like Disneyland's Tomorrowland or Epcot, which now are nostalgic looks into yesterday's view of the future—but with up-to-the-minute new technology and exhibits. This was and is very much a World's Fair for McLuhan's Global Village. You can visit this fair via your Internet connection by going to http://parallel.park.org/About/.

Dr. Thomas Furness, considered one of the fathers of virtual reality (for our purposes, we'll define virtual reality as an immersive computer simulation experienced through headgear, goggles, and sensory gloves that allow the user to feel as if he or she is present in another environment), began his work in VR creating flight simulators for the U.S. Air Force. He feels that the biggest boon for virtual reality will be how it fits into the merging of broadband telecommunications, computers, and the telephone, which are all rapidly becoming integrated via digital networks.

> "The interface for humans to that ubiquitous channel is going to be a virtual one. When you put [these different media] together, basically what you get is the 'virtuphone,' a telephone that your wear. And basically now in your home, even through coax, you have the ability to disconnect your head from your body and go places—through what we used to have as television, only television wasn't interactive. Now [this new medium] is going to be completely interactive. You'll go to work with it, you'll play with it, you'll go to school with this new medium [that is] two generations beyond the print medium. We'll be taking ourselves—head and body, because we're going to feel as if we're present—to another place."[47]

On one level, the question then becomes, with the ability to interact with 500 or 1,000 channels, what happens to our shopping malls, not to mention the local video stores? It is conceivable that more and more shopping malls will become entertainment centers. But, what happens to our transportation industry if people no longer have to travel by car, train, or plane to get to work? What happens to downtown urban areas where office buildings might, presumably, stand empty? And, in the final analysis, will people want to spend even more time in front of their television sets than they do now? Corporations are betting millions that the answer is yes.

But there are deeper, more disturbing questions to address: What happens to social interaction if you, literally, never have to leave your house? What happens to reality itself?

There is still a window of opportunity open to take VR in the direction Dr. Furness would like to see it move: a place where children can create pastoral worlds while learning about the importance of nature and ecological balance.

It seems as if we're just beginning to understand the effects television has had on us since the late 1940s, and we have little more than an inkling of what effect the new media may have. Will there be a true "democratization" of media, where people can broadcast their own programming from their homes and receive instantaneous reactions? Will McLuhan's "Global Village" come to pass, where students in the United States can communicate freely with digitally "wired" friends in Germany, China, in fact anywhere in the world? Or will the information highway be owned by corporations who will tout their own philosophies over the net, creating an electronic elite? The "Global Village" could, in fact, turn out to be more of an electronic metropolis or megalopolis, overseen by new corporate big brothers.

On a more mundane level, 500 or 1,000 channels might well offer us new experiences, opening up new vistas for our children and whole new realms of art, entertainment, documentation, and social interaction. All these new channels could also only mean that we can watch *Gilligan's Island* 999 times a day.

This is not meant to sound flippant; we are in the midst of a media and technological revolution that will, like it or not, have a profound effect on us all. Already the digital/media revolution is changing the landscape of our culture. It will certainly affect the way we interact with each other as well as the way we perceive ourselves and think. The hope is, as Isaac Asimov said, that "we do not make foolish [or trivial] use of technology. That we use technology wisely."[48]

Hopefully, we will use the new media humanely and experience the new worlds, virtual or otherwise, in a way that will help us to understand not just ourselves, but the world around us. Then, as Dr. Furness and others hope, we may truly become sensitized to the basic ecological makeup of our planet and be able to move in new and more positive directions. In this way, new technology could well assist us as a species to, at long last, mature.

Emergence of the Many-to-Many Model

The hope is that people will share information more in the form of McLuhan's Global Village. As this is happening, television news networks, newspapers, and news organizations in general are losing their power and hold on the public. There is also the danger of a fragmentation of public discourse, with discourse itself turning into a cacophony of disconnected voices, none listening to the others. We can already see this phenomenon taking place both on web blogs and on television "talk" shows where there is no debate, just rancor and propaganda.

Howard Rheingold, who describes himself as a high-tech social historian, took a more optimistic view:

"A tremendous power shift is underway, and despite the obscure or phony terminology used to describe it, this power shift is about people, and our ability to connect with each other in new ways much more than it is about fiber optic cable and multimedia appliances. The revolution triggered by the printing press was about literacy, and what literate populations are capable of doing (eg: governing themselves), long after it had anything to do with the mechanics of moveable type. The technology enabled the power shift, but the power shift was created by the people who used the tool to educate themselves."[49]

"Unlike the one-to-many model where information came from the top, news on the Internet bubbles up from the bottom and meanders its way upward. The daily reality of the many-to-many model means that the journalist now has a chance to really know and interact with his or her audience that goes way beyond traditional letters to the editor. This closer interaction should ideally lead to a better knowledge of the audience, and writing and reporting that more closely reflects readers' values and interests."[50]

One can only hope.

Endnotes

[1]Donald J. Bush, *The Streamlined Decade* (New York George Braziller 1975). The birth of planes, trains, and automobiles in the 1950s. p. 3.

[2]www.geocities.com/seattlescruff/.

[3]E.D. Hirsch, Jr., Joseph F. Kett, and James Trefil, *The New Dictionary of Cultural Literacy,* third edition. Copyright © 2002 by Houghton Mifflin Company. Published by Houghton Mifflin Company. All rights reserved.

[4]Donald L. Miller, The White City, *American Heritage Magazine,* July/August 1993, p. 83.

[5]Margaret Cheney, *Tesla: Man Out of Time* (New York: Dell Publishing, 1981), pp. 70–73.

[6]http://www.h-net.org/mmreviews/showrev.cgi?path=407.

[7]Seattle University Law Review Winter, 2005 Article *329 BEYOND THE CONVENTIONAL ESTABLISHMENT CLAUSE NARRATIVE by Richard Alpert.

[8]"The Passions of Suzie Wong Revisited, by Rev. Sequoyah Ade", *Aboriginal Intelligence,* January 4, 2004.

[9]http://www.h-net.org/mmreviews/showrev.cgi?path=407.

[10]Paul Wilborn, © *St. Petersburg Times,* published December 26, 1999.

[11]Richard Schickel, *The Disney Version* (New York: Avon Books, 1968), p. 268.

[12]Ibid.

[13]Wernher von Braun and Frederick I. Ordway III, *History of Rocketry and Space Travel,* third revised ed. (New York: Thomas Y. Crowell Company, 1975), p. 108.

[14]http://history.msfc.nasa.gov/vonbraun/disney_article.html.
"The Disney-Von Braun Collaboration and Its Influence on Space Exploration" by Mike Wright, Marshall Space Flight Center Historian.

[15]Adrian Perkins, The 1950's, A Pivotal Decade, *Spaceflight,* July/August 1983, p. 323.

[16]"The Disney-Von Braun Collaboration and Its Influence on Space Exploration" by Mike Wright, Marshall Space Flight Center Historian.

[17]Ibid.

[18]WHO STOLE Tomorrowland's SOUL? By Janelle Brown for Wanderlust Salon, http://archive.salon.com/21st/feature/1998/05/cov_28feature.html.

[19]Ibid.

[20]Ibid.

[21]Seth Schiesel, Once Visionary, Disney Calls Future a Thing of the Past, *The New York Times,* February 23, 1997.
Schiesel goes on to write: "The shift is profound for a company whose founder was one of postwar America's great popularizers of technology. And it is a reflection of the ennui that many Americans, at century's end, feel about the chips and bits in which they are immersed.

"We went to the Moon and all we got out of it was Teflon pans," said Karal Ann Marling, a professor of art history and American studies at the University of Minnesota, expressing an increasingly common attitude.

"Our goals as a people are not these pie-in-the-sky objectives that people grew up with in the 50's," said Professor Marling, who is the curator for a Montreal exhibit in June on Disney theme park architecture. "They settle now for a house in the suburbs and to hell with the Moon. What's the point of building monorails if we can hardly get the car to work?"

That was not Walt Disney's America. At the dawn of the space race, President Dwight D. Eisenhower used a Disney television program to introduce Pentagon brass to the possibilities of space travel. In the 1950's and 60's, the original Tomorrowland, at Disneyland in Anaheim, Calif., was home to Space Station X-1 and the Monsanto House of the Future. . . Nicholas Negroponte, director of the media laboratory at the Massachusetts Institute of Technology, one of whose sponsors is Disney, thinks that the company has realized that the future, as it unfolds today, is no longer good entertainment.

"The story line just doesn't carry with it the same sort of punch as going off to the Moon," he said. "Things like highly personalized information services and computer agents that do things for you just don't make a good story."

[22]Richard Schickel, *The Disney Version* (New York: Avon Books, 1968), pp. 270–271.

[23]Ibid, p. 272.

[24]From experiences of a variety of people who went to the park during its "anti-hippie" era.

[25]WHO STOLE Tomorrowland's SOUL? By Janelle Brown for Wanderlust Salon, http://archive.salon.com/21st/feature/1998/05/cov_28feature.html.

[26]Ibid.

[27]www.geocities.com/seattlescruff/.

[28]Carolyn Bennett Patterson and Thomas Nebbia, Seattle Fair Looks to the 21st Century, *National Geographic Magazine,* September 1962, p. 407.

[29]www.geocities.com/seattlescruff/.

[30]Bruce Wolcott, interview with the author, August 1995.

[31]www.geocities.com/seattlescruff/.

[32]*1965 Official NY World's Fair Guide* (New York: Time Inc., 1965), p. 90.

[33]Kendra Howe, a representative from Watts-Silverstein and Associates, in an interview with the author, spoke of how this CD-ROM product profiles a group of statistically average families from countries around the world and shows all aspects of their daily lives. It is basically an educational tool or "browsing product," with its primary target audience being families, especially those with children. In comparing and contrasting families around the world, the producers of the program thought they would find many differences and were surprised to find, in terms of overall family values, many similarities. It is interesting when browsing through the "Lifestyles" section of the "Suitcase Menu" to see six different bathrooms, from one with mink lined toilets in Kuwait to another in Uganda which is just a hole in the ground.

[34]Ibid.

[35]http://www.westland.net/ny64fair/map-docs/technology.htm.

[36]Jeffrey Stanton's website on the Fair http://www.westland.net/ny64fair/.

[37]The Official Guide New York World's Fair 1964/1965 (New York: Time Incorporated, 1964). p. 92.

[38]Bruce Wolcott, interview with the author, August 1995.

[39]Ralph J. Gleason, *The Jefferson Airplane and The San Francisco Sound* (New York: Ballantine Books, 1969), p. 3.

[40]Ibid.

[41]Barbara Kantrowitz and Adam Rogers, The Birth of the Internet, *Newsweek Magazine,* August 8, 1994, p. 56.

[42]Neil Postman, *Amusing Ourselves to Death,* p. 155.

[43]http://www.glosk.com/US/Chinatown/10781239/pages/Expo_86/40904_en.htm.

[44]Lynne S. Gross, *Telecommunications—An Introduction to Electronic Media,* plate 8.

[45]Randy Haykin, editor, *Multimedia Demystified* (San Francisco: Random House/NewMedia Series, 1992), p. 2.

[46]http://parallel.park.org/About/Fair/.

[47]Dr. Thomas Furness, interview with the author, October 1993.

[48]Dr. Isaac Asimov, interview with the author, April 1977.

[49]*CMC Magazine,* July 1, 1995, p. 7, http://www.december.com/cmc/mag/1995/jul/lapham.html.

[50]Ibid.

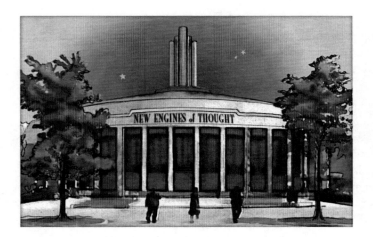

Chapter 5
New Engines of Thought: The Microprocessor, Computer, and Network

"...the steam engine was to the first Industrial Revolution what the microprocessor and the computer has been to the Information Revolution—its trigger, but above all its symbol."[1]

Peter Drucker

"The hope is that in not too many years, human brains and computing machines will be coupled together very tightly, and that the resulting partnership will think as no human brain has ever thought."

JCR Licklider, MIT (1960)

"Just when did all this computer stuff happen anyway? You know, one day I was playing Pong, the next thing I know, Wes, the gas meter guy with the eye patch, has an uplink to a satellite on his tool belt."

Dennis Miller, *American comedian*

"Any sufficiently advanced technology is indistinguishable from magic."

Arthur C. Clarke.

In the twentieth century, until the 1980s, computers combined with robotics have produced more fear than hope. In Fritz Lang's 1924 epic *Metropolis,* robot workers were to replace humans on the production line. In 1970's *Colossus: The Forbin Project,* a giant computer constructed to protect the United States from incoming Soviet missiles gets a mind of its own and takes over. It tells mankind that our lives will be better and all we'll lose is our pride. Fredric Brown probably wrote about it best: In one of his 1950s short stories, a gigantic computer, the smartest, fastest one ever built, is unveiled. All the great minds of the world have gathered to ask it the most important question of all: "Is there a God?" The punch card with the question goes into the machine; lights flicker, banks of thinking components click, switches whir, and the computer finally spits out a card with the answer on it: **"There is now."**

Foundations for the Computer and Microprocessor

Peter Drucker was a business management theorist who coined the phrase *knowledge worker,* which he used to describe an emerging computer-based workforce that does mental rather than manual tasks. Drucker saw the information and digital revolution of the late twentieth century as having as profound an effect on society as the Industrial Revolution had in the nineteenth century. The *enabling technology* that made the Industrial Revolution possible was James Watts' invention of the steam engine, which was applied to the manufacturing of textiles, leather, bricks, paper, weaponry, and many other goods.

As an example, Drucker says, ". . .the making of guns was steam-driven throughout Europe, cannons were made ten to twenty times as fast as before—the cost dropped by more than two-thirds."[1]

The social impact of the steam engine was extensive, ironically leading to an increasing reliance on slaves to harvest cotton for the highly productive textile mills and moving the average worker away from home and family on a scale never experienced before. The steam-driven railroads allowed the average person a chance to experience a wider world beyond their local community. In Drucker's view, the technological spinoffs from the steam engine weren't neutral—they changed society forever.

It was during the height of the steam-driven Industrial Revolution that the concept of the first computer was proposed by English scientist Charles Babbage and later by his pioneering software engineer Ada Augusta Byron (see Chapter 1). In 1822, his first effort was a basic calculator, a demonstration prototype made up of interlocking mechanical parts, that solved specific kinds of simple math problems. It was this device that earned him a grant from the British Government to build a more ambitious calculator, the Difference Engine. During work on this second device, Babbage came up with an idea for building a third and more versatile calculation machine in 1833, capable of handling a wide range of mathematics operations. He called it the Analytical Engine. In Babbage's plan, this device would repattern how its mechanical parts worked together through the use of step-by-step operations introduced by punched cards. Although the Analytical Engine was never completed because of manufacturing limitations of his time, Babbage's concept of how his invention worked was remarkably similar to the modern computer.

Charles Babbage's Analytical Engine (1833) consisted of the following four operations:

1) **Input**—provided by punched cards for entering numbers into the computer, a form of early *software*.

2) **Processing**—a mechanical calculator called the "mill," capable of adding numbers that were accurate up to fifty decimal places.

3) **Storage**—up to 1,000 fifty-digit numbers generated by the mill were temporarily held in the "store" for further use.

4) **Output**—a simple typesetting device for printing results.

Compare Babbage's Analytical Engine with a modern desktop computer.

1) **Input**—Multiple devices are used to transmit human actions into electronic signals that can be used by the computer, including the keyboard, joystick, mouse, light pen, voice, and so on.

2) **Processing**—The central processing unit (CPU) accepts input supplied by a user or electronic device and converts it into commands expressed in the binary language of 0s and 1s that can be executed by the computer's CPU. Software provides the instructions for how this is accomplished.

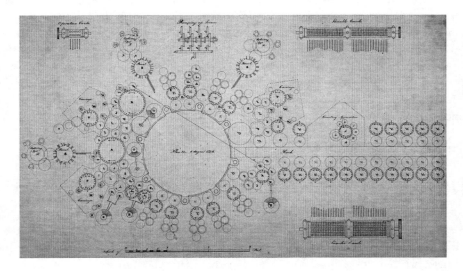

Figure 1. An illustration of the Analytical Engine by Charles Babbage (1833). Science Museum/Science & Society Picture Library.

3) **Storage**—There are multiple possible locations where information is stored on a computer, including internal hard drives, compact disks, optical disks, portable hard drives, flash drives, and older floppy disks. Read Only Memory (ROM) is permanently installed memory used to store boot up information for the computer. Random Access Memory (RAM), supports temporary storage operations for active software, and is lost when the computer is turned off.

4) **Output**—modern computers can support many different kinds of devices, including monitors, printers, fax machines, sound systems, and modems.

All computers, whether a mainframe, workstation, desktop, laptop, personal digital assistant (PDA), video game console, or smartphone perform the same fundamental operations first described by Charles Babbage. As described in Chapter 1, it was Lady Ada Augusta Byron who developed the first software concepts that provided instructions for how Babbage's Analytical Engine would work. These instructions were input into Babbage's early computer by way of cards with holes punched in them.

Today the term for a series of step-by-step instructions that carry out a specific computer task is *algorithm*—the fundamental building block for computer software applications.

What Is a Transistor?

Software-based algorithms manage the flow of two electronic states in a computer—either a "yes" or "no"—a "1" or a "0." These two states are stored in a *transistor,* a tiny switching device that is either turned on, producing the presence of a signal, or turned off, resulting in no signal. Eight bits in sequence is called a *byte.* For example, the following series of 8 bits (on/off signals)—01000001—make up a byte representing the letter "A" in a universally recognized electronic alphabet called ASCII. A computer is made up of millions of transistors that together are capable of handling very complex calculations and tasks through software-coordinated management of this *binary* or two-state form of information. Coordinated sequences of 1s and 0s stored by transistors can represent letters, numbers, sounds, and graphics.

Four Computer Functions

 **Input**

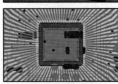 **Processing**

 **Storage**

 **Output**

Figure 2. Primary functions of a twenty-first century computer are the same as Babbage's original Analytical Engine—input, processing, storage, and output.
© Rene Drouyer | Dreamstime.com (processing photo)
© Vasiu | Dreamstime.com (input, storage, output photos)

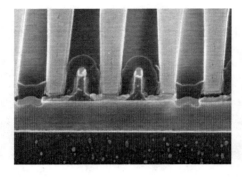

Figure 3. Microscopic view of two transistors, each of which is capable of two states, **OFF = 0 and ON = 1**. Millions of integrated transistors such as these, storing simple 0s or 1s, make complex computer tasks possible. Reprint courtesy of International Business Machines Corporation, copyright © 2007 International Business Machines Corporation.

Exhibit 1: What Is an Algorithm?

The most basic unit in software for managing human-computer interaction is the *algorithm*. The algorithm can be described as a series of discrete steps for carrying out a specific task—much like a recipe for creating a casserole.

Recipe (algorithm) for creating green bean casserole.

Ingredients:
- *Can of mushroom soup*
- *Can of green beans*
- *Can of dried French fried onions*

Instructions:
1) *Combine mushroom soup and green beans in a casserole dish*
2) *Cover with dried French fried onions*
3) *Bake at 350 degrees for ½ hour*

An algorithm consists of lines of code written in a computer programming language such as C, C++, C#, LISP, Java, or Javascript. Each algorithm instructs the computer to execute a series of steps to complete a task, such as alphabetizing a list of names from A to Z or saving a document. Thousands of integrated algorithms make up a software application such as Microsoft Word or Adobe Photoshop.

Algorithm based on programming code that responds to a keystroke

```
//if up arrow . . .
if (keyCode == 38){
if (wtEvent.getKeyState() == 1){
    //up arrow key-down
    }
else {
    //up arrow key-up
    }
```

Early Electronic Computers

"The two factors that make the computer worth using are the speed with which electricity flows, and immense amounts of data that can be handled using the binary code. For this reason the computer can be used to solve problems whose calculation would take a human longer than a lifetime."[2]

James Burke

From Charles Babbage and Augusta Ada onward, as steam was replaced by electricity and communications technologies became more diversified and ubiquitous in the nineteenth and twentieth centuries, the dream of harnessing electronic devices to augment and expand human intelligence became a major theme in the work of early computer

Figure 4. ENIAC, one of the first electronic computers, circa 1947. U.S. Army Photo.

Table 1. ENIAC vs. Intel

Characteristics	ENIAC	Intel Core Duo Chip
Introduction	1946	2006
Performance	5,000 addition problems per second	21.6 billion operations per second
Power Use	170,000 watts	31 watts maximum
Weight	28 tons	Several ounces
Processing	17,840 vacuum tubes	151.6 million transistors
Cost	$487,000	$637

scientists. Beginning in the late 1930s there were several early projects to build an electronic computational device—Atanasoff-Berry Computer at Iowa State University (1937), the Z3 computer in Germany (1941) developed by Konrad Zuse, the Colossus Mark I and Mark II (1943–1944) computers in England, and the ENIAC (Electronic Numerical Integrator and Computer, 1943). The last three were developed during World War II and used for military purposes.

The ENIAC is probably the best known of these computers and was originally built to help calculate the trajectory of artillery shells so they could hit their targets. Combat units had ground-based spotters who made use of mathematical firing tables to determine how an artillery shell would find its target based on temperature, wind speed, angle of the gun, terrain, and other variables. These tables originally were created by a group of around 100 women who were called "computers." Each trajectory required about forty hours of math calculations using electric calculators.

The ENIAC was located at the University of Philadelphia and was invented by J. Presper Eckert and John Mauchly. It was 7,200 square feet in size, weighed 60,000 pounds, and made use of 17,800 high-speed vacuum tubes. It required eight full-time technicians and had to be shut down every few hours to allow the system to cool down. The ENIAC was used after World War II to perform calculations on a variety of military-related projects, including the hydrogen bomb. It was finally put out of commission in 1955 by lightning.[3]

A recent comparison of the ENIAC with a modern desktop computer from CNET News shows just how far computers have come since 1945.[4]

As We May Think

Vannevar Bush was a scientist, inventor, and administrator whose career spanned the first half of the twentieth century. While a professor at MIT in the 1930s, he designed a large computer run by a complex assemblage of gears that he called the *differential analyzer*. During World War II he became President Franklin Roosevelt's chief scientific advisor as Director of the Office of Scientific Research and Development, where he organized the Manhattan Project (to build an atomic bomb) and other wartime scientific efforts. He was later instrumental in creating a postwar linkage of universities, corporations, and the U.S. military—which later came to be known as the military-industrial complex.

As World War II began to wind down, Bush wrote an article for *The Atlantic Monthly* magazine in August 1945 called "As We May Think." It was a remarkable document that described fundamental concepts that later became implemented in the Internet and World Wide Web. In this article, Bush's central concern was that more information was being created in the form of scientific papers and other publications than could not be adequately handled by the paper-based information storage and retrieval systems of his day. He described how inadequate traditional information storage systems had become for organizing useful knowledge. Information printed on paper required shelf space in libraries or file cabinets. These, in turn, required a system of retrieval that required numbering, alphabetizing and indexing—organized from general categories to subclasses of information. In his view, finding the paths to this information was unnecessarily slow. The amount of new published materials and data was increasing dramatically, and he thought that existing storage and retrieval systems would eventually become inadequate to handle the task.[5]

Bush expanded this idea by saying that the information storage systems of the 1940s did not support the natural way that human beings organized and accessed their thoughts. Humans organized their thoughts through associations—one idea triggering another along a pathway of related topics.

This "web of trails," whereby information could be approached from any number of start points and completed at any number of end points, was a process that Bush felt could be enhanced by the application of appropriate technology. Hierarchies of indexed data, requiring users to search through information from general categories to more specific subcategories, could be replaced by an electronically driven "web" of lateral associations. This was a way of organizing human thought through horizontal associations rather than vertical hierarchies moving from general to specific.

Vannevar Bush's proposed solution to this situation in 1945 was to have far-reaching effects. He proposed building an information storage and retrieval device called the Memex (memory extender), a machine to augment human

Figure 5. Vannevar Bush. Library of Congress, Prints and Photographs, 3a37339r.

Figure 6. Memex "desktop" machine. Illustrated by Kirsten Adams.

memory. He saw this device as an electronic library and information storage system, where a user could catalog messages, articles, books, and other forms of communication—and retrieve them quickly. Bush saw his proposed device as a way to bootstrap and augment human capacities.

The Memex as described by Vannevar Bush in 1945 strongly corresponds to today's network-ready desktop computer. It was built within a large desk, and provided a keyboard, slanting viewing screens, along with controls that would allow a user to archive and retrieve personal information on strips of film.[6]

Memex, as fully conceived by Vannevar Bush, had the following features: (1) a private library for the storage of personal records, (2) a device for the rapid navigation and access of stored information through association, (3) a device for saving these explorations as "chains of links" to share with others, and (4) an aid to human memory. Bush saw Memex users exploring associations of thought within the great storehouse of human knowledge, leaving behind "trails" of investigation that others could follow and expand on. Although Bush's Memex was never built, his ideas laid the foundation for today's networked computer, Internet, and World Wide Web.

J.C.R. Licklider: *Human-Machine Symbiosis* and Networked Computing

Like Vannevar Bush, J.C.R. Licklider gained his early association with computers through U.S. military projects. After completing his doctorate in psychoacoustics and the physiology of hearing, Licklider studied communications systems for Air Force bomber pilots in 1942 at Harvard University's Psychoacoustics laboratory. Later, during the Cold War in the 1960s, he helped create computer-enabled air defense strategies against Russian bombers while he was involved with a program called SAGE at MIT. It was here, while planning air defense systems as a human factors specialist, that he saw the need of computers to assist humans in dealing with the enormous complexity of a burgeoning technological civilization.[7]

Like Vannevar Bush, Licklider realized early on that these early electronic devices had the potential of enhancing human intelligence. In 1960, he published a paper called "Man Computer Symbiosis" that expanded on themes presented in Bush's *Atlantic Monthly* article fifteen years earlier. In it, he discusses the nature of symbiosis in biological systems and then takes the position that *computer-human interfaces should be designed to enable the gradual symbiosis between man and machine.*

Licklider's article was motivated by experiences he'd had as a clinical researcher while recording data for various experiments—how the brain and ear could interpret sound from atmospheric vibrations. He found that 85% of his working time was taken up with repetitive chores—charting graphs, doing simple mathematical calculations, referencing experimental data—tasks that Licklider described as "essentially clerical or mechanical." He felt that these repetitive jobs should be taken over by a computer so that he could spend most of his time as a research scientist interpreting data rather than preparing it. Licklider was convinced that the computer could augment human intelligence by liberating it from tedious work. Licklider was trained as a psychologist, not a computer scientist, but his insights into the future co-evolution of humans with machines broke new ground in the mid-twentieth century and proved to be extraordinarily accurate. He saw the computer of the future as not just a device for storing and retrieving data but as an interactive tool for assisting its users in understanding concepts, communicating, and making decisions. Licklider later described his excitement over this realization as the "religious conversion to interactive computing."[8]

Licklider was at MIT in August 1962, when he wrote a now famous memo that described his concept of a "galactic network"—which consisted of an interconnected matrix of computer nodes in which information and applications could be shared among its users. It was this concept that he brought with him when he was hired later that year to work at the U.S. Defense Department's Advanced Research Project Agency (DARPA). Licklider proposed that this idea be expanded as part of a "geographically distributed network of computers" that would eventually link together several major universities for the purpose of sharing computer processing time—a costly and precious commodity during that period.[9] When it was completed, this pioneering time-sharing network became known as ARPANET, the first phase of what would later become the global Internet.

Early Interfaces: Building Human-Machine Relationships

The event was the Fall Joint Computer Conference, held in San Francisco in 1968. Douglas Engelbart, a computer researcher who coordinated the Augmentation Research Center at Stanford University, presented a series of new concepts in human-computer interaction. They were packaged within an application called the Online System or NLS.

Engelbart's presentation was called "the mother of all demos," and one witness to the event referred to the demo by saying, "It was like a UFO landing on the White House Lawn." The computer interface technologies and concepts that Engelbart introduced were so advanced for the time that his audience of over 3,000 computer scientists gave him a standing ovation. His innovative methods set the direction of human-computer interaction for the next few decades. In one ninety-minute session, Engelbart single-handedly demonstrated the following technologies:[10]

1) **Hypertext**—the ability to access stored digital documents through onscreen links. Associated with this, Engelbart demonstrated the concept of the *keyword search* for locating desired electronic information.

2) **The mouse**—a navigation device that flexibly tracks hand movements, translates them to the movements of a cursor or "tracking spot," and allows a user to select items on a computer screen display. Regarding the mouse, Engelbart said: "I don't know why we call it a mouse. It started that way and we never changed it." The first widespread use of the mouse took place with the development and distribution of the Apple II computer in 1981.

3) **Word processing**—techniques for flexibly cutting, copying, and pasting text within an electronic document and saving it within a filing system.

4) **Windowing environment**—the ability to view multiple computer processes simultaneously on a screen. Text and images could be shown on the screen at the same time.

5) **Electronic mail**—the transmission of electronic messages across a network.

6) **Keyboard keystroke commands**—the use of various keystroke combinations or *chord key sets* to launch applications.

7) **Network collaboration**—the ability for two computer users to communicate and collaborate in real-time with each other across a network. In this networked environment, Engelbart provided an early example of the *paperless office,* where no paper documents actually exchanged hands. All text communications remained electronic transactions.

8) **Video and audio conferencing**—the transmission of real-time sound and television signals across a computer network.

Five years prior to his 1968 demonstration, Engelbart had written a paper expanding on ideas developed by Vannevar Bush and J.C.R. Licklider. It was called "A Conceptual Framework for the Augmentation of Man's Intellect" and advocated the use of core computer tools to help human users navigate and collaborate within complex information structures. The principles outlined in that paper became the basis for his integrated Online System. Before Engelbart's historic demo, interactivity with computers was primarily limited to punch cards, and real-time interactivity with a computer was considered science fiction. Early on, he recognized that the user interface was an essential ingredient for the successful future coevolution of humans with computers, and he saw a need to develop the electronic network as an environment for expanded social collaboration.

At about the same time Douglas Engelbart was writing "A Conceptual Framework for the Augmentation of Man's Intellect," another pioneer of human-computer interface design was inventing the first interactive graphics program called *Sketchpad.* Ivan Sutherland was in his early twenties when he created *Sketchpad* at MIT as part of his doctoral thesis, which supported the use of a light pen for creating images, grabbing and moving objects, changing image size, and using geometric constraints. Sutherland later was heard to say of his revolutionary program, "If I had known how hard it was to do, I probably wouldn't have done it."[12]

Like Engelbart, Sutherland was on the forefront of breaking the tyranny of computer punch cards and text commands to open up new vistas of exploration in the relationship of humans to computers. In fact, the development of the entire computer graphics industry can be traced to his original work.

The first interactive graphics program was developed by Ivan Sutherland for his 1963 PhD thesis. *Sketchpad* provided an early version of the graphical user interface (GUI), utilized a light pen, and set many precedents for the future development of computer graphics.

In the 1960s computing was strictly within the domain of big business, government, and academic institutions. Computers were simply too expensive for the average individual user. Mainframe computers dominated the information processing landscape. There were problems with this, of course—because computing resources were

Exhibit 2: Douglas Engelbart Interview

Figure 7. Douglas Engelbart. Courtesy of SRI International, Menlo Park, CA.

Douglas Engelbart holds the computer mouse, that he introduced at the Fall Joint Computer Conference NLS Demo in1968.

. . .I had the image of sitting at a big CRT screen with all kinds of symbols, new and different symbols, not restricted to our old ones. The computer could be manipulated, and you could be operating all kinds of things to drive the computer.

. . .I also got a really clear picture that one's colleagues could be sitting in other rooms with similar work stations, tied to the same computer complex, and could be sharing and working and collaborating very closely. And also the assumption that there'd be a lot of new skills, new ways of thinking that would evolve."

Douglas Engelbart Interview, December 19, 1986.[11] From "As We May Think" by Vannevar Bush, *The Atlantic Monthly*, July 1945. Copyright 1945 by The Atlantic Monthly. Reproduced with permission of The Atlantic Monthly in the format Textbook via Copyright Clearance Center.

scarce and demand for these resources was high, mainframe computer users often had to wait in line with stacks of punched cards to process their data. Computers could only handle one processing task at a time, which required this *first come/first served* management of information processing.

Out of this situation arose the idea of *multitasking,* where a computer could manage multiple tasks simultaneously and many users could benefit from a computer's resources through *time-sharing.* Many separate keyboards with terminals were electronically tethered to the mainframe, and each user had the illusion that they were using their own computer when in fact, they were sharing the same mainframe with many other logged in participants. The personal computer, and later the World Wide Web, were still many years away, but some people were thinking early on about the benefits of a personal multimedia computer.

One of those people was Alan Kay, who in 1969 put together a cardboard prototype of a notebook-size computer called the *Dynabook.* Kay was a big fan of Sutherland's *Sketchpad* program, and was particularly impressed by its rule-based interactive display. He wanted to extend and expand the capabilities of computer interaction so that it more fully engaged the senses of sight and sound, provided a library of easily accessed information, and was fun to use.

Kay described his concept of the *Dynabook* as follows: "Imagine having your own self-contained knowledge manipulator in a portable package the size and shape of an ordinary notebook. Suppose it had enough power to outrace your senses of sight and hearing, enough capacity to store for later retrieval thousands of page-equivalents of reference materials, poems, letters, recipes, records, drawings, animations, musical scores, waveforms, and anything else you'd like to remember and change. . ."[13] Kay had taken an original concept outlined by Vannevar Bush in 1945 and updated the *Memex* to his *Dynabook* in a form that was within reach of existing technology. Although the *Dynabook* was never built, it became a theoretical prototype for several generations of multimedia computers that would soon follow.

The Microprocessor and Moore's Law

Ray Kurzweil, a technology innovator and inventor, said, "If the automobile had made as much progress as the computer over the past 50 years, a car today would cost 1/100 of a cent and travel at the speed of light." What has caused these decades of rapid growth and development? The beating heart and task master of every computer and every digital electronic device from radios to cell phones is the *microprocessor,* a device that's been called "a computer on a chip."

Table 2. The Vacuum Tube, Transistor, and Integrated Chip

Figure 8. Three generations of electronic switching devices: The vacuum tube, early transistor, and integrated circuit (small dot to the right). Reprinted courtesy of International Business Machines Corporation, copyright 1964 © International Business Machines Corporation.

One of the key functions of a computer is the ability to represent information as a 0 or a 1 through the use of a switching device that can represent one of these two states by controlling the flow of electrical current (see Exhibit 2). In the first generation of computers, such as the ENIAC, the vacuum tube was used for this purpose. There were problems with vacuum tubes—primarily unreliability, heat, and power consumption. In 1947, Bell Labs developed the transistor, which was smaller, cheaper, and more reliable than the vacuum tube. Over time, transistors became smaller, so increasing numbers of them could fit onto a small silicon wafer, called an IC (integrated circuit) chip.

This photograph from the IBM archives shows three generations of these switching devices in 1965:

(1) vacuum tube, (2) early transistor, and (3) integrated circuit (small dot to the right).

Table 3. Early Generations of Integrated Circuits

IC chip generation and date	Description	Number of transistors
Generation 1, early 1960s	Small Scale Integration (SSI)	10 to 20
Generation 2, late 1960s	Medium Scale Integration (MSI)	20 to 200
Generation 3, early 1970s	Large Scale Integration (LSI)	200 to 10,000
Generation 4, late 1970s	Very Large Scale Integration (VLSI)	More than 10,000
Generation 5, late 1980s	Ultra Large Scale Integration (ULSI)	More than 1,000,000

In the same way that the steam engine drove the major technological and social changes of the nineteenth century, the microprocessor is transforming our own lives and times. It's worthwhile to take a look at the history of the microprocessor, which plays such a central role.

As described in Exhibit 4, the switching devices used to control the storage and manipulation of information in a computer were large and inefficient. As a result, early computers were large and inefficient compared with today's standards. Vacuum tube–based computers such as the U.S. Army's ENIAC, Remington Rand's UNIVAC I, and IBM's early mainframes in the 1950s required large physical spaces in which to operate. Purchase and maintenance costs were also high, which is why mainframes were largely used by government agencies, universities, and large corporations.

While the first transistor had been developed as early as 1947 by Bell Labs, and found early applications in small consumer radios, it was not used in mainframe computers until 1955.

Two computer scientists, Jack Kilby of Texas Instruments (1959) and Robert Noyce of Fairchild Semiconductor (1961), are credited with creating the first *integrated circuit* (IC) chips. These consist of small squares of silicon into which tiny transistors are embedded, interconnected by small traces of aluminum. As new generations of IC chips were manufactured, transistors of smaller sizes and greater numbers were created. Kilby's first integrated circuit was a simple design composited on a surface no bigger than a paper clip. Robert Noyce's first IC chip in 1961 consisted only of one transistor and four other embedded components—three resistors and one capacitor. It was the size of an adult's small finger.

Figure 9. The Intel 4004 microprocessor, a "computer on a chip" (1971). Courtesy of Intel Corporation.

As a greater number of transistors and connections were incorporated into these miniature circuits, the chips were able to handle more tasks, and at a greater level of complexity. New generations of IC circuits quickly emerged out of these prototypes pioneered by Kilby and Noyce.

These miniature electronic devices were first used by the U.S. military and space program for onboard navigation systems. As their manufacturing cost began to fall, the chips began to find their way into general consumer products, such as hand calculators and watches.

In 1971 a small California electronics company called Intel filed the patent for an integrated circuit that contained 2,300 transistors and was designed to be a general purpose programmable device called the *Intel 4004*. It was a "computer on a chip"—the size of a thumbnail and as powerful as the ENIAC .[14] This was the first *microprocessor,* and it supported all of the computer functions described by English inventor Charles Babbage in the nineteenth century: input, processing, storage, and output.

Several years later, in 1974, Intel released the Intel 8080, a milestone third generation microprocessor that worked as the *central processing unit* (CPU) for the first home hobbyist personal computer, the Altair. Ed Roberts was the president of MITS, an electronics manufacturing company located in Albuquerque, New Mexico. He had the idea of creating a do-it-yourself computer construction kit, aimed at the amateur electronics market, which he called the Altair 8800. Roberts advertised for his home assembly computer in the January 1975 issue of *Popular Mechanics* expecting to sell 800 kits at a list price of $439. Instead, by the end of February, there were 1,000 orders for the Altair. By August 1975, Roberts had sold more than 5,000 units. The first personal computer was a huge success.

The Altair was an unusual personal computer by today's standards. There was no keyboard, no mouse, no monitor, and no printer. The user interacted with the computer by flipping toggle switches on the front panel. Small lights would let the user know if a program was successful. It actually did very little, but it was a *computer,* and the fact that you could build it in your own garage added to its allure for home hobbyists.

Two young computer programmers from Seattle, Bill Gates and Paul Allen, picked up on the excitement. They contacted Roberts with a proposal to create software that would allow users to write instructions for the Altair—a computer language they called BASIC. Roberts was interested and invited them to MITS for a demonstration. At the time, Gates and Allen were students at Harvard University and had access to an early Digital Equipment Corporation minicomputer called the PDP-1. After some frantic last minute programming, Allen departed for Albuquerque with a punched tape of programming instructions to input into the Altair at MIPS. Paul Allen was pleasantly surprised when the BASIC programming instructions worked flawlessly the first time they executed.[15] Gates and Allen won a contract to develop an operating system software for the first personal computer. Soon after, they started up a new company, which they called "Micro-Soft"—now known as *Microsoft.*

Meanwhile, in California two other young computer pioneers, Steve Jobs and Steve Wozniak, were working on a do-it-yourself computer construction kit that they called the Apple I. Although the kit provided many of the important parts of the computer, such as the MOS Technology 6502 microprocessor and preassembled circuit boards, the package was not complete—users had to buy a keyboard and monitor separately. The Apple I kit was released in July 1976 for a cost of $666.66; a total of 200 were sold.

After this modest success, the two entrepreneurs went on to create a fully assembled Apple II computer (with a built-in keyboard) that was introduced at a computer fair less than a year later in April 1977. The Apple II also supported sound and graphics, which significantly added to its popularity.

Although other micro computer systems and newly started software companies began to arise during this period of time, the ground breaking work by Gates, Allen, Jobs, and Wozniak began to move computing from expensive managed mainframes in large organizations to affordable systems in the home. The era of personal computing had begun, driven by the central engine of the information age—the microprocessor.

A sense of the excitement and passion during this early period of home hobbyists and personal computers can be found in an article that was written for *Creative Computing Magazine* in November 1984 by Robert Marsh:[16]

> We didn't have many things you take for granted today, but we did have a feeling of excitement and adventure. A feeling that we were the pioneers in a new era in which small computers would free everyone from much of the drudgery of everyday life. A feeling that we were secretly taking control of information and power jealously guarded by the Fortune 500 owners of multi-million dollar IBM mainframes. A feeling that the world would never be the same once "hobby computers" really caught on.

Moore's Law: The Acceleration of Computation

In 1965 Gordon Moore, who was one of the cofounders of Intel Corporation, manufacturer of the first commercially available microprocessor (the Intel 4004), made a bold prediction: **the number of transistors per square inch on integrated circuit chips double approximately every two years,**[17] and would continue to do so in the foreseeable future. Although computer processing capacities double every twenty-four months, computer costs remain the same. This prediction has come to be known as **Moore's Law.** According to technology inventor Ray Kurzweil, if Moore's Law continues unabated, a $1,000 desktop computer (in 1999 dollars) by 2023 will provide the computational ability of the human brain.[18]

Moore's Law is significant because it implies that all industries that are tied to microprocessors, from biotechnology companies to stock market brokerage firms, will continue to experience the benefit of increased speeds and capabilities while the cost of this increased performance will remain the same. Gordon Moore himself has expressed doubt that this trend can continue forever, but so far there seems to be no end in sight.

The size of circuits and transistors continues to decrease, with a corresponding ability to integrate more of them onto tiny silicon chips. The Intel Core 2 Duo processor of 2006 is made up of more than 291 million transistors; the Intel 8088, which was the central processing unit of the first desktop PC computers in 1981, only had 29,000. In the future, a 10 GHz central processing unit, proposed by Intel, will be capable of completing 20 million calculations in the time it takes a bullet to travel 1 foot. As a result, computers can now support many different kinds of functions, from playing games and high-definition video clips, to supporting Internet-based telephone conversations. The cost of this increased performance has not gone up.

The microprocessor is now embedded in all kinds of electronic devices, such as alarm clocks, blood pressure cuffs, stop lights, automobiles, radios, televisions, thermometers, cameras, as well as computers. They have transformed even the most routine aspects our daily lives. But microprocessors and computers by themselves have not

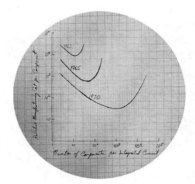

Figure 10a and 10b. This hand drawn diagram in 1965 by Intel cofounder Gordon Moore (shown above in the 1960s) predicts that computer speeds would double every two years while the cost of this increased performance would remain the same. His prediction, called *Moore's Law,* continues to be accurate to this day. Courtesy of Intel Corporation.

been the only transformative factor in the emergence of our information-based society. Their impact has been enhanced by the growth of the Internet and the World Wide Web, which provide the planet with a communications platform interconnecting over a billion participants. Since personal computers appear in many countries and cultures around the world, and information can take many different forms, it has created a social environment where there are many media producers and end users. While the early expensive main frame computers of the 1950s and 1960s with their slow data networks were only available to large corporate, academic, or government institutions, the Internet and World Wide Web have made possible bottom-up, democratic, and diverse social communications networks. Vannevar Bush's dream of a personal, networked information storage and retrieval device finally became a reality several decades after he first described the Memex in 1945.

Hypertext and Hypermedia

During the early decades of computer hardware—as interactive computer devices moved from punched tape toward a vision described by J.C.R. Licklider, Douglas Engelbart, and Alan Kay of friendlier computer interfaces and extended time-share networks—a parallel development was taking place in the realm of information management. As we've discussed, Vannevar Bush in "As We May Think" had expressed his concern that "publication has extended far beyond our present ability to make use of the record"; in other words, the volume of paper-based information was becoming unmanageable.

Bush claimed that his Memex device "affords an immediate step . . . to associative thinking, the basic idea of which is a provision whereby any item may be caused at will to select immediately and automatically another. This the essential feature of the memex. *The process of tying two items together is the important thing.*" In one short paragraph, Bush described "the essential feature" of today's World Wide Web, the ubiquitous hypertext link, an electronic synapse that allows one page on a network to instantly retrieve information from another document on the network.[19]

In the fall of 1960, a second year Harvard graduate student named Ted Nelson who was inspired by Vannevar Bush's 1945 article decided to write a software program to organize his own notes and diagrams. This was in a time before the invention of word processing, and Nelson was looking for a way of manipulating electronic text to allow authors to compare, modify, or delete text easily. There were no computers with the Memex-like storage capabilities that Nelson was seeking. He began to write his own information storage and retrieval software, and realized after writing many lines of code that it was a much more difficult task than he'd anticipated. For one thing, information storage on the Memex was based on microfilm, and Nelson wanted to create and access electronic text documents.

In addition to his interest in electronic text editing, Nelson was intrigued by the notion that ideas created in text didn't necessarily have to be accessed sequentially, as they normally are organized in a book, but could be connected in a freely associative way. This idea had been explored to a certain degree in old religious texts as seen in the illuminated manuscripts of the Middle Ages or the Talmud, where blocks of related, supplemental commentary were arranged around a central body of text. These associated blocks of information are commonly referred to as *marginalia.* Nelson wanted to push this idea further by allowing computer users to access information laterally, across documents, so that selected groups of related information could easily be accessed through links. For example, bibliographic references that an author had included in an electronic report to support an idea could be linked and directly referenced by the reader—with no waiting.

In a paper that was delivered for the Association of Computing Machinery in 1965, Nelson coined the words *hypertext* and *hypermedia* to describe his idea of associative linkages across documents. In his book *Literary Machines,* Nelson describes his idea: "By 'hypertext' I mean nonsequential writing . . . But the structure of ideas is not sequential. They tie together every which way."[20] Around the same time, Nelson began to explore the wider implications of this idea within the framework of a project he called Xanadu. This was a concept in which all documents were electronically stored in one large database, or global library, accessible to everyone on an equal basis. Xanadu carried with it a utopian idealism, as an environment in which everyone could publish, receive payments for their work, and view the work of others in a pluralistic, democratic way. By 1974, with the introduction of the first locally networked computers, Nelson saw the potential evolution of Xanadu as a *docuverse,* in which the full body of all literary, scientific, and artistic work could be accessible through hypertext or hypermedia links, a point and click information environment.

Ted Nelson worked on his Xanadu project for over thirty years, but a commercial version of it was not released until 1999, long after the advent of the World Wide Web. The writer Gary Wolf in *Wired Magazine* wrote a harsh assessment of Nelson's Xanadu project in 1995:

"Xanadu, a global hypertext publishing system, is the longest-running vaporware story in the history of the computer industry. It has been in development for more than 30 years. This long gestation period may not put it in the same category as the Great Wall of China, which was under construction for most of the 16th century and still failed to foil invaders, but, given the relative youth of commercial computing, Xanadu has set a record of futility that will be difficult for other companies to surpass."[21]

Other people have come to regard Nelson as a creative innovator who laid out a roadmap for the growth and development of what was later to become the World Wide Web.

Tim Berners-Lee: Inventor and "Patron Saint" of the World Wide Web

"First of all, I think the WWW was a brilliant simplification. As I understand it, and maybe I have this wrong, but Tim Berners-Lee came and we had lunch, in, oh I guess it was 1989, 90, something like that, in Sausalito, and I really liked the guy, and he'd done this very simple thing, and it sounded too trivial to me {laughs} but he certainly was a nice fellow and I expected to keep in touch with him, although I am a very bad correspondent, and the next thing I knew suddenly the thing had caught on."[22]

Ted Nelson

A meeting between Ted Nelson, a creative computer scientist, and Tim Berners-Lee, inventor of the World Wide Web, took place in 1992. Nelson had been working on the hypertext-based *Xanadu* concept, and while he respected Berners-Lee, he dismissed his idea of a network-based publishing system as too simplistic. Berners-Lee, in turn, had been influenced by Nelson's work and was intrigued by the notion that "there was a power in arranging ideas in an unconstrained, weblike way".[23] This idea, as in Nelson's *Xanadu*, formed a central role in the development of Berners-Lee's invention, the *World Wide Web*. These two inventors had grappled with solutions to the same problem: how to create a universal publishing environment where one electronic document could be linked to any other document on the network. One might wonder why *Xanadu*, which supported a hypertext-based model and had a longer history of development, never achieved the success of the World Wide Web.

In 1989 Tim Berners-Lee was working as a scientist at the European Laboratory for Particle Physics (CERN) in Switzerland. He was trying to resolve a situation in which various kinds of information stored by the lab had to be accessed from different computer terminals, each using different kinds of programs that were unique to each system. CERN was also bedeviled by a situation in which there was a high turnover of staff, coupled with a large amount of research information that was in a continual state of change. As part of their orientation, new employees were compelled to sort through a large amount of inefficiently organized information. A printed book was insufficient for keeping up with the large amount of information being generated. [24]

Berners-Lee had been experimenting for about ten years with a program he called *Enquire,* named after a fanciful Victorian omniexplanatory manual called *Enquire Within upon Everything*. Originally this was a program that

What Is the Difference Between the Internet and the World Wide Web?

Although the terms Internet and World Wide Web are used interchangeably, they aren't the same thing. The *Internet* has been called the "network of networks" since it has the capacity for potentially linking every computer to every other computer connected to this system around the globe. You can think of the Internet as the hardware side of the global computer network—consisting of computers, cables, routers, switches, transmitters, and receivers. The World Wide Web, on the other hand, provides a means whereby information can be published and viewed over the Internet. Through clickable hyperlinks, one Web page of information can open up any other Web page connected to the network. Over time, the World Wide Web has moved from pages supporting only text to other media such as video, animation, sound, and graphics.

enabled him to organize and access linked documents that contained information that was of personal interest; it was not designed to run on a computer network. Ten years later, *Enquire* provided the necessary conceptual foundation for Berners-Lee to resolve the information storage and access challenges at CERN. This time, the program would be accessible to multiple users on a computer network and would allow them to produce and share electronic information via hypertext links connecting one document to another. The enabling network technology upon which his software was built was the Internet. Berners-Lee settled on a name for his new network-based hypertext application—the *World Wide Web*.[25]

But Tim Berners-Lee had a wider vision—he saw his concept of the World Wide Web extending beyond the organizational requirements of CERN to a networked community—to eventually include participants from around the entire planet.

> "Suppose all the information stored on computers everywhere were linked, I thought. Suppose I could program my computer to create a space in which anything could be linked to anything. All the bits of information in every computer at CERN, and on the planet would be available to me and to anyone else. There would be a single, global information space."[26]
>
> Tim Berners-Lee

There are three fundamental concepts behind the World Wide Web as Berners-Lee initially created them. They enable network users on many different kinds of computers and running a wide variety of software programs, to publish, access, and view electronic documents across a computer network.[27]

1) **The Uniform Resource Locator (URL)**—A unique address provided for every document on a network. This was originally called the *Universal Document Identifier* by Berners Lee, but the term "Universal" was considered too presumptuous, and the name was subsequently changed.

2) **Hypertext Transfer Protocol (HTTP)**—A set of preestablished coded instructions that enables an electronic document to be downloaded from a server, where the document is stored, to a user's computer. This protocol identifies a page of electronic information as a Web document and permits the transmission of hypertext data.

3) **Hypertext**—A key ingredient for the early success of the World Wide Web. A word, line of text, or image can be activated to link to other documents on a computer network.

4) **Hypertext Markup Language (HTML)**—A set of electronic document formatting instructions that provide a way to publish and display electronic information universally across the Internet.

Berners-Lee's software was built on set of simple bracketed text commands, called *tags,* that position and format electronic text displayed on a computer screen. These tags form a simple language called HTML (for Hyper Text Markup Language). One key advantage of the HTML document is that it can be accessed across all computer platforms and networks on the World Wide Web. Another key feature is that HTML supports *hyperlinks,* which allow a user to directly link to and display other HTML documents on a network. Initially, this software was intended for use by scientists who could publish their scientific research on the Internet and set up direct electronic connections to relevant source documents.

The last missing piece of the World Wide Web system was the *browser,* an application that was designed to download and display web documents created in HTML. Berners-Lee had created an early version of a browser and HTML editor he called the World Wide Web that had limited functionality. It wasn't until the 1993 arrival of the Mosaic browser, created by students at the National Center for Supercomputing Applications (NCSA) at the University of Illinois at Urbana, that the World Wide Web began to find a wider audience.

Several members of the NCSC Mosaic production team, notably Marc Andreesson, went on in 1994 to form Netscape with former Silicon Graphics CEO Jim Clark. *Netscape* produced the first all-commercial browser, which was made available for low-cost or no-cost to its customers. Within two years, software giant Microsoft had joined the browser competition with their *Internet Explorer*. Within five years of its introduction at CERN, the growth of the World Wide Web was skyrocketing.

Tim Berners-Lee has occasionally been referred to as the *patron saint* of the World Wide Web for several good reasons. First of all, the fast growth of the web is often attributed to the fact that Berners-Lee gave the World Wide Web

```
<html>
  <head>
    <title>War of Ideas</title>
    <body bgcolor="#ffffff" align="center" vlink="#999966" link="993366" text="000000">
      <table cellpadding="0" cellspacing="0" border="0">
        <tr>
          <td>
          <img src="../graphics/splash01.jpg" border="0" />
          </td>
        </tr>
      </table>
    </body>
</html>
```

Figure 11. Example of HTML (Hypertext Markup Language).

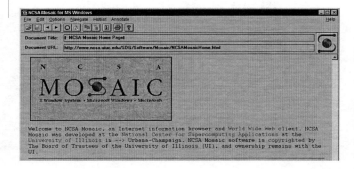

Figure 12. The NCSA Mosaic browser, first introduced in 1993. Courtesy of the National Center for Supercomputing Applications (NCSA) and the Board of Trustees of the University of Illinois.

software away—he decided to let it remain part of the public domain. Its value was instantly recognized, and it was universally adopted. Berners-Lee stood to gain financially if he made the World Wide Web a proprietary software product, but he chose to let it remain as a public good, without cost to its users. In contrast, the *Xanadu* hypertext model developed by Ted Nelson was based on a proprietary technology where the universe of available digital information was located on a centralized source as opposed to distributed nodes of information access across a network as provided by the World Wide Web. In Nelson's system, users were charged a fee for information access and all network publishing had to be conducted through the *Xanadu* company. An act of public-spirited generosity on the part of Tim Berners-Lee is largely credited for the rapid growth and acceptance of the World Wide Web system.

Berners-Lee left CERN in 1994 to help create the World Wide Consortium (W3C), which is currently on the MIT (Massachusetts Institute of Technology) campus. The W3C consists of corporations, nonprofit agencies, and universities from around the planet that are making decisions about the future of the Web. He has dedicated a large part of his life to help guide the direction of the World Wide Web so that it remains an open, interactive public resource and does not fall under the proprietary influence of a few individuals or companies.

"If we succeed, creativity will arise across larger and more diverse groups. These high-level activities, which have occurred just within one human's brain, will occur among ever-larger, more interconnected groups of people acting as if they shared a larger intuitive brain. It is an intriguing analogy. Perhaps that late-night surfing is not such a waste of time after all: It is just the Web dreaming."[28]

Tim Berners-Lee

The initial idea of technology-augmented human intelligence, as articulated by early pioneers like Vannevar Bush, J.C.R. Licklider, Douglas Engelbart, Alan Kay, and Ted Nelson was largely manifested by a general acceptance of Berners-Lee's World Wide Web. But we're not only talking about the enhancement of human intelligence through the use of hyperlinks and rapid information access, but also about the advantages provided by large numbers of network-connected participants engaged in a continuing exchange of ideas. According to the Ethernet inventor and engineer Bob Metcalfe, *the usefulness of a network corresponds to the square of the number of network users,* which is also known as *Metcalfe's Law.* A network consisting of four people will be four times more valuable than a network of two people, because there are four times the number of interconnections and contacts possible. From an information exchange standpoint, the worth of a network grows exponentially. The Internet constitutes the largest network and was estimated to have reached a billion users worldwide by the year 2005.[29]

The growth of the World Wide Web as a universal publishing medium has been accompanied by a transformation of text, images, video, animation, and sound from analog experiences recorded on many different media to a single digital representation as 0s and 1s. In this digital form, these various media can be edited, combined, and presented in a flexible way on the World Wide Web. Web users can download programs, view information, interact collaboratively, and produce their own ideas.

Andy Covell[30] describes these unprecedented self-publishing capabilities as being enabled through *digital convergence* and summarizes this development as the ability to:

1) Represent all media experiences (sound, text, video, and images by using the common substrate of binary digital data) as 1s and 0s.

2) Manage, edit, combine, and transmit or publish this information via the Internet.

3) Incorporate interactivity and two-way communication within this communications environment.

New Directions: Web 2.0 as a Many-to-Many Communications Medium

As the process of digital convergence continues, the distinctions among the television, telephone, fax machine, computer, game console, and DVD player have become blurred. Information continues to be delivered in an expanding array of different formats. Since its introduction in 1993, the World Wide Web has changed from an electronic publishing environment with static web pages, hyperlinks, and images, to an interactive domain of news feeds, digital movie clips, image catalogs, music, video conference calls, and games. Internet search companies such as Google, Yahoo! Search, Ask.com, Wikia Search, and Live Search (formerly MSN Search), have also provided a way for web users to easily find the specific content they're looking for.

In October 2004, there was a brainstorming session between Tim O'Reilly (of O'Reilly Media) and MediaLive International. Major changes were taking place in how certain new innovative websites were delivering information and services to their audiences. The term **Web 2.0** was used to describe these generational changes—a new and improved version of the World Wide Web. What are some of the characteristics of this latest generation of websites?

Probably one of the significant features of Web 2.0 sites is the fact that the user is no longer a passive observer, but an active participant and a contributor. Every Internet user is a potential viewer *and* producer of information. Traditional media, including newspapers, radio, television, movies, and the first generation of World Wide Web sites (Web 1.0), assume that the audience will take on the role of a passive observer (a *one-to-many communications model*) where a small group of producers create content for a large number of receivers.

Think of a city newspaper, which gathers in information from news services, maintains a group of reporters to write about local events, and is managed by a team of editors who determine what information will be included in the final printed copy. The newspaper is distributed by trucks to newsstands, homes, and vending machines. Readers either buy or subscribe to the newspaper, but they can't change the content of the paper. Later, a reader may send a letter to the editor to discuss an issue of importance to them that appears in the newspaper, but it must be approved by the paper's editorial staff before it goes to print. The day's news is unchangeably inked to paper and can't be altered. Information is permanently embedded into the medium that delivers it, and content is managed from the top-down. The newspaper is a one-to-many communications medium (see Chapter 4).

Wikipedia is a Web 2.0 website that provides a prime example of a *many-to-many communications model* as described in Chapter 4. Wikipedia describes itself by saying, "Wikipedia is an online encyclopedia that can be edited by anyone."[31] The plan behind Wikipedia is to build a worldwide encyclopedia in multiple languages that's created not by a team of specialists but from website users. Users also can correct and update information that's posted by other content authors. One might think that a publically created encyclopedia would be filled with inaccuracies and poorly written content, but Wikipedia has proved itself to be almost as accurate as the *Encyclopedia Britannica.*[32] The philosophy behind this open-authorship model is that eventually errors will be self-correcting as more users review and make contributions to the articles. It should also be noted that newly created content for Wikipedia is checked by a group of volunteers called "new page patrollers" to protect the encyclopedia from vandalism and invalid content.

Don Tapscott and Anthony Williams in their book *Wikinomics* describe the power and effectiveness of Wikipedia in delivering an up-to-the-minute news report after a bombing in the London subway system in 2005.

> "On July 7, 2005, at 8:50 A.M., the city of London, England, came to a standstill as four synchronized bombs exploded in its transportation system. Eighteen minutes later, as media outlets scrambled to cover the story, the first entry appeared in Wikipedia, a free online encyclopedia that anyone can edit. Morwen, a wiki enthusiast from Leicester, England, wrote: 'On July 7, 2005, explosions or other incidents were reported at various London Underground stations in central London, specifically Aldgate, Edgware Road, Kings Cross St. Pancras, Old Street, and Russell Square tube station. They have been attributed to power surges.'
>
> "Within minutes, other community members were adding information and correcting her spelling. By the time North Americans woke up, hundreds of users had joined the fray. By the end of the day, over twenty-five hundred users had created a comprehensive fourteen-page account of the events that was much more detailed than the information provided by any single news outlet . . . demonstrating that thousands of dispersed volunteers can create fast, fluid, and innovative projects that outperform those of the largest and best-financed enterprises."[33]

The first article for Wikipedia was posted on January 16, 2001; on February 12, almost a month later, there were 1,000 entries. By September 7 of the same year, the count was up to 10,000 articles, and after one year of operation, Wikipedia had more than 20,000 encyclopedia entries. As of April 2008, there were *10 million* articles posted to the site.[34]

What distinguishes Wikipedia from a print-based encyclopedia is that it is an open, editable body of information capable of accepting infinite updates, corrections, and improvements. Despite this fact, it should be noted that many librarian professionals, researchers, and academic institutions do not wholly support the user-derived information on Wikipedia, and some think that it should not be referenced at all for serious publications.

Wikipedia is one of many successful Web 2.0 websites that have emerged over the past few years. Below is a chart showing some of the most well-known of the better-known sites that draw on user-generated feedback and participation.

All of the Web 2.0 websites listed above have several features in common:

1) They all deliver their services and content over the Internet—they are network-based.

2) They actively encourage and support participation as well as engagement from their users. Content is often generated by viewers.

3) Some or all of their services require no financial transactions—they are free of cost, but may require their users to view advertising or web links that are tailored to their interests.

4) Web 2.0 websites tend to build communities of common interest, creating groups of individuals who consistently return for updated information.

5) They are accessible and easy to use, without requiring advanced programming or other technical skills.

There is the assumption in the Web 2.0 model that websites are "platforms for participation," where there is a collective intelligence that generates useful information through social networking and collaboration. The philosophy is that the wisdom of the crowds (when that wisdom is accessible and well presented) can lead to beneficial results for participants and successful online businesses; a "win-win" situation. Tim O'Reilly of O'Reilly Media sums up the Web 2.0 viewpoint by saying:

> "Web 2.0 is the understanding that network is the platform. And on the network as platform, the rules for business are different. And the cardinal rule (for this networked platform) is this one, 'users add value'. And figuring out how to build databases that get better the more people use them is actually the secret sauce of every Web 2.0 company."[35]

Just as it has been important in the past for people to become skilled at writing and speaking, it is becoming increasingly important to learn digital communications media, networking technologies, and their implementation

Table 4. Web 2.0 Websites

Web 2.0 website	Web 2.0 features
AMAZON http://www.amazon.com	Provides ways for users to give feedback on book titles and purchases. Provides suggestions for new online purchases based on previous purchases.
FLICKR http://www.flickr.com	Provides an online service that allows users to post, organize, and share photographs and videos on the web.
PANDORA http://www.pandora.com	Gives music listeners the ability to choose music that is tailored to their specific tastes and to create "radio stations" that play customized song lists.
MYSPACE http://www.myspace.com	Users create customized personalized websites and can develop friends lists for online social networking. FACEBOOK is another popular social networking site.
DEL.ICIO.US http://del.icio.us	A service that lets users post their bookmarks to favorite websites and see what sites other users are visiting. Calls itself a "social bookmarking site."
GOOGLE http://www.google.com	Google began as an Internet search engine company, but has now expanded into other online services, including email, document creation, blogs, and news—among numerous others. It is often referred to as the leading example of a Web 2.0 company.
YOUTUBE http://www.youtube.com	A 2.0 generation website, now a subsidiary of Google, that gives users the ability to shoot video clips and publish them on the Internet.

on the World Wide Web. These skills are valuable not only for accessing information online, but also for meaningfully participating in a society that is progressively more dependent on digital telecommunications. Business and political consultant Ben Rigby claims that when many people begin using these new Web 2.0 tools, it will lead to beneficial results:

> "It's clear that tectonic shifts are well under way. Alternative media are flourishing. It's easier to communicate with close friends and relations alike, which is strengthening the wide diversity of social bonds. The range of information available to average people is growing rapidly. Significant hurdles exist, of course, such as a lack of access to computing resources among many of the world's poorest populations. However, on the whole, these changes are improving our quality of life and engendering a more vital, engaged, and democratic citizenry."[36]

A new generation of Web 2.0 technologies is poised to transform our society and institutions in unexpected ways. Stay tuned.

Endnotes

[1] Ibid.

[2] James Burke, *Connections* (New York: Simon & Schuster, 2007), p. 116.

[3] Michael Kanellos, A Computer Is Born, *CNET News*, February 13, 2006, http://www.news.com/ENIAC-A-computer-is-born/2009-1006_3-6037980.html.

[4] Ibid.

[5] Vannevar Bush, As We May Think, *The Atlantic Online*, July 1945, http://www.theatlantic.com/unbound/flashbks/computer/bushf.htm.

[6] Ibid.

[7] Scott Griffin, *Internet Pioneers*, http://www.ibiblio.org/pioneers/licklider.html, http://www.ibiblio.org/pioneers/author.html.

[8]Howard Rheingold, *Tools for Thought: The People and Ideas of the Next Computer Revolution* (New York: Simon & Schuster, 1985), Chapter 7, http://www.rheingold.com/texts/tft/.

[9]ARPA Does Windows: The Defense Underpinning of the PC Revolution, *Columbia International Affairs Online*, August 2000, http://www.ciaonet.org/isa/fog01/.

[10]Tim Lenoir, Stanford University, "The Demo," *The Mouse Site*, http://sloan.stanford.edu/mousesite/1968Demo.html.

[11]Douglas Engelbart, Interview 1, December 19, 1986, http://www-sul.stanford.edu/depts/hasrg/histsci/ssvoral/engelbart/main1-ntb.html.

[12]Rheingold, http://www.theatlantic.com/unbound/flashbks/computer/bushf.htm.

[13]Ibid, Chapter 11, http://www.rheingold.com/texts/tft/11.html.

[14]Mary Bellis, Intel 4004—The World's First Single Chip Microprocessor, http://inventors.about.com/od/mstartinventions/a/microprocessor.htm.

[15]Paul Allen, excerpt from a dinner talk, *Triumph of the Nerds: Part I*, Ambrose Video, April 1996.

[16]Robert Marsh, 1975: Ancient History, Creative Computing, Vol. 10, no. 11, November 1984, p. 108 http://www.atarimagazines.com/creative/v10n11/108_1975_ancient_history.php.

[17]Gordon Moore, as summarized on the Intel Corporation website, http://www.intel.com/technology/mooreslaw/index.htm.

[18]Ray Kurzweil, *The Age of Spiritual Machines* (Penguin Books, Non-Classics,1999), p. 278.

[19]Bush,

[20]Ted Nelson, *Computer Lib* (Tempus Books of Microsoft Press, 1987), p. 29.

[21]Ibid.

[22]Ted Nelson, "Orality and Hypertext: An Interview with Ted Nelson," interview with Jim Whitehead, 1996, http://www.ics.uci.edu/~ejw/csr/nelson_pg.html.

[23]Tim Berners-Lee with Mark Fischetti, *Weaving the Web* (San Francisco: HarperCollins Publishers, 1999).

[24]Tim Berners-Lee, Proposal to CERN for the World Wide Web Software, 1989–1990, http://www.w3.org/History/1989/proposal.html.

[25]Berners-Lee, Fischetti, *Weaving the Web*, pp. 10–15.

[26]Ibid, p. 4.

[27]James Gillies and Robert Calliau, *How the Web Was Born* (Oxford University Press, 2000), pp. 206-208.

[28]Berners-Lee, Fischetti, *Weaving the Web*, pp. 201–202.

[29]David M. Ewalt, Report Predicts a Billion Web Users by 2005, *Information Week*, February 8, 2001, http://www.cconvergence.com/article/IWK20010208S0002.

[30]Andy Covell, *Digital Convergence* (Newport, RI: Aegis Publishing Group, 1999), p. 17.

[31]Wikipedia, History of Wikipedia, http://en.wikipedia.org/wiki/History_of_Wikipedia (accessed May 23, 2008).

[32]Jim Giles, Internet Encyclopaedias go Head to Head, *Nature Magazine*, no. 438 (December 15, 2005), pp. 900-901.

[33]Don Tapscott and Anthony D. Williams, *Wikinomics* (Portfolio, a member of Penguin Group, 2006), p. 65.

[34]Wikipedia, History of Wikipedia, http://en.wikipedia.org/wiki/History_of_Wikipedia (accessed May 23, 2008).

[35]Tim O'Reilly, What Is Web 2.0? *Kamla Bhatt Show*, May 21, 2007, http://www.youtube.com/watch?v=CQibri7gpLM&feature=related.

[36]Ben Rigby, *Mobilizing Generation 2.0: A Practical Guide to Using Web 2.0*, (Jossey-Bass, A Wiley Imprint, 2008), p. 257

Chapter 6
The Hall of High Definition

Beavis: "I wonder what people did before television."
Butthead: "Don't be stupid, Beavis! There's always been television! There's just more channels now."
Beavis: "Oh, yeah. Progress is cool. Heh heh."

Beavis and Butthead episode, writer Mike Judge

Timeline of Advanced Television Technologies

1927—Philo Farnsworth, at twenty-one years old, successfully demonstrates the first successful electronic television in San Francisco. While in high school, Philo Farnsworth was obsessed with the idea of creating an electronic device that could capture live action and transmit it as a signal over a distance using radio waves. His approach is to scan a scene electronically, encode that scanned information as pulses of electronic information that, in turn, paint a reconstructed picture on a light sensitive screen. Just after Farnsworth completes a working television camera prototype, an investor asks, "When are we going to see some dollars in this thing, Farnsworth?" In response, the young inventor points his early TV camera at a dollar sign.[1]

1957—Philo Farnsworth appears on Gary Moore's television show *I've Got A Secret* where he discusses the future of television. His predictions are remarkably accurate regarding developments taking place several decades later with the emergence of high definition television (HDTV).

Transcript of television show, *I've Got A Secret* with host Gary Moore, on July 21, 1957:

Gary Moore:	As I understand it, sir . . . there have been television sets of sorts before you came along.
Philo Farnsworth:	Yes. There had been attempts to devise a television system using mechanical disks, rotating mirrors, and vibrating mirrors—but all mechanical. My contribution was to take out the moving parts and make the thing entirely electronic. That was the concept I had when I was just a freshman in high school.
Gary Moore:	How many patents do you hold in the television field?
Philo Farnsworth:	I hold something in the neighborhood of 165 American patents.
Gary Moore:	Let's go from the past . . . to the future. What are you working on now?
Philo Farnsworth:	In television, we're attempting to make better utilization of the bandwidth—because we think we can eventually get in excess of 2000 lines, instead of 525—and do it on even a narrower channel, than we're doing on the current television—which will make for a much sharper picture. We believe in the picture frame type of a picture where the visual display will just be a screen.[2]

1969—Alan Kiron, a staff scientist at the U.S. Patent Office, coins the term *domonetics* to describe the interaction between culture and technology. Combining the words *domicile, connections,* and *electronics,* Kiron used the term to describe how work and living patterns would be reshaped by the new computer and other communication tools. Telephones, televisions, video games, computers – linked by wires, fiber optics, switches, and wireless connections, provide the central nervous system of the domonetic world.

Television is a broadcast medium shaped by the characteristics of the vacuum tube and the radio frequency spectrum. Thus, both the power and limitations of television as an information medium and a cultural force were decided as far back as the 1930s when the new technology was being invented. Television was and is a "master-slave" architecture—a top to bottom technology with a few broadcasters creating programs for millions of passive viewers (what the industry referred to as "dumb terminals").

With the development of new technologies, the Television Age began to give way to the Digital Age:

- The transistor in 1948.

- The microchip in 1958.

- Fiber optic cable in the 1970s—glass wires the width of a human hair that could bear billions of characters of information per second, sending out data in digital form on a laser diode. The signals could be stored and manipulated without deterioration. By the 90s it was possible to produce TV sets that could create, perfect, store, and even transmit signals of their own.

By radically changing the balance of power between the distributors and creators of culture, the merging of television and the Internet (dubbed the "telecomputer" by George Gilder, also called "Web TV" and a variety of other names) is breaking the broadcast bottleneck. There are potentially as many channels as there are computers attached to the global network. People order what they want, when they want, rather than settling for what is dished out to them. Participants in the new global digital communications network are also its content producers.

1990—In his book *Life After Television,* George Gilder writes about what he sees as the future of interactive technology and the "telecomputer":

> "Create a school in your home that offers the nation's best teachers imparting the moral, cultural, and religious values you cherish. Visit your family on the other side of the world with moving pictures hardly distinguishable from real-life images. Have your doctor make house calls without leaving his office. Give a birthday party for Grandma at her nursing home in Florida, bringing her descendants from all over the country to the foot of her bed in vivid living color. Watch movies or television programs originating from any station or digital database in the world . . . Order and instantly receive magazines, books, or other publications from almost anywhere in the world, edited to your own taste. You could potentially call up any of these functions and unlimited others, through listings on a telecomputer menu . . . through the alchemy of sand and glass in computer and fiberoptic technology."[3]

2000—Television sets become flatter and wider. DVDs are quickly replacing VHS tapes as the choice of what type of technology to own. We are now, officially, in the Digital Age.

2007/2008—According to www.msnbc.msn.com: "As the final weeks of the 2007/2008 television season unfold, one theme keeps reappearing in news reports: We're watching less TV . . . Decreased ratings have many causes, but what underlies them all is that television is undergoing a fundamental change that was highlighted—and maybe even accelerated—by the recent writers' strike . . . There has been significant change in recent years, especially as viewers have fled from network TV to cable, where there are hundreds of choices. That fragmentation of audience means lower ratings for some shows . . . The overall shift to cable may introduce some viewers to new shows, but it also means quality programming has a more limited audience."[4]

"Network TV is becoming a repository for more simple-minded comedies and reality television," said Eric Deggans, the TV and media critic for the *St. Petersburg Times,* while "very complex, big ticket dramas are on cable . . . I think that's a loss because people who can't afford cable are going to end up being deprived of great television. . . When viewers do tune in, it's increasingly on their own schedule, whether that's the result of renting an entire season of a show on <u>DVD</u> or just waiting a few days before watching a program recorded on DVR."[5]

2009—The <u>Digital Television Transition and Public Safety Act of 2005</u> requires full-power television stations to cease analog broadcasts and switch to digital after February 17, 2009. Antenna signals for Standard Def television will be all digital. CATV and SAT users do not have to change anything. Converter boxes are available in order for older analog TVs to continue to receive digital broadcast signals.

From Analog to Digital

"One machine can do the work of fifty ordinary men.
No machine can do the work of one extraordinary man . . ."

Elbert Hubbard, *American author*

The late 1980s and early 1990s saw more and more consumers using the term *digital*. The word was connected to another corresponding term that arose at the same time—namely, *analog*. Despite the fact that these terms have been around for several decades, most people on the street today might still have difficulty understanding the difference. The analog system, the aim of which is to replicate sound or images via transmitted waves, had been around since 1887, when Edison captured and stored sound on tinfoil cylinders. With digital technology, signals or data are represented as a series of on/off impulses, with information being stored in "bits" rather than in a continuous wave. Sound and image quality is much better. (You might thinks of an analog system as someone tracing an image with a piece of tracing paper—no matter how steady the artist's hand, the replica image still will not be exact. Now, compare this with, say, a digital scan or photocopy of the original image. In this case, you couldn't tell the original from the copy.)

George Gilder further describes the distinction between analog and digital technologies:[6]

"Analog signals are application specific. Like the grooves of a vinyl record, the helical print on a videocassette, of the chemical patterns on film, they directly mimic the shape, timing, and character of the content of the signal they record. Thus analog signals must be played in "real time", at the same pace they were recorded. Analog signals mostly tie the receiver to the transmitted rendition of the signal. **It is the medium for a world of few transmitters and many receivers.**"

"Digital signals are all homogeneous bits and bytes, on-off codes that can easily be stored, compressed, error corrected, edited, and manipulated. Rather than incompatible, single purpose functions, digital signals can carry many different kinds of audio and visual information. **The distributed intelligence of digital systems is appropriate for world with as many transmitters as receivers.**"

The following diagram shows how analog signals are characterized by a continuous representation of information as recorded by audio tape, vinyl records, or emulsion-based film (analog media). Computer-based digital media, on the other hand, record all information in discrete steps, because digital information must be represented by separated values generated by 1s and 0s, the binary language of microprocessors.

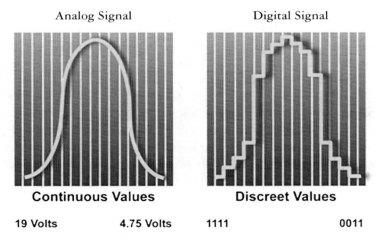

Figure 1. Analog versus Digital signals. Illustration by Kirsten Adams.

"Digital technology is the same revolution as adding sound to pictures and the same revolution as adding color to pictures. Nothing more and nothing less. . ."

George Lucas, *Wired* magazine, *February 1997*

For over ten years, the manufacturers of video equipment have been trying to make video cameras more like film, but to no avail. For their part, companies like Kodak tout slogans like "The Power of 16 mm—The Better Video." But video, even if shot with an Ikegami EC-35, is still an electronic process as opposed to the chemical process of film. The differences in image quality are still very much in evidence. Yes, film may be "the better video," and most who have worked with film and video still prefer film. Those who work continually in film are loath to work with videotape. With video, dramatic productions, no matter how well done, tend to look like either soap operas or game shows (or sometimes a combination of the two, in which case you get episodes of *Dr. Who*). But film is still very expensive (prohibitively expensive for most consumers and small production houses). With the advent of digital technology merging with photography and moviemaking, a major change in the way movies are made and a leveling of the playing field for independent producers is now taking place.

The quality of the digital image is much closer to film. You can use numerous lighting techniques (for example, Rembrandt lighting), which is difficult with video because of limited contrast. In much the same way digital audio has replaced analog sound, the digital image is superseding the video image.

"By the year 2015, Hollywood as we knew it in the 1990's may have undergone a change so profound that its impact will be equivalent to the advent of *talkies*, television, and home video combined. A major paradigm shift in Hollywood film, television, and video production is evolving, powered by new technologies in computers, digital film, compact discs, interactive multiplayers, and new delivery systems including fiber optic cable. . ."[7]

Joyce A. Shwarz, Joyce Communications, *Multimedia—Gateway to the Next Millennium*

A Brief Overview of Video Production Formats

With the introduction of videotape in 1956, the beginning of the end of what is known as The Golden Age of Television (as in live broadcasting) began. As film was used for motion pictures, so video was now used for television shows. The technology of videotape would define the entire medium of television for decades.

Like filmed movies, videotaped shows could be shot out of sequence and edited, special effects (although primitive by our standards) could be added, and laugh tracks could be added. The first video recorders used 2-inch tapes on large reels that had to be threaded much like early audio tape. Video tape recorders and video cameras were large, ungainly, and expensive.

By the late 1960s, largely because of strides made by the U.S. space program to enable crews to broadcast from outer space and the moon, smaller video cameras began to be manufactured. The real breakthrough for independent producers came with the introduction of 3/4-inch video cassette tapes in 1970. Besides being much easier to use (no more threading, you just "popped" a video cassette into a deck) and much smaller than recorders and players for 2-inch tape, 3/4-inch allowed corporate and industrial producers to create products primarily for training and documenting purposes. It also became easier for news organizations to capture events as they occurred live, the new cameras being lighter and more mobile. That same year, various companies were experimenting with home video equipment. As already noted, in the November 1970 special issue of *Look* magazine, John Kronenberg wrote an article titled "Push Button Movies: The Video-Cassette Revolution" where he predicted a time eight years in the future when consumers would be able to pop a cartridge of their favorite movie into a video machine and watch it whenever they wanted to. At the time, the only cassette machines available were crude, with tapes offering only fifty minutes of grainy black and white video and twenty-five minutes of color video. Kronenberg did, however, see a day when a home video cassette revolution would occur. However, the final question his article asked was who would be providing the content. "Will it be what is still called Hollywood?"[8]

The answer, of course, was a resounding "yes," for the content still had to be shot on film before being transferred to video. The cost of film equipment, film stock, and lighting equipment was still prohibitively expensive and out of reach for all but those people lucky enough to have either financial backing from a major Hollywood studio or a presale agreement.

The video cassette revolution really began some five years after Kronenberg's article in 1975, when <u>Sony</u> introduced its Betamax video recorder and player.

A year later, Matsushita introduced a cassette recorder with half-inch VHS (video home system) tape that could record for up to two hours. The deck was marketed through JVC.

In competing for consumers, the Betamax format soon was also able to record for two hours. By early 1980, a host of features had been added to both VHS and Betamax machines, including pause buttons, slow-motion effects, and different taping speeds. In 1984, home video cameras, or camcorders, were introduced into the marketplace.

Betamax and VHS machines and tapes were not compatible. Even though the Betamax machines were superior, Sony refused to share its technology with other companies. Thus, many more companies created VHS-compatible decks and motion picture companies distributed many more titles for VHS decks than for Betamax. The end result was that, by the late 1980s, Betamax machines were quickly being phased out and VHS machines and tapes became the home standard. Around the same time, low-cost editing equipment for the home became available. Sony, which ironically had begun marketing its own VHS machines, introduced Video-8 in 1985, followed four years later with Hi-8, a format that could be used by both consumers and professionals because of its high-quality resolution.[9]

In the meantime, new tape formats were being developed for professional recording and broadcasting that soon overtook both 3/4-inch tapes and decks as well as 1-inch professional equipment. Sony's Betacam (and later Betacam SP, or Betacam Superior Performance, with an improved image) was the clear winner. Television news producers in particular quickly switched from 3/4 to the Betacam format. In fact, Betacam cameras, with a variety of filters and three **CCDs**,[10] soon replaced 16 mm film as the format of choice. It was less expensive, could be edited quickly, and for what was being aired, provided image quality as good as most 16 mm films. Filters could give the Beta image a more dramatic quality, taking some of the harshness away from the video image. With silicon chips replacing the older tube technology cameras used, annoying problems such as comet tailing or a streaking glare caused by things like headlights were done away with.

Film, of course, is a chemical process. The "film look" was one of capturing shadow details and texture lost on video, a completely electronic process. Likewise, film had a subtler color quality and a greater tonal range than even the best video. Video, on the other hand, was immediate; you could conceivably begin editing right after wrapping a shoot. With film, you'd have to send the material into a lab, have it developed, look at it, then have a workprint made before editing actually began. In fact, by the mid-1980s, a variety of production facilities were shooting 16 mm film ps and transferring the film immediately to Betacam tape. Although the film could never be projected, when broadcast or shown on a video player, the images still looked like film. Other problems inherent with video (for example, the "bleeding" of overexposed areas into adjacent areas) could also be alleviated by this process.

Finally, companies such as Ikegami Electronics were designing new video cameras, which aimed to eliminate the problems inherent in video while achieving the tonal subtleties of the film image. Cameras like Ikegami's EC-35 used devices such as an automatic beam control circuit, which sensed overexposure, calculated the extent of the overexposure, and increased the strength of the electron beam in that area to ensure the erasure of comet-tailing, bleeding, or afterimage.

At the same time the video revolution was taking place, the same technology that helped create this revolution was enabling an exponential leap to take place in the world of home computers and special visual effects.

In 1988 the movie *Willow* introduced a new special effect called **morphing**. With this technique, it became possible through a computer to transform one shape seamlessly into another.[11] A year later, the film *The Abyss* made more extensive use of morphing technology, special effects having gone as far as they could using state-of-the-art stop-motion and prosthetics. In 1991 morphing gained worldwide notoriety because of its use in the popular film *Terminator 2*. By 1993 this technology became available to the home computer user for the affordable price of $150.00. So, it now became possible to sample a voice, digitize a body image, and create an ersatz actor on a computer—an actor totally controllable by the user.[12]

Computer programmers became more and more involved in special effects for motion pictures. Richard Brestoff has written, "In the movie *The Babe,* 1,000 extras were turned into 200,000 screaming baseball fans, using sampled and digitized people. These digitized human beings are now being used not only for extras, but also for stunt work. Why endanger a human being when a computer simulation can take the punishment risk free?"[13]

By the mid-1980s, the merging of computer technology and video technology had already become a reality: Microprocessors, silicon chips that contain the central processing unit (CPU) or the "brains" of the computer, were now an integral part of all video equipment. Microprocessors were helping to create, enhance, and manipulate both video images and sound. Computers had also become essential tools for scriptwriters, production managers, location managers, and accountants, becoming a new source of information management.

PCs were also being used as the interface between the machines and the people who used them, in effect taking over many of the tasks once performed by equipment operators (in fact, some small affiliate stations' news programs had only three people on the floor, along with the on-camera news people). Nowhere was this more evident than in the editing suite.

Computer-assisted editing units facilitated the normal editing process of searching as well as marking edit-in and edit-out points. Along with that, these editing units were also able to store and memorize all edit points, as well as transition effects such as dissolves and superimpositions. All of the information was stored on a floppy disk, which could then be taken to the **online editing** suite.

One of the first of these new, computerized, editing stations was the **CMX editor.** Even though the CMX editor could nonlinearly and randomly access video for editing purposes, traditional editors did not find it user-friendly, and its prohibitively high cost put it out of the reach of independent filmmakers and videographers. After this, the nonlinear idea fell into disuse for close to a decade, with most agencies and production houses using the standard linear editing systems available. However, by 1986, CMX editing was back with a vengeance because of the proliferation of home computers. Basically, the CMX allowed **desktop editing,** whereby the director or editor of a project could literally type onto a floppy disk everything from cuts to dissolves to overlapping sound. The floppy was then taken to a CMX online facility, where it was inserted into the editing machine. The CMX editor would then be able to find all edit points on the master videotapes, saving hours of searching to find the material. A major problem would ensue if the director or editor typed a number wrong into the home PC, cueing the tape at the wrong place during the online edit. Then, just as many hours saved might be necessary to number-crunch in order to get the online edit back on track.

After the CMX, the next big step came in the form of the Montage Picture Processor and Ediflex systems. Montage gave the user the ability to select takes via light pen and see the various takes one after the other. The user then selected a text menu command like Splice, Dissolve, Insert, Discard, and so on, and the Montage would cue up videotape machines to show the edited sequence. This was still not a digital system. This first wave of nonlinear systems had a **wait state** built in to allow videotape decks to cue to the right spot for playback. Ediflex became popular on episodic television because it incorporated script integration. With studio television series being script-driven, it made sense to be able to follow a script, issue a Play command at a particular point, and see the related takes.

By the early 1990s advances in desktop computing had made it possible to seamlessly process full-motion video using a Mac or PC. Especially important in this desktop video is the notion that the manipulation of the video is not only simple and fast, but because it is in digital format, it is **nonlinear.** In contrast to editing analog videotape, desktop video allows the editor to move instantly from one image or sequence to another, to remove, add, resequence, or modify any images in a database or image file in the same manner a writer can edit text in a word processor.[14] This soon became known as Random-Access or nonlinear editing.

The first company to gain a foothold in the market and sell their nonlinear systems industry-wide was <u>Avid Technology</u>. Consumer versions of this technology were developed in programs such as Adobe Premiere and Apple iMovie. In recent years, Apple came up with a system called <u>Final Cut Pro</u> that continues to challenge Avid as the industry standard because of its ease of use and relatively low cost.

Back in 1981 Sony had introduced Betacam videotape, a professional version of their home 1/2-inch Betamax videocassette. Five years later, in 1986, with Betacam SP (for superior performance), the quality of the Betacam image was improved to the extent that it now rivaled (some say exceeded) the quality of 1 inch broadcasting tape. Betacam quickly replaced 16 mm film as the medium of choice for news, television documentaries, and particularly industrial and corporate video, where it rang a death knell for the old standby, 3/4-inch tape.

In 1994 Sony, which had pioneered professional Betacam tape, introduced digital Betacam cameras. Along with the digital cameras, digital tape (the **D** format) was also introduced, and a number of different formats emerged.

According to Ron Whittaker in his text *Video Field Production,* digital video recording can be copied over and over without any apparent loss of quality and exceeds the best analog recordings.

In the meantime, sales for higher-end consumer and pro-sumer video cameras and recorders began to drop. To avoid the problems that beset the video industry back in the late 1970s and early 1980s, 55 companies formed a

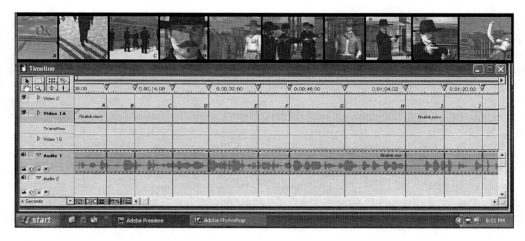

Figure 2. Non-linear digital video editors as represented by this screenshot sample from Adobe Premiere, provide powerful tools for editing visual sequences, adding special effects, and synchronizing audio tracks.
© Wade Chitwood.

Figure 3. The Sony Betacam SP, an early commercial grade camera once and for all replaced 16mm film as the medium of choice for news and documentary footage.
© Openko Dmytro | Dreamstime.com.

consortium to develop a new digital video format for consumers. First called DVC (Digital Video Cassette) and soon shortened to DV, consumer digital cameras were introduced in late 1995, first by Panasonic (the DVCPRO), followed a year later by Sony's DCR-VX1000, which incorporated a 3-CCD imaging system. The DV format offers a virtually unbeatable performance-to-cost ratio. In fact, the consumer DV camera was as good as any "pro" model, and the pricing in some cases was almost identical. Charlie White's article "Digital Cameras in Focus" from the February 1996 issue of *DV Magazine* put it this way:

> "the [consumer DV] format matches or exceeds the specs of the television industry's workhorse format and touchstone of broadcast quality Betacam SP. Will the DV format replace the stalwarts of professional video production? Let's put it this way: If you were to put winds of change into a weather forecast, the Emergency Broadcast System would now be posting a category five hurricane warning."[15]

Due to the fact that the consumer DV cameras had image quality as good as or superior to that of Betacam SP, as well as the fact that their performance was virtually identical with pro digital formats, a year after Sony's DV camera was introduced an unprecedented step was taken by the Sony company. A number of people were already claiming that DV video was a format that had "escaped the labs prematurely, before marketing managers could 'dumb it down.'" Perhaps, but what *did* happen was that companies with an established presence in the industrial video and professional area quickly saw the sales of their higher priced units dwindling as organizations like CBS or BBC started buying Sony's first consumer DV camera, the VX1000, in wholesale fashion.

In the early fall of 1997, Sony pulled the VX1000 and began advertising "professional" variants of the VX1000 which were, of course, much more expensive. A more consumer-oriented digital camera was then unveiled by Sony, which was not compatible with the pro-cameras. Now the differences between professional and consumer cameras have narrowed, and many television production companies are using high-end consumer models rather than paying for the more costly professional ones.

There are no pixels or lines of resolution, as in video. When transferring to 16 mm film, the effect is extremely good (although still expensive). The final product often looks as if it had been shot in film to begin with. If you realize that 400 feet of 16 mm negative gives you eleven minutes of film time and costs upwards of $50 to purchase, another $50 to print, and yet more money to make a workprint, magnetic 16 mm stock for sound, edge coating, and so on, and you compare this with a digital tape that costs $19 or less and gives you one hour of screen time, the cost benefits become very apparent. The look of film and digital imagery is also getting closer, although adherents of film say it can never be replaced. We shall see.

The goal of videotape and video camera manufacturers has, for a long time, been to eventually replace film. In the final analysis, what may actually happen in the future will be the disappearance of videotape all together, while digital imaging and film merge, creating an entirely new process for creating motion pictures and home theater shows.

As noted in our timeline, with the development of new technologies, the Television Age began to give way to the Digital Age. The hope of people like Kiron and later George Gilder was that people would one day be able to decide individually what they wanted to watch and could also create their own programming.

"There could be as many channels as there are computers attached to the global network. People will be able to order what they want, when they want, rather than settling for what is there."

George Gilder

According to George Gilder in his book *Life After Television:*

"Rather than exulting mass culture, the telecomputer will enhance individualism. Rather than cultivating passivity, the telecomputer will promote creativity. Released from the restrictions of mass media, American culture could attain new levels in both the visual arts and literature . . . The possibilities are endless: Create a school in your home that offers the nation's best teachers imparting the moral, cultural, and religious values you cherish. Visit your family on the other side of the world with moving pictures hardly distinguishable from real-life images. Have your doctor make house calls without leaving his office. Watch movies or television programs originating from any station or digital database in the world. Order and instantly receive magazines, books or other publications from almost anywhere in the world, edited to your own taste. All of these functions are possible today through the alchemy of sand and glass in computer and fiber-optic technology—A crystalline web of glass and light."[16]

High-Definition Television (HDTV)

Along with new forms of television, viewers and manufacturers have long looked forward to a better overall image. HDTV attempts to improve picture quality in terms of resolution (resolution being the sharpness or crispness of a TV or video image created by pixels, the smallest single picture element, which form the "lines" of resolution). European television has the potential to broadcast 625 lines of resolution (as opposed to U.S. TV, which has a potential of 525 lines). HDTV can increase the lines of resolution to 1,125 or even higher.

In 1968 research into HDTV was started by Dr. Takashi Fujo of NHK, the Japanese state broadcasting company. Then, in 1981 Sony unveiled the first HDTV system in Tokyo. The event was attended by Francis Ford Coppola who hoped to be able to shoot his next film, *Tucker,* entirely in high-definition video and transfer it to film to only make release prints, but the technology wasn't advanced enough yet.

In 2001 a Federal Communications Commission ruling stated that cable companies only must carry one digital channel per station. In 2005, in a four to one vote by the FCC, the ruling was upheld.

"Digital broadcasts offer sharper pictures than the traditional analog transmissions used in most TV sets in American homes. A digital signal also can carry more information without using any more space on the broadcast spectrum. Some stations have chosen to use their digital signals for crystal-clear, high-definition broadcasts, while others have established multiple channels."[17]

Cable operators have voluntarily agreed to carry multiple digital channels in some cities, but broadcasters say making it a requirement would benefit the public by giving them more programming choices. The cable industry

What Is HDTV?

Back in the early days of television, before World War II, various television manufacturers were competing to see whose manufacturing standards would prevail. For example, RCA wanted a 441-scan line standard for its television sets, while Philco wanted to increase the number of scan lines to between 605 and 800. The National Television System Committee was set up by the Federal Communications Commission (FCC) in 1940 to address these differences and establish industry-wide manufacturing standards for televisions. For many decades the NTSC standards held sway in the United States and provided a template for how television sets should be made. Accommodations were made for color television when it was introduced in the 1950s, but few changes were made in the beginning, even after Sony's introduction of the first HDTV prototype in 1981. The reason? No one could agree on broadcast standards for the new technology.

As HDTV technology improved over time, it became clear that the benefits of this new television standard would inevitably supersede the older NTSC guidelines. The first HDTV broadcast in the United States covered the launch of John Glenn into space in 1998.

The Advanced Television Standards Committee (ATSC) has set newer guidelines for how audio and video are converted and transmitted as digital signals. The FCC has now mandated that all television broadcasters are required to support the HDTV technology, and all television viewers will need to have digital-to-analog converter boxes to enable them to view HDTV broadcasts on older, predigital televisions. All NTSC broadcasts will be shut off on February 17, 2009. In the long run, the result will be that viewers will have better video and audio quality, as well as the many benefits that digital television can provide.

What are the differences between the older NTSC analog technology, and the newer ATSC high-definition television standards?

Notice in the illustration the differences between the traditional NTSC television screen versus a current HDTV display. The HDTV picture is wider (9 units wide by 16 units across) and contains about ten times the information on the screen. This is also because there are more pixels (picture elements) of electronic information packed on the screen; the picture quality in HDTV is sharper and clearer as a result. Because HDTV signals are digital, many additional functions are potentially available to viewers. Among these functions: the ability to pause TV programs and to continue viewing them later, to see multiple television programs simultaneously onscreen (picture-in-picture), interactive purchasing, polling, the ability to receive Web broadcasts, and the capacity to switch between a computer and television display.

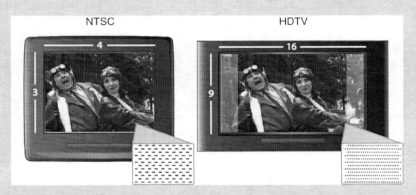

Figure 4. NTSC versus HDTV screen formats. Illustration by Kirsten Adams.

has argued that the First Amendment gives the operators, and not the government, the power to decide what channel to carry. Requiring up to six digital channels would take up valuable space because there is room for only a limited number of channels, cable operators say. As noted, four out of the five FCC commissioners sided with the cable companies.[18]

In the final analysis, digital television, whether using HDTV or not, will make manipulation and the faking of events much easier. The question then arises: what will we be able to believe? News alone will suffer an upheaval once the validity of tape and film becomes questionable. Also, will people really want their media to be "interactive"? Will new digital media in the end make us even more passive, or will it truly create a democratization of media, what Celia Pearce back in 1997 labeled "Digital Socialism." Pearce found ADD (attention deficit disorder) to be more of a positive technological mutation than a negative mental problem. In her text *The Interactive Book,* she stated that major revolutions are characterized by three things:

1) The rise of an educated intelligentsia
2) The ability to form a coherent community
3) The ability to leverage the prevailing media distribution technology[19]

She felt all of this is happening in the new interactive age. The hope is that we will all be educated in the ways of this new media because, ultimately, verification of falsehoods and reality could be up to each individual.

"For my experience in humanities computing has convinced me that some kinds of knowledge can be better represented in digital formats than they have been in print. The knowledge of a foreign language, for instance, can be better conveyed with examples from multiple speakers in authentic environments than with a list of words on a page. The dramatic power of Hamlet's soliloquies is better illustrated by multiple performance examples in juxtaposition with the text than by the printed version alone."

From *Hamlet on the Holodeck* by Janet H. Murray

Janet H. Murray notes that interactive television will eventually change the language of television and film and eventually lead to interactive holographic drama.

Innovations were also continuing to take place on the Internet and the computer. In the twenty-first century, streaming video for the web quickly became a new arena on which both film and video technicians and craftsmen could set their sights. Likewise, the web itself is now being used to advertise theatrical releases. This has opened up an entirely new kind of advertising, as seen with *The Blair Witch Project.*

"In October of 1994, three student filmmakers disappeared in the woods near Burkittsville, Maryland while shooting a documentary. A year later their footage was found." This solemn pronouncement appears on an opening screen of a fictional horror movie made in 1999 called *The Blair Witch Project,* created by independent film directors Daniel Myrick and Eduardo Sánchez.

The Blair Witch Project styled itself as a documentary about a young group of three college students who go into Maryland's Black Hills Forest to shoot a film about a mysterious character called the "Blair Witch." According to local legend in the nearby town of Burkittsville, the witch is responsible for numerous ghastly murders that have taken place since the eighteenth century. The students interview the locals and then proceed into the woods, where they are never heard from again, until their unprocessed film footage, sound recording, and hi-8 video is found. The film is a visual diary, which documents their increasing panic and subsequent deaths by certain undefined (and largely unseen) forces in the woods.

According to one of the film's directors, Eduardo Sánchez, the film's success largely resulted from the fact that it told a supernatural story under the guise of being a documentary about a "real" event.

Director Eduardo Sánchez: "We didn't want to tell people that it was real, but we didn't want to tell people it was fake, either. We wanted to walk that line, you know? Also, the only thing we thought when we started talking to people, and when we and later Artisan started doing the web site, was that we didn't want to give anything about the real film away. We wanted people to go in and get a fresh look at it. Artisan has been doing a really good job walking the line between reality and fiction, and when people ask us straight out, we never lie to them. We say it's a film, a fictional film."[20]

The Blair Witch Project was a meme[21] produced by amateurs using 16 mm and hi-8 digital cameras to produce a full length motion picture on a minimum budget. The meme satisfied a public need and caught on, and the film was wildly successful. *The Blair Witch Project* was shot with an initial budget of $35,000; its final box office returns were over $248 million, making it the most successful independent film in history.

The film used successful advertising techniques to first of all build a *brand,* a world that people could identify with, and used that brand to "leverage" products. This is similar to popular movies, such as *Shrek, Toy Story, The Lion King,* and *Star Wars,* that use outlets like McDonald's, Taco Bell, and Burger King to sell brand-related products.

In the final analysis, cinema history will not remember the movie so much as its advertising campaign, which revolutionized new ways of attracting an audience. Another movie, shot in a very similar way, did not rake in millions of dollars. Unlike the team that created "Blair Witch," this film about the so-called New Jersey Devil did not use the net for advertising.

Soon there was a surfeit of "Blair Witch" type advertising on the web, as well as similar projects done by independent film and video makers.

A new venue for independents appeared in mid-February of 2005 with YouTube, a website where users are able to upload and share video and film clips. Adobe Flash technology is used to display a variety of both corporate-made (and copyrighted) material along with user-generated content. Suddenly, users had that very outlet George Gilder had written about over fifteen years earlier with which to "broadcast" their own shows, editorials, music videos, and dramatic projects.

YouTube videos take up an estimated 45 terabytes of storage (about 5,000 home computers' worth) and require several million dollars' worth of bandwidth a month to transmit. Those costs are one reason that some predict YouTube will collapse under the sheer weight of providing a haven for every teenager with a cellphone camera eager to be famous for fifteen minutes of video.[22]

By August 2006, YouTube was hosting about 6.1 million videos and had about 500,000 user accounts. This has, no doubt, increased exponentially since then.[23]

By November 2006, Google Inc. acquired YouTube.

YouTube soon became a major tool of American politicians. Negative campaign ads, editorials, and politicians' and candidates' own ideas and views can now be seen on YouTube. "In March 2008, YouTube launched 'High Quality' versions of its videos."[24] In the meantime, both computer and television screens have gotten flatter and wider.

Along with the larger screens have come better sound systems. In the early 1970s, television shows, particularly those on PBS in the United States, used to broadcast concerts simultaneously with stereo radio broadcasts. Sometimes, the program was slightly out of sync with the sound, but when it worked, it worked beautifully. By the fall season of 1985, NBC had a number of shows, including *Miami Vice,* with its music video style and Jan Hammer theme and incidental music, broadcasting in stereo. People who had their televisions and hi-fi VCRs hooked into their stereo amplifier were able to enjoy this new addition to the television watching experience—quite a change from just a few years earlier when sound was one of the most unimportant aspects of a television set. Often, even the largest of Sony Trinitrons had a speaker no better than that of an old transistor radio. Stereo television sets were available in the mid-1980s but were very expensive. By the mid-1990s, most television sets came with two stereo speakers.

Where television used to be a more intimate experience, where the close up ruled as opposed to the epic sweep of a major motion picture, the time will soon come when wide screen epic applies to both motion picture screens and television. When that happens, "going to the movies" will take on a whole new meaning.

New Technologies and Screen Formats

Television sets have been slowly taking on the appearance of movie screens for more than a decade. Now image quality is matching the size of the screen, and the more than 100-year-old fantasy of Albert Robida, the French science fiction illustrator whose telephonoscope illustration appears in Chapter 1, is now a reality, although I don't think even Robida thought that some of these giant screens would be light enough to hang up like a poster on the wall.

Right now, the two combating technologies are plasma and LCD screens.

Whereas plasma screens use a matrix of tiny gas plasma cells charged by electrical voltages to create a picture, LCD (liquid crystal display) screens are made up of liquid crystal pushed in the space between two glass plates. Images are created by varying the amount electrical charge applied to the crystals. LCD screens essentially have a backlight shining through the LCD layer of the screen.

At the moment, plasma screens display blacks better than LCD screens, giving better contrast in dark movie scenes (such as those in the opening scenes of *The Godfather*). However, LCD contrast continues to improve. Both plasma and LCD screens have reasonably comparable and good viewing angles (a tip—if you're shopping for LCDs, check the refresh rate. The lower it is, the better the image quality in fast-moving scenes). [25]

LCDs do tend to have more pixels on the screen, which is important if you're really interested in high-definition television. Plasma screens can last anywhere between 30,000 and 60,000 hours. LCDs, on the other hand, are guaranteed for 60,000 hours.[26]

The Great Convergence

In Chapter 3, we discussed how the digital telephone has now become part of a larger cluster of integrated technologies in a process that has been called *digital convergence*. The delivery of text, graphics, telephone, audio, video, and data communication through single media devices by means of a digital network, is where we seem to be heading. It appears that a significant part of this digital convergence process is also happening with the rapid public acceptance of high-definition television, along with its interactive capabilities and spectacular visual display. High-definition television is becoming an important hub for integrating with all digital media—cell phones, PDAs, computers, video game consoles, as well as local, cable, and satellite-based broadcasts. It allows users to switch easily between these multiple sources of information. As a result, television viewing, telephony, gaming, social networking, news, work, and everyday personal business activities such as shopping and banking can now be centered on the core interactivity provided by what George Gilder termed the "telecomputer" back in the 1990s. HDTV and its affiliated cluster of technologies is rapidly becoming a central driving social force behind the technology-augmented societies of the twenty-first century.

No one is completely certain in what ultimate direction these new digital high-definition technologies are taking us, but some of its main features will include the following:

- **The TV will merge with the computer**—The computer and television will be one multifunctional system for entertainment, work, information access, and network collaboration. IPTV (Internet Protocol Television), Internet TV, and on-demand online services are leading the commercial developments in this direction.

- **The network is the computer**—Think of the Internet as your hard drive. The traditional model of using a personal computer was to load software applications onto your local storage drive and use it from there. The approach now is to provide software applications, such as word processing, database management, email, and image processing programs, off the local computer, providing them as free or low cost services delivered from the Internet. Also in this model, entertainment packages such as films, video games, music, and so on, can be rented or purchased online and played back via a home computer. There will be a progressive blurring of boundaries between activities once associated with work, communications, and entertainment.

- **Ubiquitous computing**—According to Intel corporation, a leading manufacturer of microprocessors, we are entering the age of ubiquitous computing, where every processor will contain a wireless transceiver capable of both wirelessly receiving and transmitting information. This means that every electronic device from a toaster to a cell phone will be able to "talk" with every other device. Recently, Microsoft has

Figure 5. The telecomputer, a convergence of multiple digital communications technologies.
© Bánhidi Zsolt | Dreamstime.com.

demonstrated how a cell phone can communicate automatically with a tabletop digital touch screen by merely placing it on top of the display—transmitting phone messages, reservations, and text messages directly to a computer's database.

- **Increasing network and computer speeds:** Moore's Law (see Chapter 3) states that computer processing speeds are doubling every two years, with no corresponding increase in cost. There is no foreseeable change in this law in the future. For online delivery of information, the speed of the computer networks making up the Internet is also increasing, allowing the delivery of higher quality content at faster speeds. *Wired Magazine* reported an achievement in fall 2003, where network speeds in an experimental laboratory pointed the way to faster possible content delivery times in the future:

> "CERN, whose laboratories straddle the Franco-Swiss border near Geneva, said it had sent 1.1 terabytes of data at 5.44 gigabits per second to a lab at the California Institute of Technology, or Caltech, on Oct. 1 (2003). This is more than 20,000 times faster than a typical home broadband connection, and is also equivalent to transferring a 60-minute compact disc within one second—an operation that takes around eight minutes on standard broadband."[27]

> *Wired Magazine,* October 15, 2003

The trend is toward increasing speed, and the ability to transmit and receive rapid streams of information wirelessly from any location. What many are hoping for (and some are fearing) is the attainment of this ultimate digital convergence. The fear, as expressed by critics like Neil Postman and Todd Gitlin, is that the torrent of information already coming to us at incredible speed cannot be properly digested or analyzed, that we have become a country (perhaps a world) of consumers (as opposed to citizens) who want nothing more than to be entertained, and that our attention spans are getting shorter with each new technological breakthrough.

At a recent educational technology conference that the authors of this book attended, the topic of Moore's Law was brought up. The concern was that the consistent drumbeat of change and increasing processing speeds brought on by new communications technologies were making it difficult for schools and libraries to keep up with the pace. A member of the audience made the statement, "There is no social equivalent to Moore's Law." At some point, the question needs to be raised: is this accelerating technological change beneficial? Is there a downside to large numbers of people in our society watching highly captivating multisensory experiences by way of large HDTV screens and the "telecomputer"? We will be examining some of those social issues more closely in Chapter 9.

Endnotes

[1] Mitchell Stephens, www.nyu.edu/classes/stephens/History%20of%20Television%20page.htm.

[2] Gary Moore and Philo Farnsworth, on the "I've Got a Secret" television show, July 21, 1957 http://www.youtube.com/watch?v=pKM4MNrB25o.

[3] George Gilder, *Life after Television* (New York: WW. Norton & Company, 1992), p. 41.

[4] Andy Dehnart, MSNBC contributor, *Strike not to blame for drop in TV viewership: Everything from Internet to lack of good shows to viewing habits play part,* May 5, 2008, http://www.msnbc.msn.com/id/24458848.

[5] Ibid.

[6] George Gilder, Life After Television, WW. Norton & Company, New York, 1992 pp. 115–116.

[7] Joyce A. Swhwarz, *Hollywood, USA Creative Approaches To New Media Production,* Multimedia Gateway to the Next Millennium, AP Professional, New York , 1994 p. 47.

[8] John Kronenberger, Push Button Movies: The Videocassette Revolution, Look Magazine, New York, November 3, 1970 p. 94.

[9] Resolution: the sharpness or crispness of a received image measured by the number of horizontal lines that make up one image frame or complete picture.

[10] CCD stands for "Charged Coupled Device." CCDs are sensors used in digital cameras and video cameras to record still and moving images. The CCD captures light and converts it to digital data that is recorded by the camera. For this reason, a CCD is often considered the digital version of film – from The Tech Terms Computer Dictionary (http://www.techterms.com/).

[11] Richard Brestoff, *The Camera Smart Actor* New Hampshire, Smith and Krauss, Inc., 1994), p. 199.

[12]Ibid.

[13]Ibid.

[14]John V. Pavlik, *New Media Technology* (Boston; Allyn & Bacon Press, 1996), p. 75.

[15]Charlie White, Digital Cameras in Focus, *DV Magazine*, February 1996.

[16]George Gilder, *Life after Television* (New York: W.W. Norton & Company, 1992), p. 41.

[17]Copyright 2005 The Associated Press.

[18]Ibid.

[19]Celia Pearce, *The Interactive Book* Indiana, Macmillan Technical Publishing, 1997), p. 180.

[20]Joshua Klein interview with Eduardo Sanchez, *The Blair Witch Project*, July 22, 1999, http://www.avclub.com/content/node/22980/print/

[21]"A **meme** consists of any unit of cultural information, such as a practice or idea, that gets transmitted verbally or by repeated action from one mind to another. Examples include thoughts, ideas, theories, practices, habits, songs, dances, and moods and terms such as "race," "culture," and "ethnicity." Memes propagate themselves and can move through a "culture" in a manner similar to the behavior of a virus. As a unit of cultural evolution, a meme in some ways resembles a gene. Richard Dawkins, in his book, *The Selfish Gene*, recounts how and why he coined the term "meme" to describe how one might extend Darwinian principles to explain the spread of ideas and cultural phenomena. He gave as examples such as tunes, catch-phrases, beliefs, clothing-fashions, and the technology of building arches. (Source: http://en.wikipedia.org/wiki/Meme.)

[22]Gomes, Lee, Portals: Will All of Us Get Our 15 Minutes On a YouTube Video?, The Wall Street Journal Online, Dow Jones & Company, August 30, 2006.

[23]Ibid.

[24]http://en.wikipedia.org/wiki/YouTube#cite_note-35.

[25]Randolph Ramsay on January 31, 2006, CNET.com Plasma Vs. LCD: Which Is Right For You?

[26]Ibid.

[27]Data Faster Than a Speeding Bullet, *Wired Magazine*, October 15, 2003, http://www.wired.com/techbiz/it/news/2003/10/60833.

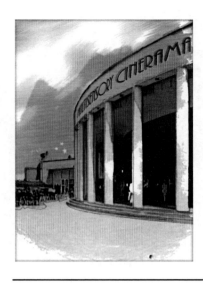

Chapter 7
Multisensory Cinerama Exhibit

"It would hardly be believed how different an effect is produced by a longer or shorter exposure to the light and also, by mere variations in the fixing process by means of which almost any tint, cold or warm, may be thrown over the pictures, and the effect of bright or gloomy weather may be imitated at pleasure . . . All of this falls within the province of the artist to combine and to regulate; and if in the course of these manipulations, he . . . becomes a chemist and an optician, I feel that such an alliance of science and art will prove conducive to the improvement of both."

Henry Talbot, English photography pioneer, 1841

"Bold indeed was he who first ventured on this orchestral union of music, poetry, architecture, sculpture and painting in the ancient theater, that together they might produce on the multitude a harmonious sentiment, a homogeneous emotion."[1]

Eugene Emmanuel Viollet-Le-Duc, 1875

"To remove the barriers between sight and sound, between the seen world and the heard world! To bring about a unity and a harmonious relationship between these two opposite spheres. What an absorbing task!"

Sergei Eisenstein, *The Film Sense*[2]

Early Forms of Multimedia: Art, Technology, and the *Synchronization of the Senses*

In 1859 a famous Parisian art gallery called the Paris Salon displayed a collection of early photographs, twenty years after the French inventor Louis-Jacques-Mande Daguerre created the first photograph, later known as the *daguerreotype*.

This collection of photographs at the Paris Salon is significant, because it represents one of the first instances where the technology of photography was held to be on the same level as traditional fine art. A cartoon published in a Parisian newspaper announced the event by showing a traditional artist's color palette walking arm-in-arm with an early box camera. It symbolized a long continuing relationship between art and technology that evolved in the late nineteenth century and throughout the twentieth century.

By the 1970s, the term *multimedia* was first used to describe the integration of sound, graphics, film, and text by means of early microprocessors—often controlled by signals generated from punched computer tape. Professor

Figure 1. Cartoon from a Paris newspaper, circa 1859. An artist's palette walks arm-in-arm with an early box camera. Illustration recreated by Kirsten Adams.

Robert Bell from San Francisco State University wrote that multimedia is a "technological loom that weaves media together." Motion pictures, starting in the late 1920s, integrated sound with moving images and pioneered early special effects techniques. Later, increasing flexibility was provided by early computer technologies. Atari's *Pong* and the Magnavox *Odyssey* video game consoles in 1972 expanded this relationship between early computing and sensory experiences even further by making it possible for viewers to interact in real-time with sound and visual events on a video screen. The World Wide Web and the ubiquitous Internet increased these capabilities even further by making it possible to share three-dimensional perceptual environments with thousands of other participants in cyberspace in virtual social spaces called *persistent worlds,* typified by networked games such as *World of Warcraft, Eve Online,* and *Halo 3,* and by cyberspace societies such as *Second Life.*

Finally, traditional movies are being integrated with games—made possible through the use of emerging forms of artificial intelligence. Peter Jackson, director of *Lord of the Rings* and *King Kong,* recently described his interest in this new entertainment medium: "What I'm interested in doing is looking at the technology, at Xbox 360 and Live, and the way that that universe of technology is being created. At the moment it's primarily used for playing games but what's interesting is the challenge of finding a method of conveying stories on that technology that will allow an interactive component but they're not movies and they're not games . . . There's room for another form of entertainment that is on par with watching a movie or reading a book, an alternative for people who are interested in story and who want to engage with characters."

The development of technologies to simultaneously engage multiple senses and to simulate perceptual worlds marks the character of multimedia technology and its descendants. The term *multimedia* itself has become somewhat old fashioned, because it is most strongly associated with twentieth century technologies. It is useful for the purposes of this chapter, however, because it links earlier developments with our own twenty-first century multisensory devices—often referred to as real-time interactive computer simulations, virtual worlds, or more simply, video games.

Opera, Film, and Other Multimedia

In 1849 the German opera composer Richard Wagner wrote an essay called "The Artwork of the Future" in which he proposed the creation of a *Gesamtkunstwerk,* or *great work,* which would encompass and synthesize multiple art forms simultaneously. In his mind, these art forms included aspects of architecture, painting, dramatic arts, sculpture, music, and dance. He felt these artistic disciplines should all be present in equivalent amounts before a performance could be called a *Gesamtkunstwerk.* He himself worked to create this fusion of artistic disciplines in his own works of opera and musical theater.[1]

---

[1] In 1849 the German composer Richard Wagner wrote a treatise called *The Artwork of the Future.* He laid out a theory in which he described how the expressive arts of painting, music, dance, and drama could be synergistically brought together within the framework of architecture to create what he called the *Gesamtkunstwerk* or *total artwork.* "Architecture can set before herself no higher task than to frame for a fellowship of artists . . . the special surroundings necessary for the display of the Human Artwork." The aim of his *Gesamtkunstwerk* was to create a theatrical environment where the audience "forgets the confines of the auditorium and breathes now only in the artwork which seems to it as Life itself." Wagner was describing an early version of *worldbuilding,* where a story represented in the multisensory virtual environment of a theater was made to seem more compelling than the real world itself.

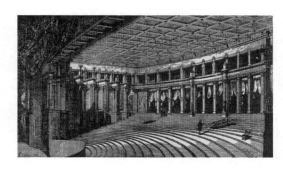

Figure 2. German composer Richard Wagner opens a technically advanced opera theater called the Festspielhaus in Bayreuth, Germany (1876).

In 1876 Wagner completed building his Festival House Theater (Festspielhaus) in Bayreuth, Germany. Here, he experimented with his own forms of *Gesamtkunstwerk* and initiated such theatrical innovations as wrap-around sound, eliminating balconies and box seats to create Greek-style amphitheater seating. He also dimmed auditorium lights to total darkness just before a performance, which was considered a highly innovative concept. Wagner had designed one of the most technologically sophisticated theaters of his time.

Because of financial difficulties, Wagner was able to hold only two opera festivals at Bayreuth, but he succeeded in successfully demonstrating his concept of *Gesamtkunstwerk*. Music, architecture, dance, story, and environmental atmospherics created one of the first examples of technologically enhanced multisensory experience, or multimedia.

Ten years before Wagner wrote his essay "Artwork of the Future," the French inventor Louis-Jacques-Mande Daguerre took one of the first photographs in history. It is a photograph of a street in Paris in 1839, from a second-story apartment window. It shows a Parisian boulevard and a man getting his shoes shined. The street appears empty because a long exposure time was required to capture objects on the photographic plate—only stationary portions of the image could be recorded. The image was etched in light through a focusing lens onto a silver-coated copper plate treated with iodine vapor that was placed within a black box called a *camera obscura*. This early photograph came to be known as a *daguerreotype*, a brittle and perishable medium.

In 1891 the American inventors Thomas Edison and W.K.L. Dickson patented the first motion-picture camera (the Kinetograph) and projector (the Kinetoscope). This was made possible after numerous innovations in photographic cameras, film emulsions, chemical processing, and lenses. A few years later, a World's Fair was held in Chicago that gave more than a glimpse at what the coming century would offer. This fair, the World's Columbian Exposition of 1893, exhibited many new inventions and was perhaps the first time that the technology which would eventually evolve into movies and multimedia was shown to vast audiences in one particular location.

Interestingly enough, the same year the Chicago fair opened, H.G. Wells' *The Time Machine* appeared in *Strand* magazine. Inventor and early film pioneer Robert Paul took note of the novella and contacted Wells. Initially, Paul was intrigued that Wells used certain "cinematic," or kinetoscopic, techniques in his story. Note this section, when the time traveler first begins his trip through time:

> "The Laboratory got hazy and went dark. Mrs. Watchett came in . . . and walked toward the garden door. I suppose it took her a minute or so to traverse the place, but to me she seemed to shoot across the room like a rocket."[3]

Later on in the story, the narrator describes Mrs. Watchett going backward, much like a film in reverse. As Robert Paul noted, such "time traveling" could be accomplished with the magic of moving pictures, as this anonymous editorial from the *St. Louis Post-Dispatch* notes:

> "The kinetoscope, we are told, has recently been made to run backwards, and the effects of this way of running it are truly marvelous. . . . The effect is said to be almost miraculous. In the process of eating food is taken from the mouth and placed on the plate."[4]

The kinetoscope of that era was considered a poor person's form of entertainment and was usually on display in arcades, much like video games are today. Wells and Paul hoped to go one better than just linear moving pictures that moved forward or backward. They attempted to create a device that would allow paying customers to visit the past, present, and future. In 1895, Wells and Paul patented their "novel form of entertainment," a machine that might easily have shared space with the wonders of the Chicago fair two years earlier. The hope was to liberate the spectator from the instant of the Now. Wells and Paul wanted to be able to lead their audience at will "back and

Figure 3. H.G. Wells and early cinematographer Robert Paul hoped to create the equivalent of a Victorian interactive multimedia presentation through the use of moving platforms, magic lantern projections, and moving pictures. This "Time Machine" was never built. Illustration by artist Kirsten Adams.

forth along the infinite line of time."[5] The plan was to give the spectator the ability to travel from past to future to present in any order. It would be achieved by a series of moving platforms, magic lantern slides,[6] projected motion pictures—"successive instantaneous photographs after the manner of the kinetoscope," Paul called it—and sound effects. What Wells and Paul were hoping to create was nothing less than a Victorian interactive multimedia presentation. Alas, this "Time Machine" was never built. In this way, Wells' and Paul's Time Machine was not unlike the Difference Engine, a computer conceived by Charles Babbage in 1822. In both cases, neither machine was constructed because the components to make them work could not be fabricated.[7]

One might be correct in assuming that this shows that no idea is really new, just the technology that can make it a reality.

The actual process of the evolution of "successive instantaneous photographs after the manner of the kinetoscope" really wouldn't begin until 1904 with Edward Porter's *The Great Train Robbery,* and 1908, when D.W. Griffith began to assemble the mechanical and optical properties of the motion picture into a new dramatic technique and art form.

In 1900 L. Frank Baum's *The Wizard of Oz* was published. One of the memorable parts of Baum's work has always been the wonderful atmosphere he creates in his books, much like Tolkien does in *Lord of the Rings.* The images work powerfully with text to create his world of Oz. In 1906 Frank Baum decided to present his Oz stories in a form he called *Fairylogue and Radio-Plays.* Baum's shows combined a live orchestra, actors on stage, Baum himself as narrator, magic lantern slides, and hand-colored motion-picture film (and, by the way, the word *Radio* in the show's title refers to Michael Radio, a Frenchman who invented a way to hand-color the moving footage). Although successful with audiences and critics alike, the show closed in New York City in 1908 because of the expenses involved in producing the little extravaganza.[8] These *Fairylogues* might be tagged as the first on-the-road multimedia presentations. Baum's original and inventive technical innovations (such as two strips of film used to show Dorothy being flung about in the open sea) were soon outstripped by new technologies that were being continually introduced during the early years of the century.

There was a continuous experimentation with early media technology forms as they emerged. As an example, Frank Baum's best-selling *The Wonderful Wizard of Oz* book was illustrated by William Wallace Denslow in 1900. Denslow was able to make use of the early color printing technology available at the time to enliven his illustrations. Because of the limitations of early color reproduction, these illustrations were limited to just a few basic flat colors, as seen in Denslow's first book cover of the Oz series in 1900.

The thirty-five Oz books in the series that followed were illustrated by John R. Neil, who was able to take advantage of the maturing capabilities of color printing technologies to add more expressiveness to his artwork in the form of gradients and an expanded color palette. This can be seen in Neil's cover illustration for Baum's *The Emerald City of Oz,* published a decade later in 1910.

In the meantime, experimentation with television broadcasting had been going on for quite a few years. As early as 1884, Paul Nipkow created a mechanical scanning wheel. The wheel, containing tiny holes, was set in front of a picture, and as the wheel turned, each hole scanned one line of the picture (see Chapter 1, page 7). By the 1920s, Ernst Alexanderson, working for General Electric, was utilizing the scanning system in a new way. Using the

Figure 4. Cover of Frank Baum's *The Wonderful Wizard of Oz,* 1900. Illustrated by William Denslow.

Figure 5. Cover of Frank Baum's *The Emerald City of Oz,* 1910. Illustrated by John R. Neil.

system, he created a science fiction show of a missile attack on New York by scanning an aerial photo of the city that moved closer and closer and then disappeared in an explosion.

In 1927 the first commercial film with synchronized sound was released—called *The Jazz Singer.* The first half of the twentieth century was a time of experimentation with these new technologies that allowed the choreography of moving images with sound. Early film directors like Orson Welles, Alfred Hitchcock, and Frank Capra began to discover the potential of creating compelling narratives using the integrated audiovisual language of cinema.

One of these early pioneers in the new medium of cinema was the Russian film director Sergei Eisenstein. His films included *The Battleship Potemkin, Ten Days that Shook the World, Strike,* and *Alexander Nevsky.* He made numerous discoveries about the motion-picture medium that he describes in his 1942 book *The Film Sense.* One of these is *montage,* in which the meaning of a message conveyed by moving images can be changed by how these frames are positioned in relation to one other. For example, the close-up shot of an actor with a neutral facial expression can be interpreted as jealousy, shock, surprise, or indifference depending on what scene was shown directly beforehand. A second key idea of Eisenstein is what he calls the *synchronization of the senses.* Here, Eisenstein claims that it a characteristic of audiences to synthesize all information that they are given into an integrated perceptual experience. All perceptual elements that are introduced into a film—color, the pacing of visual events, music, camera angle, frame composition, lighting, and acting style—contribute to an overall aesthetic result.

In Eisenstein's view, it is the job of a film director to choreograph these elements to achieve a desired emotional response. In his book *The Film Sense,* Eisenstein takes twelve shots from his movie *Alexander Nevsky* in which Russian soldiers wait nervously on the shores of the frozen Lake Chudskoye for an attack of Teutonic knights on horseback. He shows a diagram to demonstrate how musical events correspond with visual sequences in a carefully synchronized way to create the desired mood of fearful anticipation. The music and visuals reinforce each other and together create an overall effect that neither could achieve independently.

This "blockbuster" state propaganda film was commissioned by Soviet Premier Joseph Stalin as a cautionary tale about the potential threat of Nazi Germany in the years preceding World War II. The movie is most widely recognized for its carefully choreographed battle scenes that take up half the story. Both director and composer closely collaborated to find a perfect integration of music with moving images.

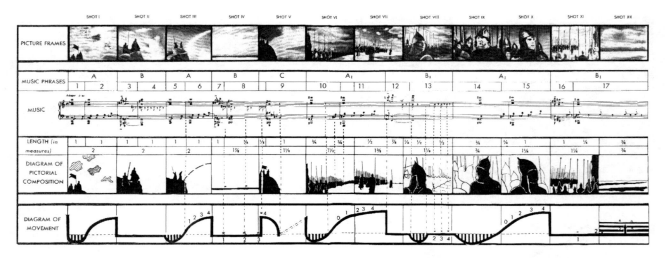

Figure 6. A multisensory scene diagram from Sergei Eisenstein's movie *Alexander Nevsky* (1938). Edits, frame composition, and music are carefully scored to achieve a "synchronization of the senses." Diagram from *The Film Sense* by Sergei Eisenstein, translated by Jay Leyda, copyright 1942 by Houghton Mifflin Harcourt Publishing Company and renewed 1969 by Jay Leyda, reprinted by permission of the publisher.

Visual Effects and the Movies

A history of multisensory technologies of the twentieth century should include mention of the rich and varied growth of synthetic motion-picture experiences, usually under the description of "visual effects" or "special effects." Only some of the major milestones of this history are shown here, because of the complex woven tapestry of this development.

1895—While Thomas Edison was developing his kinematoscope in the United States, two brothers, August and Louis Lumière, had created their own motion-picture camera and film projector system in France. The first public demonstration of their new invention took place in Paris on December 28, 1895. In the audience was a Frenchman who was later to become one of the early masters of visual effects in film, Georges Méliès. His account of this experience typified the disbelief and wonder that the new medium of film invoked in its audiences: "No sooner had I stopped speaking when a horse pulling a cart started to walk towards us followed by other vehicles, then a passerby. In short, all the hustle and bustle of a street. We sat with our mouths open, without speaking, filled with amazement."[9]

1902—Méliès himself became an accomplished filmmaker and had built a motion-picture studio in Paris. It was here that he filmed *A Trip to the Moon,* a science fiction movie that tells the story of a group of men who travel to the moon and confront many dangers and challenges. Méliès developed many visual effects for this movie, including moon creatures that disappear in clouds of smoke, flying comets, women's faces appearing in stars, and a famous scene showing the man in the moon getting hit in the eye with a space capsule. He made numerous films that made use of a variety of new techniques. Some of these were very simple according to today's standards, such as stopping the camera, replacing an object with another one, and then restarting the camera, which would create the magical illusion of instant transformation. According to Méliès, ". . . I introduced into the cinema the tricks of machinery, mechanics, optics, prestidigitation, etc. With all these processes mixed one with another and used with competence, I do not hesitate to say that in cinematography it is today possible to realize the most impossible and the most improbable things." At the root of all visual effects technologies is the construction of synthetic perceptual environments, which is as true today as it was when Méliès made his films.[10]

1903—Edwin S. Porter, working for Edison Studios, directs the first cowboy Western feature, *The Great Train Robbery,* which runs about twelve minutes. It includes some of the earliest special effects, including one scene where two robbers blow up a safe in a railway car, while speeding trees rush by outside an open door. There are actually two separate film sequences that are fit together like pieces

Figure 7. Poster for the first feature film, *The Great Train Robbery* (1903). Library of Congress, Prints and Photographs, 1994001839

of a jigsaw puzzle in postproduction—masks were used to provide clear areas for portions of the frame that needed to be exposed. Because early film stocks were all black and white, red dye was manually applied to individual frames to provide color for the explosion.

1927—German director Fritz Lang went through elaborate preparations to build a futuristic cityscape for his science fiction classic film **Metropolis** set in the year 2026. His constructed city set consisted of looming skyscrapers, stadiums, elevated expressways filled with cars, buzzing airplanes, immense scale, and an atmospheric sense of foreboding. In one scene, during the Frankenstein-like creation of a female robot, rings of light move up and down her body in a show of extraordinary early visual effects. The long-term influence of this movie, in terms of special effects, dark urban environments, and its theme of the merging of humanity with machines can be seen in later films, especially *Blade Runner* (1982) and *The Matrix* (1999).

1933—Arguably, the most famous early visual effects movie is **King Kong**, with special effects pioneer, Willis O'Brien. O'Brien made use of a flexible miniature model of the gorilla character King Kong, and developed its movements through a painstaking process called *stop-motion* animation, where objects and characters within a scene are moved slightly, shot in a single frame, and then moved and photographed again in subsequent frames. O'Brien also integrated his miniature King Kong model into elaborate movie sets with live action sequences from actors who were filmed separately.

Mid-Twentieth Century—Two major figures in the history of visual effects appear in science fiction and fantasy movies from around 1950 to 1980. These were the special effects innovators **Ray Harryhausen** and director **George Pal.**

Ray Harryhausen gained his early experience working with Willis O'Brien of *King Kong* fame and went on to create special effects for many different movies. These included *Jason and the Argonauts,* where he choreographed a sword battle between live actors and several animated skeletons, and *Earth vs. the Flying Saucers,* where alien spaceships destroy large government buildings in Washington, DC.

George Pal was a Hungarian-born film director, producer, and animator who became involved in numerous science fiction and fantasy movies that made extensive use of visual effects—*Destination Moon* (1950), *When Worlds Collide* (1951), *The War of the Worlds* (1953), and *The Time Machine* (1960)—that used time-lapse photography to accelerate and decelerate viewers backward and forward in history.

1968—The science fiction film *2001: A Space Odyssey,* directed by Stanley Kubrick and with special photographic effects by Douglas Trumbull, received an Academy Award for visual effects and in 2002 was voted as one of the top ten films of all time by a group of leading film critics. The film concerned humanity's first contacts with extraterrestrial intelligence and pioneered the use of a technique called slit-scan photography, where a motion-controlled camera photographs narrow slits of light as it moves along a track.

Its use of advanced camera and effects techniques introduced a new generation of special effects films.

1977—*Star Wars Episode IV: A New Hope* was a surprise science fiction hit created by a relatively unknown young director, George Lucas. Because this film required the construction of an entire fictional universe, Lucas set up a new company in San Rafael, California, to build the models and sets and create the visual effects needed for the film. The company was called **Industrial Light and Magic (ILM),** and it went on to become one of the preeminent visual effects production houses for the motion-picture industry, creating custom visual sequences for more than 100 major motion pictures. From the very beginning, when ILM made use of a computer-controlled camera called the Dykstraflex for space battle scenes in the first Star Wars movie, the company became famous for its numerous innovations in the motion-picture special effects industry.

One of ILM's most notable technical achievements in visual effects can be seen in the movie *Terminator 2: Judgment Day* (1991), directed by James Cameron. In this movie, a murderous robot assassin from the future, played by Robert Patrick, is sent back in time from a future Artificial Intelligence race to kill a young boy in the twentieth century. For the first time in history, *Terminator 2* made use of an all-computer-generated leading character and pioneered a technique called motion capture—where live human movements can be recorded by computers and mapped onto three-dimensional animated models. The film also used a process called morphing, where Patrick's character changed from molten metal to human flesh.

1986—Steve Jobs, one of the founders of Apple Computer, purchased the computer graphics division of Lucasfilm, Ltd., from filmmaker George Lucas. It was established as an independent production company and was named Pixar. From the very beginning, under the creative leadership of animator John Lasseter, Pixar was very successful. Pixar presented a short animated film in Dallas, Texas, at SIGGRAPH, a conference held every year for computer graphics professionals. The film was called *Luxo Jr.,* and while it was only two and a half minutes long, it demonstrated the potential of computer-generated images for creating compelling stories and images. This short animated film was about the relationship between two desk lamps, a child, and a parent. What made the movie so unique at the time was how lifelike these computer-generated "inanimate objects" were and how effective digital lighting and shadowing could be.

Pixar went on to become one of the leading all-digital animation production studios in the world. After creating several highly acclaimed short animated films, as well as many state-of-the-art digitally animated ads for television, Pixar partnered with Walt Disney Studios in producing several of the most successful animated feature-length films in motion-picture history: *Toy Story* (1995), *A Bug's Life* (1998), *Toy Story 2* (1999), and *Monsters Inc.* (2001). Together, these four films brought in box office revenues exceeding $1.5 billion.[11] After these early successes, Pixar continued to produce popular and profitable films, including *Finding Nemo* (2003), *The Incredibles* (2004), *Cars* (2006), *Ratatouille* (2007), and *WALL-E* (2008).

The first *Toy Story* distinguished itself by being the first all-digital feature-length motion picture. Every character, environment, lighting effect, and object in the movie was virtual—constructed from a 3D model.

Multimedia after 1960

The idea of creating perceptual environments within a theatrical setting using preprogrammed audiovisual technologies simultaneously evolved with the growth of visual effects and began to appear in the mid-twentieth century in the form of theme parks such as Disneyland and Universal Studios, as well as in larger scale public multimedia events.

Here are some examples, based on the authors' firsthand experiences.

The Family Dog

During the height of the LSD-inspired psychedelic rock music movement of the late 1960s, a San Francisco group called The Family Dog sponsored multimedia music concerts in various cities in the United States. Luria Castell of The Family Dog described what was going on to writer Ralph Gleason:

"We want to bring in the artistic underground, use light machines, boxes projecting a light pulse from the tonal qualities of the music . . . I think that rock 'n' roll people are just starting to know how to use their instruments. They're doing new things in electronics, the generation brought up in the insanity . . . young people today are torn between the insanity and the advances of the electronic age."[12]

One event in particular would influence numerous "hippie" artists who would one day be on the front lines of digital communication: the Trips Festival, a three-day event held in January 1967 at the Longshore Hall.

It boasted a multimedia light show that Ralph J. Gleason immortalized in his book *The Jefferson Airplane and The San Francisco Sound:*

> "There were five movie screens up on the wall and projectors for the flicks and other light mixes spread around the balcony. A huge platform in the middle of the room housed the engineers who directed the sound and the lights. Loudspeakers ringed the hall and were set up under the balcony and in the entrance. . . Stroboscopic lights set at vantage points beamed down into the crowd and lissome maidens danced under them for hours, whirling jewelry. . ."[13]

The Family Dog music concerts took place in a large dance theater, where participants were submerged in a sensory mix of projected movies, slides, strobes, colored lights, fog, and sound effects. No attempt was made to connect or synchronize any of these spatial events—the result was spontaneous, improvised, and without an overall plan. It was the recreation of a psychedelic trip on LSD in audiovisual form.

The Scopitone Visual Jukebox

In the late 1960s promotional films were being made for a variety of acts like Nancy Sinatra, who performed *These Boots Are Made for Walking.* Some of these films were made for visual jukeboxes, an experiment whereby people could pay not just to listen to music but to see a *high-fidelity* performance as well.[14]

Originally called scoop-a-tunes, and later Scopitones, these were productions captured on color 16 mm film and synced with a magnetic soundtrack. The first Scopitones were made in France around 1960, and the Scopitone craze spread throughout Europe (particularly in West Germany and England) before crossing the Atlantic to the United States in mid-1964. They were originally intended to capitalize on the dance craze called the Twist, but everyone from Neil Sedaka to Della Reese to The Turtles to The Beatles attempted to take advantage of the new medium. Scopitone films really are the mid-1960s precursors to today's music videos.

> "A revolutionary coin-operated system blending the best features of music, motion pictures and television for the finest in public entertainment. A combination of the richest high fidelity sound and synchronized living color motion pictures."
>
> From a Scopitone 1966 brochure

Between 1964 and 1969, American, British, and European acts performed on these video jukeboxes. Unfortunately, the technology was noat yet perfected and the jukeboxes more often than not didn't work. By the end of the 1960s they were gone.[15]

Can Man Survive?

In 1970 the Museum of Natural History in New York City, in honor of the first Earth Day, hosted a temporary exhibit called "Can Man Survive?" Audiences walked into a series of enclosed tunnels filled with the sounds and images of industrial society. Looped audio tapes and a series of looped sixteen-millimeter films showed everything

Figure 8. A Scopitone jukebox machine. Illustration by Kirsten Adams.

Figure 9. Kodak Slide Projector, used in early multi-image shows. © James Steidl | Dreamstime.com.

from garbage dumps to tree planting ceremonies. The final image audiences saw as they exited the exhibit was a piece of scrawled graffiti on the wall that read:

"We have met the enemy and he is us—Pogo Possum."

Motiva, Ltd.—New York City, 1975

Starting in the early 1970s, media production companies began to experiment with the concept of using computers to synchronize sound and visual events as a form of public theater. One of these companies was Motiva, Ltd., in New York City. In 1975 Motiva produced public multimedia displays using slide projectors that rear-projected their images onto a grid of integrated screens called a matrix module. Visual changes were triggered by holes punched in a wide strip of mylar that was run through a simple computer called a synthesizer. When light passed through a hole in the strip, it would trigger a command to make an image change at a specified slide projector. The command strip was synchronized with a soundtrack to integrate visuals with audio events. The multiple screen format enabled a presentation to move flexibly in time and space, much like animated comic strip panels. Motiva produced public programs for Penn Station, the Museum of Natural History, the City Museum of New York, and the Galleria shopping mall in Houston, Texas.

Before 1970, computers were too large, expensive, and inaccessible to be useful for the production of multimedia. Beginning in the early 1970s, simple computers in the form of punched tape—initiated programming equipment, as seen in the Spindler and Sauppe Media Mix programmer, enabled producers to synchronize slide projectors, motion pictures, ambient lighting, and sound into coordinated audiovisual public events. This technology made it possible for media designers to flexibly work with 35 mm slide imagery, graphics, and sound bytes to experiment with a wide variety of perceptual effects. From the 1970s through the early 1990s, this technology, referred to as "multi-image," became integrated with the newly introduced personal computer. It was primarily used in public contexts such as conventions, tourist attractions, or sales presentations.

One of the limitations of large format multi-images was that it required the precise coordination of specialized equipment to make it work—display screens had to be erected, projector bulbs in multiple slide projectors replaced, sound systems tweaked, sufficient electricity supplie d, and enough space allocated for it to be staged. Teams of specialized professionals were also needed, working in various media—sound, programming, photography, typesetting, staging, graphics, and special optical effects. Because of the wide variety of media and skills required, production costs were high. Another limitation was the audience—everyone had to be at the same place at the same time.

During the mid-1970s, a multimedia event produced by Paul Heller, called *The New York Experience,* opened in Rockefeller Center. It was a carefully choreographed event that simulated life in New York City, using multiple movie projectors, slide projectors, lighting effects, and surround-sound to put an audience in the midst of downtown Manhattan. The show incorporated the sound of Revolutionary War Cannons, smoke, and even the hanging execution of Nathan Hale.

These early computer multimedia technologies were exploring ways in which several media (multiple slide projectors, music, narration, lighting, motion-picture projectors) could be engaged to construct an experience or tell a story using electronic devices to coordinate the complexity of this task. From the 1970s through the mid-1990s, computer-based multimedia shows, using audiovisual presentation equipment, became a popular and widely used commercial production format.

Multimedia Production in the 1970's—Bruce Wolcott

In 1975 I worked in a multi-image production company called Motiva in New York City. It was considered a state-of-the-art multimedia production company at the time. Motiva produced multi-image slideshows for clients such as the New York City Museum, the Museum of Natural History, Dupont, and the Galleria shopping mall in Houston, Texas.

The heart and soul of Motiva's presentation came from two innovations: (1) The "matrix module," a screen display consisting of multiple windows with slide projectors casting their images onto the screen from behind. With this screen configuration it was possible to show separate images in relationship to each other or composite images for panoramic and close-up views. This made it possible for ideas to be represented in an interesting way and to move flexibly through time. (2) The synthesizer. This was a custom-made box of electronics that sent signals out to trigger off visual events in synchronization with a soundtrack. The way this worked is that a stiff toll of card stock paper was punched with holes and fed through an optical reader. When a hole passed over the optical reader, it initiated a signal to a projector to display an image on the screen. The movement of the punched strip of card stock was synchronized with sound signals being sent out by an audio track. In this way, the synthesizer coordinated sound events to closely correspond to visual events on the screen.

Motiva hired freelance scriptwriters, graphic designers, sound producers, photographers, and special effects camera operators to create their shows. These specialized skills were brought together in a flexible way whenever a new project was being developed. A freelance crew was also on hand to maintain the multiple multi-image installations that Motiva had set up—equipment would break down, bulbs would burn out, and slides would get jammed in projectors.

I remember being particularly impressed with a multimedia presentation for the New York City Museum. It showed a history of New York City during the Revolutionary War. The story was "unstuck in time" in that it moved from year to year and location to location without disorienting the viewer. Sound cues and subtle visual effects, such as a flickering projector to show distant cannon fire, were often used to tell the story, often with a minimal amount of information. The screen matrix and close coordination with a soundtrack seemed to make all of this possible.

Motiva created an early form of computer-based, multisensory design that worked very well.

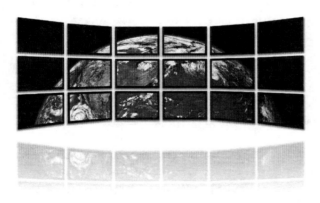

Figure 10. Multi-image shows from the 1970s through the 1990s often contained multiple projection screens along with sound-synchronized slide and film projectors. © Erik Reis | Dreamstime.com.

Interactivity and Audience Participation

Interactivity: a cyclic process in which two actors alternately listen, think, and speak.

Chris Crawford[16]

Movies, novels, and plays, despite their indisputable narrative power, don't allow an audience to interact with the story. In the traditional forms of these media, a single chain of events is created, and the viewer vicariously participates in those events while empathizing with the story characters. In Hitchcock's classic movie thriller *Psycho,* when lead character Vivienne Leigh checks in to the creepy Bates Motel and then steps into a shower, the audience is unavoidably pulled along to witness her gruesome murder at the hands of a psychotic killer, played by Anthony Perkins. No amount of foot stomping, pleading, or shouting from the audience will save her life—the movie always leads to her inevitable violent death. In *Psycho,* Hitchcock takes the unorthodox step of murdering his heroine halfway through the story and temporarily disorients his audience in the process. Hitchcock is a masterful storyteller, however, and the narrative continues successfully by switching from the story of a woman embezzling money to the twisted worldview and motivations of a demented killer. Hitchcock as a director makes interesting choices here by steering the direction of his narrative in unexpected ways, but as strongly as we may be emotionally affected by the series of events, as an audience we are always observers, not participants. Hitchcock takes us where he wants us to go; we've just come along for the ride.

In traditional theater, this separation between a performance space and the audience is known as the *fourth wall.* The fourth wall can be imagined as a large, transparent screen that separates the stage action from an audience. The actors don't acknowledge the presence of the audience, and viewers sit in an imagined space not physically represented on stage. The fourth wall is only broken at the end of the play when performers take their bows, or on occasion when the audience responds spontaneously to something they've seen on stage. The fourth wall is a picture window that puts viewers in the role of being outsiders and voyeurs to the ongoing dramatic action.

Digital World-Building and Interactivity

In the case of human-computer interaction, the computer acts as a management tool for staging the unfolding narrative.[17] Here interactivity refers to a human participant inputting information to the computer and the computer interpreting the action and responding in a way that is dramatically satisfying to the user. Interactivity also refers to computer-mediated communication between human participants on a network, as seen in the new generation of multiparticipant online games.

To engage an audience emotionally, the digital storyteller encounters the same issues found in improvisational theater. Randy Dixon, an improvisational actor/director in Seattle, describes these issues as they apply to a live improvised performance. "It's simple from an audience viewpoint. What keeps me watching? What do I care about? What has been set in motion that I want to see completed? Where are the actors taking me? Then, how well did they meet my expectations? If the audience doesn't have something to care about from the beginning, they will not engage in the story."[18]

These are questions that require the following: (1) an understanding the rules and principles of dramatic engagement (i.e., what are the ingredients of a good story and sustained interest?), and (2) the knowledge of how to apply these rules to digital storytelling technologies. These are issues that are both technical and artistic.

One of the earliest experiments in computer interactivity took place at Massachusetts Institute of Technology (MIT), when the computer scientist Joseph Weizenbaum in the years 1964 through 1966 created an experimental program called ELIZA in an attempt to mimic a conversation between a human and a computer. The human user would type in a question or comment on a computer, and the computer would process the message using a limited set of rules (algorithms) and then return a typed response to the computer screen. Weizenbaum's program made use of a technique used by psychotherapist Carl Rogers, in which the therapist both asks questions and repeats statements provided by a person being interviewed in order to bring out additional information.[19] This approach created the illusion that the computer actually understood the typed questions and statements of the user and was responding intelligently as a wise and all-knowing psychologist. In his book *Computer Power and Human Reason,* Weizenbaum provides an example of an early "conversation" between a woman (shown in lowercase letters) and ELIZA (shown in uppercase letters):

> *Men are all alike.*
> *IN WHAT WAY?*
> *They're always bugging us about something or other.*
> *CAN YOU THINK OF A SPECIFIC EXAMPLE?*
> *Well, my boyfriend made me come here.*
> *YOUR BOYFRIEND MADE YOU COME HERE.*
> *He says I'm depressed much of the time.*
> *I'M SORRY TO HEAR YOU ARE DEPRESSED.*

One of the unexpected results of this automated conversation program was a response that later came to be called the *ELIZA effect.* People who used the program began to have long, intimate conversations with ELIZA and asked for privacy when "talking" with the program. Weizenbaum was amazed that his own secretary and even his colleagues, who should have known better, were giving undue authority to a machine that was blindly following a set of preprogrammed conversational rules. In actuality, the program looked for keywords in the user text input, like *depressed, always,* or *everyone,* or statements of opinion that the program would then restate to the user, often as a question, to elicit further input.

You give me good advice.

OH. I GIVE YOU GOOD ADVICE.

You are very attentive.

DOES IT PLEASE YOU TO BELIEVE THAT I AM VERY ATTENTIVE?

Everyone says so.

CERTAINLY NOT EVERYONE.

ELIZA demonstrated early on that cleverly planned and executed algorithms, or fundamental rules of interaction, could engage and sustain human attention in a human/computer relationship, even on the level of simple text interactions. You could say that ELIZA was one of the first programs to identify and make use of some basic rules of conversation that felt natural and satisfying to its users—rules that provided the beginning groundwork for an evolving interaction between humans and computers.

The ability to communicate with a computer, where it responds and changes according to our input, offers the possibility of more intense and sustained levels of *immersion*[2] than is available through a movie, novel, or play where we remain as spectators to events outside of our control. The rapid growth of graphics-based video and computer games since the 1970s, the era from Atari's *Pong* to Blizzard's Web-based *World of Warcraft,* provides a prime example of this movement toward increased interactivity, where humans and computers—through digital entertainment technologies—are finding a common ground of interaction and enhanced communication.

A Short History of Video Games

As discussed in Chapter 5, Charles Babbage and Ada Augusta Lovelace worked on developing the first computer, the Analytical Engine. Although the Analytical Engine was never built during their lifetimes, Babbage and Lovelace shared a common passion for mathematics and games of chance. Together, they dabbled in creating mathematical systems for beating the odds at horse racing and even constructed a tic-tac-toe machine as a children's novelty. None of these schemes brought them any kind of financial success, however, and at one point Ada was even forced to pawn family jewelry to pay off her gambling debts.

More than 100 years after Charles Babbage and Ada Lovelace experimented with game theory at the horse races, the intimate relationship between computers and gaming was reignited with the introduction of electronic computing in the mid-twentieth century.

Starting in the late 1950s and 1960s, experiments with early computer games eventually led to the development of commercial game delivery platforms that now play a major financial role in the entertainment industry. There are three broad categories of game platforms: (1) **Consoles,** which are controller boxes that can control games played back through a television set using a joystick or other interactive device. (2) **Arcade games,** which are generally coin-operated and found in public locations. (3) **Computer-based games,** which are played on personal computers and handheld devices. The following is a short list of some of the major developments in the history of video games. A number of significant events are left out of this account in order to cover the history efficiently.

1958—William Higginbotham and Robert Dvorak of the Brookhaven National Labs hook up a computer to an oscilloscope, a device that shows electronic diagnostic information on a screen. Two handheld controllers equipped with a button and a dial move an electronic "ball" back and forth over a vertical line representing the "net." They call the game *Tennis for Two,* and it is set up along with other exhibits at a Brookhaven open house. People stand in line for hours to play the game, which is displayed on a 5-inch oscilloscope screen.

---

[2]**Immersion:** The illusion that you are within an environment created by a computer and not just looking at it on a screen.

1961—Digital Equipment Corporation (DEC) donates its state-of-the-art computer, the PDP-1, to MIT. The PDP-1 is one of the first computers to support a video screen. Programmer Steve Russell, while exploring the graphics capabilities of the PDP-1, creates the first interactive computer game, called *Spacewar*, where two spaceships try to blow each other up by firing electronic pellets as they circle around the screen. The game is an instant hit among the handful of other university and corporate mainframe computer users across the country.

1972—Magnavox releases the *Odyssey* home video game console for $100. The *Odyssey* is designed to generate electronic game displays on a television screen, and it is packaged with controllers, play money, a scorecard, and a pair of dice. Users are required to write down their scores and use transparent screen overlays to simulate graphics.

1972—Nolan Bushnell had been a computer graphics student at the University of Utah and was familiar with Steve Russell's *Space War* game. Along with programmer Alan Acorn, Bushnell creates an electronic simulation of the game of Ping-Pong. The concept is simple: two players control vertical bars on opposite sides of a computer display that bounce an electronic "ball" back and forth across the screen. The game, called *Pong*, is built into a rugged arcade game cabinet with the following instructions: "Ball will serve automatically. Avoid missing ball for high score." The first *Pong* arcade game is installed in a Los Angeles gas station, and it is forced to shut down during the first night of operation because its change box is filled to capacity with quarters. A home video game version of *Pong* is also released.

Pong is the first successful commercial video game, and Bushnell's new company, Atari, begins to compete with older pinball arcade machines. In a 1995 *New York Times* article, Bushnell described the circumstances surrounding the release of the world's first commercially successful video game: "You had to read the instructions before you could play, people didn't want to read instructions. To be successful, I had to come up with a game people already knew how to play; something so simple that any drunk in any bar could play."[20]

1976—Atari employees Steve Jobs and his friend Steve Wozniak complete work on *Breakout*. The game is well received, and a year later the two young game developers go on to create Apple Computers. William Crowther creates the first text-based adventure game called *Colossal Cave Adventure*, a single-player exploration and puzzle-solving game.

1977—The first distributed online game, called *Zork*, appears on early computer networks. The game is created by MIT students in their spare time, and it is accessed over the early Internet from a school's computer. Although this early interactive adventure is text-based and relies on the human imagination rather than displayed graphics, it sets the stage for online role-playing games.

1978—*Space Invaders*, created by Taito/Bally/Midway, becomes the first "blockbuster" electronic arcade game. The player must defend himself by blasting wave after wave of attacking aliens, who approach with increasing levels of speed and stealth. *Space Invaders* incorporates music to build dramatic tension. Extensive use of this arcade game causes a coin shortage in Japan.

1979—To counter the success of *Space Invaders*, Atari creates the game *Asteroids*, where a spaceship must blow up floating asteroids to avoid being destroyed.

1980—Atari creates the first game with a fully interactive 3D environment using simple line shapes. *Battlezone* is the original *first-person shooter*, where the game user must shoot at enemy tanks and an occasional flying saucer while defending his own tank. The U.S. Army is so impressed with the game that they adapt a version for training soldiers in tank combat. *Battlezone* became the great granddaddy of first-person 3D shooter video games.

1980—*Pac-Man* is released by Namco. The game is based on a traditional Japanese story. The main character devours power pellets in a maze and avoids getting eaten by "ghosts." The Pac-Man character becomes a celebrity, appearing on magazine covers, on t-shirts, in cartoons, and in a hit song.

1981—Nintendo began as a playing card company in 1889, eventually branching out into toys and electronics. In 1981 they introduce the video arcade game *Donkey Kong*, in which a character named Jumpman overcomes obstacles thrown out by a large ape. Later, Jumpman takes on the name Mario and becomes one of the most popular video game characters of all time. Peter Main, vice president of marketing at Nintendo, talks about the value of Mario as a brand based on a virtual character: ". . .if you take 120 million pieces of software and you multiply it by an average of . . . say, thirty dollars, in order to have accomplished that with other people's characters, were we able to sell that many games, you would've had to pay somebody else roughly 15 percent of that amount . . . It's over half a billion dollars that would've been paid to somebody else." By 1990, one survey indicates that more American children recognize Mario than Mickey Mouse.

1981—Microsoft distributes an interactive game called *Flight Simulator* to show off the graphics capabilities of IBM's first personal computer.

1982—Namco and Atari release the first race car driving game, *Pole Position,* and create a new genre of 3D interactive gameplay.

1983—George Lucas' *Star Wars* movie series is one of the most successful film franchises of all time. The first video game based on this George Lucas film series is *Star Wars* by Atari, starting a long tradition of creating Hollywood movies with associated video game spin-offs.

1989—As processing speeds increase on personal computers, more traditional arcade games as well as new computer-based game offerings begin to move into interactive entertainment. Developer Will Wright creates *Sim City,* where players build and manage a city and simulations of real-life situations initiate an innovative category of gaming for personal computers.

1993—Cyan Software produces a CD-ROM–based adventure game called *Myst* for the personal computer. Players explore a beautiful and mysterious 3D world to solve an elaborate, interlocking set of story puzzles.

1996—Young twenty-something programmers at id Software, John Carmack and John Romero, produce a first-person shooter game that can be played on the Internet with other networked users. The game is called *Quake,* and it makes use of realistic environments and characters in a highly interactive 3D virtual environment. This development was made possible by earlier successes that id Software had in developing the 3D first-person shooter genre in games such as *Castle Wolfenstein* (1992) and *Doom.*

1996—Eidos Interactive introduces the video game *Tomb Raider* for the Sony Playstation gaming console. *Tomb Raider's* protagonist, Lara Croft, is a female James Bond who fights her way through crowds of bad guys in exotic locations. Croft becomes the first virtual female actor to be represented by a talent agency. Six years after the release of the first *Tomb Raider,* products sold under the Lara Croft brand generate more than $1.2 billion. The motion picture *Lara Croft: Tomb Raider,* starring Angelina Jolie, becomes a box office hit, worth $300 million in ticket sales.

1996—A small company called Archetype Interactive releases the first massively multiplayer online game (MMOG), called *Meridian 59,* which allows large numbers of game players to interact in a single "persistent world." Although this game was popular, it had limited financial success, and it was quickly followed by Origin System's *Ultima Online* in 1997, a medieval sword and sorcery themed virtual world based on Richard Garriot's *Ultima* game series. This game eventually attracts 400,000 subscribers.

1998—Sony's massively multiplayer online role-playing game (MMORPG) called *EverQuest* is introduced on the Internet. This networked game features an immense virtual world consisting of five continents. In their *EverQuest* adventures, players engage in combat, practice a trade, converse, or go on quests where they encounter fantasy creatures such as gnomes, elves, wizards, and trolls. *EverQuest* builds a subscriber base of more than 400,000 users, becoming the most successful MMORPG up to that time.

2000 and beyond—One of the most dramatic developments taking place in the arena of video games since the beginning of the twenty-first century is the release of high-performance and relatively low-cost game consoles produced by Microsoft, Sony, and Nintendo. As of 2009, three game consoles dominate the market:

Nintendo Wii

Nintendo has always specialized in games for general family entertainment. The Nintendo Wii game console, since its release to the public in 2006, has consistently outsold other competing platforms on the market.

Figure 11. Microsoft Xbox 360. Photo by Benjamin Hollis.

It features a wand that can interact with objects on a video screen in three dimensions and has released an interesting new generation of sports and home exercise games. Nintendo also manufactures handheld game devices such as the Nintendo DS.

Microsoft Xbox 360

Microsoft's Xbox 360 game console was first made available in November 2005. As of the first quarter of 2008, Microsoft claims to have sold 19 million units worldwide.[21] Xbox 360 supports high-resolution graphics and fluid gameplay. One of the strong attractions to this platform is the availability of *Xbox Live,* a Microsoft online service that allows gamers to buy products, download games, view game statistics, and play networked games with other Xbox users. The sales of the Xbox consoles have been strongly supported by well-designed game software such as Bungie's science fiction themed series called *Halo.* The third game of the series, *Halo 3,* generated $125 million within the first twenty-four hours of its release in September 2007.

Sony Playstation 3

Sony released its first Playstation (PS1) console in late 1994. A second-generation Playstation console (PS 2) came out in March 2000 and sold more than 127 million units by January 2008, making it the most widely sold game console in history. As a consequence, Sony Playstation has a strong group of loyal users, many having used the console for years. Playstation 3, the third generation of Sony consoles, was released relatively late, in November 2006. Besides supporting a high level of game performance, the PS3 includes a Blu-Ray DVD player and access to an online networked community called *Home,* where users can talk with each other, play video games, create virtual apartments, watch movies, and buy products. Sony also sells a handheld game device—the Playstation Portable or PSP.

Current Trends in Video Gaming

Moore's Law (see Chapter 5) states that computer processing speeds double every twenty-four months while the cost of this increased performance remains unchanged. The impact of this law on electronic game devices is that they have consistently achieved better performance without users having to pay more money for this improvement. This has been a major factor in stimulating the rapid growth and maturation of video games. For example, the Atari 2600 home game console sold in 1977 for $199.00, contained 128 *bytes* of RAM memory, and was able to support only sixteen colors. It was the most popular game console of its time. Almost twenty-five years later, in November, 2001, the first Xbox game console was released by Microsoft which ran almost ten times faster, contained 64 *megabytes* of RAM memory, supported 3D polygon objects, and displayed millions of colors. The cost: $199.00! Also, compare the original second-generation Atari 2600 with the Nintendo's powerful seventh-generation Wii game console, which can be purchased for around $250. For more than a quarter century, the customer's cost for vastly increased performance remains almost unchanged. Because of the highly competitive nature of the commercial game console industry and the ongoing consumer demand for high performance at a low cost, this trend will undoubtedly continue.

A second factor in the growth of video games is the introduction of *high-bandwidth* network connections that allow game developers to create increasingly realistic real-time interaction among game users over a network. High-bandwidth connections through telecommunications services such as cable modems, wireless, and digital subscriber lines (DSL) permit increasing amounts of data to be passed through an Internet connection. It was discovered early on that the ability to play games and participate in shared virtual worlds with other network users provides a major incentive for getting involved and staying involved with games. The sense of participation in a larger community of common interest is as powerful a lure to a gaming experience as gameplay itself. Both console games and computer-based games have strongly entered this market. For the past several years Microsoft has provided a subscription service for the Xbox console that enables users to talk to each other as they play games on the Internet.

Arcade games have also moved into large-scale public entertainment centers such as Gameworks, formed from a business partnership between Steven Spielberg and Dreamworks, Universal Studios, and Sega. Located in five cities, GameWorks provides its customers with access to cutting-edge arcade games that are bigger and better than anything available on consoles or personal computers. These include larger-than-life race car simulations, tank combat scenarios, downhill skiing, hang gliding, as well as first-person shooters.

Commercial video games during their successful thirty-five-year history have not always been taken seriously. Atari founder Alan Bushnell describes an early experience he had convincing people that video games were an important industry. "You'd go to these . . . multimedia conferences, and they'd say, 'What's the killer app?' And I'd say: 'Guys, the killer app for multimedia is games. . .' And then they'd say, 'But what's *really* going to be important?' . . . People would look at you like you had three heads."[22]

By 2001 the situation was very different. The financial return from video games as well as related hardware amounted to $9.4 billion in 2001, which exceeded box office returns from Hollywood movies—$8.4 billion. Video games had hit the big time.[23] By the year 2012 it is estimated that the global sales for the video game industry will reach $68.3 billion.[24] It's projected that the revenue from mobile handheld games alone will reach $3 billion.[25]

Although it's true that game sales are increasing every year, it's equally true that video games are in an early phase, and there is an increasing demand for more compelling characters, stories, interactivity, gameplay, and software that brings increasing sophistication to the player's experience.

Peter Molyneaux, president of Lionhead Studios in Guilford, England, and one of the industry's most innovative game designers, describes this situation well by saying, "We are just getting out of the circus tent and into the cinema. But we're not even in the talkies yet."[26]

Lorne Lanning, the creator of the Oddworld video game series and now working on a new video game and film project called *Citizen Seige,* sees a lot of room for improvement in gaming, particularly in the areas of artificial intelligence and in the merging of motion pictures with video games. Here, he talks about his early experience with using artificial intelligence in the Oddworld games *Munch's Oddysee* and *Abe's Oddysee:*

"We're dealing with artificial intelligence at such a mundane level, with collision detection problems, that it's like herding hamsters. If the characters were as smart as a protozoa, I'd be ecstatic! They're not. And if you don't understand those limitations, you can have a lot of lofty ideas that'll never see the light of day."

"We're still in an age where the majority of coding time is going towards efficiency. The concerns for running a better frame rate while casting shadows and deforming skin and calculating collision detection . . . are more pressing today than those of making characters more believable in their personalities. In the end, the more convincing characters can become . . . the more the audience is going to identify with them. Which means it will be more rewarding for the user."[27]

Artificial Intelligence Applied to Storytelling and Dramatic Action

In their earlier games, Oddworld began to explore the possibilities of engaging an audience through the use of characters that operate independently from the direct control of a video game user. Character autonomy and believability is one aspect of a more comprehensive application of artificial intelligence to storytelling and dramatic action. Another important aspect involves the ability to understand the fundamentals of human psychology and apply that understanding to programs that enable computers to create dramatically compelling stories.

Interactive story designers Michael Mateus and Andrew Stern, formerly of Carnegie Mellon University's *Oz* project, characterize this form of computer-mediated interactive storytelling as a way of "building dramatically interesting virtual worlds inhabited by computer-controlled characters, within which the user experiences a story from a first person perspective." The interactive world design they describe has the following characteristics[28]:

1) **The story**—It is artistically complete and dramatically satisfying.

2) **Animated characters**—Real-time animated characters have convincing emotions, personality, and the ability to speak.

3) **Interface**—First- and third-person perspectives are controlled by the user with mouse and keyboard commands.

4) **Dialog**—The user can engage the story characters in active conversation. The game is provided with a sufficiently large database of AI responses to make the dialog convincing.

5) **Interactivity and plot**—The player can change the outcome of the story through his or her choices. The story can be "rewound" and played multiple times with different outcomes, based on the user's interaction with story characters.

A key concept in their approach to computer-enhanced interactive storytelling is the *dramatic beat,* which they describe as an event that changes the property of a character or a relationship within the story. For example, sharing a secret with a character is a story event that can increase the property of trust, whereas finding a note that indicates a betrayal of love is a dramatic event that decreases the same property. The dramatic beat becomes the smallest unit of dramatic change in a computer-driven story, in much the same way that a pixel is the smallest unit of display on a computer screen. They are the "fundamental building blocks of the interactive story . . . the fundamental unit of character guidance."[29]

Character motivation and the story plot are woven together through the use of the dramatic beat. The coordination of user input with character responses, the history of dramatic beats, and the adjustment of the story path according to user decisions is all carried out by the *drama manager,* an artificial intelligence program working "behind the scenes."[30] An example of Mateus and Sterns' work can be found in the interactive story called *Façade,* which is located on the World Wide Web at http://www.interactivestory.net.

A long-term interest of game developers is how stories, dramatic action, and relationships with characters can be integrated into interactive virtual environments. Concurrently with Mateus' and Sterns' work with interactive drama in *Façade,* other game production companies have been exploring the use of artificial intelligence in games with the goal of providing the illusion of freedom of choice for a player while guiding him or her through a satisfying story and set of emotional experiences.

In 2007 the video game company Bioware released a story-based game called *Mass Effect.* It explores the idea that nonlinear interactive game environments can also incorporate story themes and characters in an effective way—in the same way that twentieth century movie directors presented compelling stories to their audiences despite the inherent limitations of early motion-picture technologies. Bioware is able to accomplish this in the game by using an artificial intelligence storytelling software "engine" that provides a series of dramatically satisfying choices to game players.

In *Mass Effect,* the lead character, Commander Shepard, interacts with members of his crew, as well as a variety of alien personalities. The player, who takes the role of the commander, must make difficult choices here that will determine the outcome of the game. Rather than dictate specific spoken words, *Mass Effect's* dialog system presents a series of possible psychological attitudes or postures the lead character can follow when responding to various decision points that arise. The conversational content is based on the characters' emotional interactions. As Commander Shepard, you navigate through the galaxy in a starship called the *Normandie*, negotiating with extraterrestrial species and striving to protect galactic civilizations from destruction.[31]

Online Worlds and MMOGs: Massively Multiplayer Online Games

"Hiro's not actually here at all. He's in a computer-generated universe that his computer is drawing onto his goggles and pumping into his earphones . . . Hiro is approaching the Street. It is the Broadway, Champs Elysees of the Metaverse.

It is the brilliantly lit boulevard that can be seen, miniaturized and backward, reflected in the lenses of his goggles. It does not really exist. But right now, millions of people are walking up and down it."[32]

Neil Stephenson

When Neil Stephenson published these words in his novel *Snow Crash* in 1992, they were science fiction. The Internet had not yet become a public utility, and the World Wide Web was still in its infancy. Stephenson coined the term *"Metaverse"* to describe a society consisting of computer-generated landscapes, buildings, and inhabitants that millions of human beings plugged into on a daily basis by means of a global electronic network. It was a collective virtual world in which people conducted business, found employment, developed relationships, and found entertaining diversions. Stephenson's lead character, Hiro Protagonist, is a computer hacker who lives in a dingy rented storage container in the "real" world, while maintaining a luxurious mansion and a high social status in the Metaverse. The millions of inhabitants in this shared electronic hallucination take the form of "avatars," three-dimensional characters that speak, make gestures, wear custom-made costumes, and are the electronic representations of their human hosts who invisibly control the avatar's actions from home computers.

For more than two decades before Stephenson's book, people had been communicating and playing games with each other over computer networks, primarily with written text, but not at the immersive level or scale that Stephenson described. In 1994, two years after Stephenson published *Snow Crash,* an early version of the Metaverse was released in the form of *WorldsChat* by Worlds Inc. In this three-dimensional chat environment, online participants would first enter a room where they could choose from a variety of pre-prepared avatars—Alice in Wonderland, a space alien, Count Dracula, and some other less recognizable characters. After choosing a preferred persona, users would be "teleported" to a space station where they could wander around various rooms, much like being at an interstellar cocktail party, and talk with other avatars from around the world. As conversations were typed on a keyboard, corresponding words appeared in balloons over the head of each speaking avatar. Sound effects accompanied the opening and closing of doors as well as other events, and music wafted through the corridors of the virtual space station.

Soon afterward, Worlds Inc. changed its name to ActiveWorlds and released its first version of AlphaWorld, an expanded version of WorldsChat in which users logged on as citizens and were given the ability to build their own landscapes and buildings. After its public release in 1995, AlphaWorld grew over the next few years to a 3D multi-user virtual environment larger than the state of California. Over the years, virtual builders in AlphaWorld have created an airport, a monorail system with 40 stations covering 27 square kilometers, a replica of the Titanic, and a forest containing more than 1 million objects, primarily trees!

ActiveWorlds has become a platform for building worlds for personal entertainment as well as commercial and educational applications. In the ActiveWorlds *Eduverse,* students or faculty are able to build their own museums, libraries, lecture halls, and simulations. A recent virtual worlds educational project in Bergen, Norway made use of a three-dimensional interactive environment that was created in the style of Van Gogh.

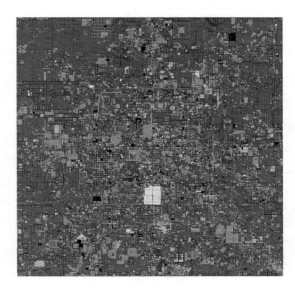

Figure 12. ActiveWorlds virtual world, birds-eye view, in August 2001. Each colored section represents 3D virtual buildings, forests, lawns, lakes, and other features all built by users. Courtesy of Activeworlds, Inc.

Figure 13. Avatar residents of Second Life. Second Life is a trademark of Linden Research, Inc. Certain materials have been reproduced with the permission of Linden Research, Inc. Copyright © 2001-2008 Linden Research, Inc. All Rights Reserved

Virtual Societies

Since the early days of virtual social networking worlds in the mid-1990s, several other companies specializing in supporting user-created worlds on the Web, including *There, Kaneva, IMVU,* and *Second Life* have emerged on the Internet. Arguably, the most well known and publicized of these online societies is *Second Life,* owned by Linden Labs. Like other virtual worlds societies, *Second Life* requires users to sign on as a new resident and choose an avatar, or a 3D virtual character that will be their graphic representative in the world. While using these characters as an identity, the users of *Second Life* have the ability to build an alternate existence for themselves in the virtual world. While residents are in the virtual world, they can modify their appearance, talk to other inhabitants, engage in a variety of entertainment activities, conduct business, and build, buy, and trade virtual objects. According to reports in *Second Life,* one enterprising resident built a flying saucer that enabled him to fly over and abduct other community members.

Residents can purchase various items, including real estate, clothing, furniture, and various services using Lindens, the unit of currency for the *Second Life* economy. Lindens can be converted to real currency, with a current rate of US$1 for each L$270 (Linden dollars). Chief Financial Officer John Zdanowski of Linden Labs says that a substantial number of residents make income from their activities within *Second Life:*

> "We have about 45,000 profitable business owners—accounts that have positive monthly Linden flow. That's up from about 25,000 in February. About 150 of them make over US$5,000 dollars within a single month."[33]

Since its online opening on June 23, 2003, Linden Labs claims that there are more than 14 million residents enrolled in the virtual world, with approximately half a million users logging in every week.[34]

Massively Multiplayer Online Games (MMOGs)

The early Web-based shared social environments such as WorldsChat and ActiveWorlds led the way to the creation of networked games called massively multiplayer online games (MMOGs). These differ from networked social worlds like *Second Life* in that subscribers participate in online quests, battles, role-playing, and forms of organized gameplay. They act out their roles and make choices as individual characters or in active collaboration with others in large-scale three-dimensional graphic game environments.

Richard Garriot's *Ultima Online* was one of the first successful graphically based MMOGs that required players to choose characters and gain additional points and capabilities as they played through a variety of designer-created quests. They were also able to join collaborative groups with common aims and objectives. When Origin

Systems opened up the graphically based *Ultima Online* in July 1997, the technological challenges involved with gathering together thousands of virtual characters all sharing the same environment as *avatars* within a single game-playing environment were daunting. Because this was one of the first networked games of its kind to be released, many unexpected problems arose when *Ultima Online* went live on the Internet. Thousands of beta testers entered the world at the same time, and commenced "killing" every virtual object or entity in sit—plants, animals, creatures, and non-player characters. The impact of thousands of players interacting with the virtual world was too much for the software engine running the world to withstand.[35] Ultima Online game designer Richard Garriot likened it to migrating 100,000 people into a city the size of Garriot's home town of Austin, Texas overnight.[36]

Table 1

Multimedia Fundamentals (Packer and Jordan)	Corresponding Features of Massively Multiplayer Online Games (MMOG)
Integration: "The blurring of traditional boundaries between disciplines—such as the arts and science—or between discrete media."	An MMOG creates an aesthetic, social, and game environment with a "look and feel"— composed of integrated music, sound effects, color, atmospherics, landscapes, architecture, characters, animation, and stories. This is similar to Richard Wagner's concept of the *Gesamtkunstwerk,* an endeavor that requires cross disciplinary expertise in engineering, architecture, music, art, kinesthetics, drama, and business management.
Interactivity: Computer/human communication. "Reciprocal exchange between the viewer and the artwork, the ability to manipulate media and objects intuitively and with immediacy."	New MMOG environments, such as the Sony Playstation 3 *Home,* allow users to manipulate objects, talk in real-time, play interactive games, create living spaces, watch movies, and adjust the appearance of their own virtual character.
Hypermedia: Collaboration and links to extended resources. "The non-sequential linking of information, events, and discrete media."	Participants in MMOGs are able to access information about their player status, communicate online, download virtual items, and conduct financial transactions within the online game environment.
Immersion: Enhanced engagement with a computer-simulated experience. "The experience of entering a multi-sensory representation of three-dimensional space."	MMOG environmental design is much like traditional theatrical stagecraft, in that it makes use of graphical styles, lighting, shadowing, weather effects, color, and sound to invoke emotional experiences, and a *feeling of place* to match the dramatic setting. The virtual world allows you to move in 3D space and explore the territory.
Narrativity: Storytelling, nonlinear narrative, and the flexible use of time. "Interactive, branching forms that lend the user control over the narrative, diminishing the traditional primacy of the author's voice."	Historical context and narrative form the foundation for the imaginary worlds of MMOG game experiences. For example, the story of *World of Warcraft* begins with this sentence: "Four years have passed since the mortal races have banded together and stood united against the might of the burning legions. . ." However, participants aren't limited to a single story line, but are presented with a wide range of possible narrative choices available within the context of a virtual game space. No player will have exactly the same experience.

Since *Ultima Online* debuted in 1997, there have been hundreds of multiparticipant online games created. The most successful to date is Blizzard's *World of Warcraft,* which was launched in November 2004. As of January 2008, there were more than 10 million *World of Warcraft* subscribers worldwide, with 5.5 million of those in China alone.[37]

MMOGs like *World of Warcraft* and *EverQuest* are transforming not only how we communicate with each other but also how we think and process ideas. The virtual world can be seen as a *theater of the mind* in which networked users interact with each other and with artificial intelligence agents (called *bots* or *nonplayer characters*) that facilitate human-to-game communication. The virtual world provides an umbrella where various media types—text, graphics, animation, 3D environments, and sound—are seamlessly integrated. It supplies a context for an amplified language of *perceptual form,* engaging the entire perceptual field to represent our thoughts. The closest familiar analogy to this is theater, but electronically mediated theater with greater flexibility, interactivity, and precision. Brenda Laurel describes this as using ". . .drama and theater as tools for thought. . ."[38]

With the introduction and growth of MMOGs also came the emergence of highly sophisticated digital multimedia technologies that required a century's worth of development, as described earlier in this chapter. Randall Packer and Ken Jordan have identified the characteristics of developed multimedia systems as the following: **integration, interactivity, hypermedia, immersion,** and **narrativity.**[39] The following chart shows how these fundamentals of multimedia work within an MMOG.

When we use the term *world-building,* we mean more than the representation of concepts by means of traditional methods of communication—spoken words, gestures, written text, and pictures. We're talking about the synergic formation of ideas shaped by moving images, text, sounds, rhythm, lighting, texture, 3D spatial cues, scale, and dynamic interaction with co-participants within a digital network. The human mind creates an ongoing simulation of events in response to sensory experience. Virtual worlds communication seeks to modify the character of that simulation by shaping perceptual experience via multiple sensory channels.

A key idea here is that traditional communication methods engage only a subset of the full human sensorium. Real-time interactive multimedia technologies are expanding the perceptual range and flexibility of how we communicate ideas and interact with them. In the next chapter we'll explore how the ongoing evolution of multimedia technology is leading to forms of representation that create direct relationships between artificial intelligence, new immersive delivery platforms, the human central nervous system, and through cybernetic extensions, our social lives.

Endnotes

[1] Eugene Emmanuel Viollet-Le-Duc, *Discourses on Architecture,* translated by Henry Van Brunt (Boston: James Osgood & Co., 1875), p.14.

[2] Sergei Eisenstein, *Film Sense,* translated by Jay Leyda (New York: Harcourt Brace & Company, 1975).

[3] H.G. Wells, *The Time Machine,* in *3 Prophetic Science Fiction Novels of H.G. Wells* (New York: Dover Publications, Inc., 1960), p. 278.

[4] Terry Ramsaye, "Paul and the Time Machine," *Focus on the Science Fiction Film,* ed. William Johnson, (New Jersey: Prentice Hall, 1972), p. 24.

[5] Ibid., p. 21.

[6] The Magic Lantern is the earliest form of slide projector . . . With the advent of photography in the mid-1800s, it became possible to produce black-and-white images on glass in greater numbers . . . Until movies came along, in the mid-to-late 1890s, the magic lantern was the sole projection device available. Though glass slides would indicate a still image, many innovations in magic lantern design and construction, as well as slide design (moving layers of glass images), allowed dissolving images, movement, and special effects. Thus, the magic lantern became "the Father of motion pictures, and the Grandfather of television." From Magic Lantern Castle Museum, http://www.magiclanterns.org/.

[7] John Clute, *Science Fiction: The Illustrated Encyclopedia* (London: Dorling Kindersley, 1995). If you want to explore what might have happened had the technology been available, you might read William Gibson's and Bruce Sterling's *The Difference Engine,* a novel about an alternate world where the industrial and the computer revolution occurred at the same time.

[8] Angelica Shirley Carpenter and Jean Shirley, *L. Frank Baum: Royal Historian of Oz* (Minneapolis: Learner Publications, 1992), p. 96.

[9]The Missing Link, "Méliès and Early Films," http://www.mshepley.btinternet.co.uk/melies2.htm.

[10]Ibid.

[11]Pixar Animation Studios, http://www.pixar.com/companyinfo/history/index.html.

[12]Ralph J. Gleason, *The Jefferson Airplane and the San Francisco Sound* (New York: Ballantine Books, 1969), p. 3.

[13]Ibid.

[14]Gert J. Almind, "Scoop-a-Tunes for Audio/Visual Jukeboxes," http://juke-box.dk/gert-scoop-a-tunes.htm.

[15]Bob Orlowsky, "Scopitone Archive," http://scopitone.tripod.com/.

[16]Chris Crawford, *The Art of Interactive Design* (San Francisco: No Starch Press, 2002), p. 3.

[17]Brenda Laurel, *Computers as Theater* (Addison-Wesley Publishing Company, 1991), p. ix.

[18]Randy Dixon, personal interview with the author.

[19]Joseph Weizenbaum, *Computer Power and Human Reason* (San Francisco: W.H. Freeman, 1976), pp. 2–3.

[20]Samuel Hart, "A Brief History of Home Video Games", citing Nolan Bushnell, http://www.samhart.com/vgh/first/atpongarc.shtml

[21]Bob Purchese, "Xbox 360 Passes 19 Million Mark," *Eurogamer,* April 25, 2008, http://www.eurogamer.net/article.php?article_id=134387.

[22]Nolan Bushnell, "The Revolutionaries: On Turning Inspiration into Innovation in Silicon Valley," interview with Joyce Gemperlein, *San Jose Mercury News,* January 19, 1997, http://www.thetech.org/revolutionaries/bushnell/i_c.html.

[23]NintendoWorldReport, "Lots of Moola!" February 7, 2002, http://www.nintendoworldreport.com/newsArt.cfm?artid=6969.

[24]Paul Bond, "Video Game Sales on Winning Streak, Study Suggests," *Reuters,* June 18, 2008, http://www.reuters.com/article/technologyNews/idUSN1840038320080618?pageNumber=1&virtualBrandChannel=0.

[25]MobileGamesBlog.com, "Juniper: North American Games Market Worth $3bn by 2012," http://mobilegames.blogs.com/mobile_games_blog/2008/01/juniper-north-a.html.

[26]Peter Molyneux, quoted in "Games Get Serious," *Red Herring,* December 17, 2000, http://www.redherring.com/Home/2405.

[27]Lorne Lanning, interview with authors Michael Korolenko and Bruce Wolcott, June 19, 2002.

[28]Michael Mateas and Andrew Stern, "Towards Integrating Plot and Character for Interactive Drama," *Working Notes of the Social Intelligent Agents: The Human in the Loop Symposium,* AAAI Fall Symposium Series (Menlo Park, CA: AAAI Press. 2000).

[29]Ibid

[30]Ibid.

[31]Bioware, Mass Effect Promotional Video, 2007, http://masseffect.bioware.com/gallery/gallery_archive.html.

[32]Neil Stephenson, *Snow Crash* (New York: Bantam Books, 2000), pp. 22–23.

[33]Erica Naone, "Making Money in Second Life: Linden Lab's CFO Explains How the Economy Works in the Virtual community," *Technology Review,* published by MIT, August 14, 2007, http://www.technologyreview.com/Biztech/19242/?a=f.

[34]Second Life, "Economic Statistics," http://secondlife.com/whatis/economy_stats.php (accessed July 10, 2008).

[35]Brad King and John Borland, *Dungeons and Dreamers: The Rise of Computer Game Culture from Geek to Chic* (McGraw-Hill/Osborne, 2003), p. 158.

[36]Ibid.

[37]MMOGCHART.com, "World of Warcraft Hits 10 Million," January 30, 2008, http://www.mmogchart.com/2008/01/30/world-of-warcraft-hits-10-million/.

[38]Brenda Laurel, *Computers As Theater* (Reading, MA: Addison-Wesley Publishing, 1991), p. 40.

[39]Randall Packer and Ken Jordan, "Teacher's Guide: From Wagner to Virtual Reality," http://www.artmuseum.net/w2vr/Teachers.html.

Chapter 8
Looking Glass Worlds Pavilion

"Shows there will certainly be in great variety in the modern civilization ahead, very wonderful blendings of thought, music and vision; but except by way of archaeological revival, I can see no footlights, proscenium, prompter's box, play-wright and painted players there."

H.G. Wells, *A Modern Utopia, 1905*

". . . certainly by the end of this decade, we'll have a very high bandwidth connection to the Internet at all times; we'll be in full immersion visual and auditory virtual reality. The electronics for all of this will be invisible, so small, they'll be in the glasses or woven in your clothing, and the nature of websites will be virtual reality environments, and going to a website will mean entering a virtual reality environment."[1]

Ray Kurzweil, *2000*

The Knowledge Navigator

In 1987 former Apple CEO John Sculley wrote a book called *Odyssey* in which he introduced the idea of a *knowledge navigator,* a portable device that could access a large library of electronic resources and make use of intelligent software agents that would help users find the information that would be most useful to them. Following up on these ideas, Apple employees Hugh Dubberly and Doris Mitsch conceived of a future scenario taking place in 2010 that became series of videos in which Sculley's knowledge navigator idea was fully developed. The intent was to develop a vision of the future that would help guide the direction of Apple computer interface design. The future vision provided by these videos is striking today, because so many of the predictions contained in them turned out to be true.

One of these videos shows a university professor using a folding book-sized portable computer with an interactive touch screen. The computer is wireless; provides access to written articles, images, and movies; and enables the user to communicate by way of video conferencing. Probably the most startling feature of this retro-futuristic 2010 computer is a helpful agent with a bow tie who is enhanced with artificial intelligence that allows him to converse directly with the professor. This agent also works as his personal secretary, providing useful reminders, interacting with callers, and assisting in searches for information on a network.

Much of this seems ordinary today, until you realize that the Internet in 1987 was still mostly used by large corporations, universities, and government agencies. The World Wide Web had not yet been invented, search engines were yet to be developed, connection speeds were mostly wired and exceedingly slow, and laptop computers were in their infancy. The knowledge navigator video seems to have gotten it right for everything except the intelligent agent, whose human-like helpfulness exceeds anything provided by today's computers—but that may be changing. Artificial agents now take airline reservations over the telephone, drive cars, and predict stock market trends. They may not be humanoid in appearance, but they can handle complex tasks in a way that seems very human-like.

The central interest of Apple in producing these futuristic scenarios was to set some guidelines in terms of how computers should interact with their human users. The quest for creating interfaces that allow computers to more effectively engage their capacities to meet human needs is an ongoing process and is a central theme of this chapter. This falls under the general category of human interface design.

Recently, the eminent physicist Stephen Hawking said, "We must develop as quickly as possible technologies that make possible a direct connection between brain and computer, so that artificial brains contribute to human intelligence rather than opposing it."[2] More than most people, Hawking understands very well the value technology provides in unlocking human potential.

Hawking is one of the most prominent astrophysicists living today and is known for his theoretical work in the field of black holes, or gravitational singularities. When he was a student at Cambridge he began showing symptoms of Lou Gehrig's disease, a condition that leads to a loss of muscle control. Over time, Hawking became almost completely paralyzed, losing the use of his arms, legs, and eventually his voice. Paradoxically, one of the greatest scientific minds in the world became locked in a physical body that no longer functions.

To a large degree, Hawking is able to overcome his severe disability through the use of a computer interface that allows him to spell out words by lifting his cheek to manipulate a switch located in his glasses. The switch gives him the ability to navigate in his wheelchair, communicate via emails, and even compose public talks through a text-to-speech conversion software. He's won numerous scientific awards, writes academic papers, and is well known for his three books, including the best-selling *A Brief History of Time*. Hawking is married and has three children.

Hawking's ability to rise above the limitations imposed by his disease through the use of a computer interface begs the question: how can computer technologies engage, expand, and augment the abilities of a normally functioning, healthy human being? Interestingly, the bootstrapping of human abilities through a progressive merging of human intelligence with computer capacities has been a long-standing dream of the most forward-thinking computer scientists right from the very beginning.

Norbert Wiener, Cybernetics, and the Human-Friendly Computer Interface

Norbert Wiener was a professor of Mathematics at MIT from 1919 to 1964. He was a child prodigy who began high school at age eleven and graduated from Tufts College by fifteen. After completing his PhD, Wiener taught philosophy at Harvard starting at age 20. During World War II, he helped develop mathematical models that would help antiaircraft weapons target enemy planes through radar feedback loops. These provided an ongoing stream of updated aircraft tracking information, which in turn guided the antiaircraft weapons. Weiner saw these feedback loops at work not only in automated mechanical devices like a thermostat—which turns on or off based on the temperature of a heated space—but also in biological organisms. He coined the term *cybernetics* to describe the study of self-regulating systems—both human-made and those found in nature. The term *cyber* is derived from the ancient Greek word for a ship's steersman or navigator.

William Gibson coined the word *cyberspace,* derived from Wiener's term, in his early novel *Neuromancer.* In 1986 Gibson talked about the powerful attraction that computer games had on their users—providing us with the perfect example of a human-computer feedback loop in the process. He described his experience in a video game arcade where an interactive electronic simulation had pulled the gamers' attentions into its powerful embrace.

> "I could see in the physical intensity of their postures how rapt these kids were . . . you had this feedback loop with photons coming off the screen into the kids' eyes, the neurons moving through their bodies, electrons moving though the computer. And these kids clearly believed in the space these games projected."[3]

Several questions arise: Is there a clear separation between a video game and the gamer's central nervous system, or have they merged into an integrated system? Can the same question be asked of any electronic device with a human interface? Are we moving toward a progressively more intimate relationship between humans and software-driven digital devices? Certainly, the seeds for this evolving human-computer relationship were put in place in 1944, when Norbert Wiener met with other colleagues to create the Teleological Society for the purpose of exploring "communication engineering, the engineering of control devices, the mathematics of time series in statistics, and the communication and control aspects of the nervous system."[4]

By introducing the discipline of cybernetics, Wiener led the way for succeeding generations of scientists to think of computers and their interfaces as a means to expand human capabilities.

As described in Chapter 5, the innovative computer scientist Douglas Engelbart took computers out of the era of punch cards and tape by introducing input devices that made computers more user friendly, such as the keyboard, tracking mouse, application windows, screen cursor, text editing, keyword search, and network-based real-time communication. All of these tools provide ways in which human action (pressing a key, moving a mouse) can be translated into a binary code of 1s and 0s so that it can be interpreted and processed by a computer. The only language a computer understands is a stream of numerical data. For example, when the letter *A* is pressed on a keyboard, the ASCII numerical translation of this letter is interpreted by a computer as the following combination of 1s and 0s: **01000001**.

Since the late 1960s, when Engelbart first introduced his early interface concepts, other forms of interactive devices have been developed, including the trackball, joystick, optical mouse, and wireless keyboard. These information input tools are not enough, however, to complete the cycle of a successful interactive relationship between the user (audience) and a computer. The computer must also translate data from these devices and create a response that is interesting and useful to the user. In many applications, such as word processing or database management, a text or numerical result is sufficient. However, for more complex interactive situations, such as a video game, the computer must deliver its responses in a dramatically compelling way in order to capture and hold the attention of its audience.

While the growth of personal computers and video games drove the development of human interface design on the commercial side, another important area of technology growth has taken place in the field of multisensory virtual worlds environments, commonly referred to as *virtual reality.*

What Is Virtual Reality?

"Virtual Reality represents the convergence of computer simulation and visualization into a single, coherent entity. It also encompasses an attempt to eliminate the traditional separation between user and machine and to provide a means of naturally and intuitively interacting with information."[5]

Ivars Peterson

On one level, virtual reality (VR) is the use of a variety of interconnected digital sensory interface devices to place a computer user into an artificial world, a simulation that interacts in real-time with gestures, movements, voice commands, and more recently, *thoughts.*[6] It differs from movies or television in the sense that the user can influence ongoing events and experiences a greater sense of *immersion,* or the felt sense of actually being present in a synthetic world. Essentially, VR provides the user with the ability to interact with data in a way that enables "entering" and navigating through a computer-generated 3D world or environment. Within the VR world the user can change his or her viewpoint and interact with objects within that world. Historically, computers were not powerful enough to support the number of calculations needed to display continually changing photorealistic immersive sensory experiences, but newer generations of microprocessors and video cards are changing that. VR is becoming more portable, affordable, and accessible to the average user.

Beyond these technical considerations, virtual reality also implies the ability to use very precise tools to engage and measure the characteristics of the human central nervous system, especially those aspects that are involved with one of the most important activities of our lives, making sense of the world and making our way through it. It's a powerful tool for understanding and shaping human cognition and awareness.

Dr. Thomas Furness, one of the earliest pioneers in virtual worlds technology, describes it this way:

"What do we mean by virtual? Virtual comes from the concept in optical physics of virtual images—virtual images are images that you see that appear to be located somewhere in space but aren't really there. A mirror does this—it's basically an illusion of yourself in the mirror—that person really isn't there—that is a virtual image. We can create virtual acoustics. We can do this tactilely—touch things that appear to exist but don't really exist. Something that appears to be there but isn't really there. VR is the technology that applies stimuli to human senses—that mirror real world experience. What it does is create an alternative real life experience."

Interest in immersive multisensory experiences has been around for a long time, as seen in the following timeline of virtual reality.

Timeline of Virtual Reality

1883—Early World-Building—Panorama of the Battle of Sedan

In 1883 the Prussian government commissioned the creation of an exhibition in Berlin to commemorate their 1870 victory over the French in the Battle of Sedan during the Franco-Prussian War. The exhibition included a photorealistic 360-degree painted panorama of the battle that covered 7,000 square feet. Within this panorama were shrubbery, stones, weapons, cardboard soldiers, and accompanying sound effects. One Berlin newspaper of the time described the exhibit by saying, "At first the visitor is startled, he is surprised, and naturally keeps a distance. He is afraid to collide with the horses and feels inclined to move backwards. The air seems to be filled with swirled-up dust and mist. Trumpets sound and drums beat." Another reported, "It is as if one were standing amidst the awful battle."[7]

1929—Edward Link patents the first flight simulator, built to train new pilots. The wooden simulator is mounted on an organ bellows to simulate movement as the pilot trainee adjusted the tilt and roll of the airplane.

1931 through 1932—Aldous Huxley writes about *feelie movies* in his science fiction novel *Brave New World.*

1961—Morton Heilig patents the *Sensorama,* which gives people a full sensory experience of riding a motorcycle through Brooklyn, a bicycle ride, a helicopter flight, and a belly dancer. The simulation is based on watching a 3D film in an enclosed space—movement, sounds, winds, and smells were all added to the experience to provide additional realism.

Michael Noll develops the force feedback joystick.

Myron Kruger publishes papers on artificial reality, describing a device providing input to computers for video mapping.

Douglas Engelbart develops the first pointing device, or mouse.

1965—Ivan Sutherland's paper "The Ultimate Display" inspires others to continue work in the field of VR. He also develops the first head mounted display, or HMD, in 1966. Sutherland is also credited with implementing the first computer graphics software in a program called *Sketchpad* in the 1960s.

1968—Sutherland describes the first Head Mounted Display (HMD) device, which tracks a user's movement and shows a re-rendering of that movement on a stereoscopic display.

1970—Sutherland's paper becomes the basis for Fredrick Brooks' combined computer graphics and forced feedback.

1970s—Thomas Furness develops the Super Cockpit flight simulator for fighter pilots. This work is initially classified but forms the foundation for later scientific research and commercial applications in virtual reality.

1985—Enabling technology allows Thomas Zimmerman and Jaron Lanier to create VPL Research. Their first product is the Data Glove, which tracks hand movements and translates those movements into controlling a synchronized virtual hand. Lanier invents the term *virtual reality.*

Mid-1980s—At MIT's Media Lab, the Vivarium is created. Vivarium means "an enclosed environment for life," and the lab creates an area where school children can invent and then unleash realistic "organisms" in whole "living" computerized ecologies. The organisms they create behave, "learn," and even evolve independently. Marvin Minsky, a cofounder of *artificial intelligence,* is very much involved in the Vivarium.

1989—Autodesk creates a Virtual Bicycle Ride and a Virtual Racket Ball Game.

1989—Dr. Thomas Furness begins work at the Human Interface Technology Laboratory, a research facility he established to investigate virtual worlds technologies and find *real-world* applications for them at the University of Washington.

Late 1980s/Early 1990s—SIMNET becomes the world's largest immersive simulation. Personnel at military bases throughout the United States and Europe jointly participate in maneuvers on the same simulated battlefield and wage war games on a massive scale entirely within computer-controlled and networked tank, helicopter, and fighter-bomber simulators. The simulation is so real that, on at least one occasion, a soldier jumps out of his virtual "tank" to take a compass reading because the tank is "lost."

Early 1990s—Virtual World Entertainment creates Battle Tech Tank Simulator.

Disney Tours creates a fantasy ride based on the motion control platforms of flight simulators.

1992—Work begins on a networked multiplayer system.

Mid-1990s—*Chemistry World* allows users to pick up electrons, protons, and neutrons in order to build atoms in a virtual world. Discussion continues as to whether or not this is a better way to teach fundamental chemistry than the traditional way.

1995—The *GreenSpace* project takes place at the Human Interface Technology Laboratory (or HIT Lab) at the University of Washington in December. A person in the HIT Lab in Seattle walks into a virtual "room" where he works together with a man thousands of miles away in Japan. The two feel as if they are together in one room, helping each other contain tiny butterfly-like beings with virtual Ping-Pong paddles. Travel time is nonexistent as the two meet in virtual space.

The Future—Thomas Furness continues work on replacing HMDs with Rear Retinal Displays using microlasers that will "write" an active matrix image on the retina of the eye, and he helps to set up new virtual reality labs internationally. Furness is also working with motion picture effects wizard Douglas Trumbull on developing new uses for VR for both entertainment and education in the twenty-first century. In Japan, ATR Systems Research continues research on wireless VR. Microvision, Inc., a visual display company in Redmond, Washington, continues their development of *mobile device eyewear,* which promises wireless augmented reality experiences, with lightweight glasses that can project screen displays directly onto the retina of the eye—merging virtual information worlds with real-world experiences.

Virtual reality research centers now operate in the United States, Canada, Japan, Australia, Korea, Europe, and New Zealand. Virtual reality is now being used for many purposes, some of which will be described more fully in this chapter; these include, pain management, the treatment of phobias, education, engineering, surgery, architecture, scientific visualization, and emergency response.

Dr. Thomas Furness: Early Virtual Reality Pioneer

By the late 1980s, designers and engineers of military jet aircraft were trying to solve a difficult problem. Pilots of powerful new military jets were involved with flying tasks that were becoming too complex to manage using a traditional aircraft instrument panel. Military pilots had to fly the plane at speeds where decisions had to be made quickly and weapons systems accurately controlled. The F16 fighter jet, for example, had fifty different computer systems running simultaneously, each monitoring a different aspect of the plane's performance. Because the high-performance F16 was flying at speeds faster than the speed of sound, the pilot had difficulty dividing his attention between the instrument panel and visually flying the airplane through a cockpit window. Life and death decisions had to be made quickly and without errors.

Tom Furness, as a young Air Force officer working as an engineer for the Air Force, decided that it was time to revamp aircraft instrumentation so that a pilot could be oriented with visual and sound cues in a *heads-up* display that he could view while flying the plane. Furness' goal was to "increase bandwidth to the brain," meaning that the changing data streams needing the pilot's attention needed to be displayed in such a way that he or she could manage the plane's complex information systems without undue stress or hazard. Three-dimensional graphics displays as shown below were found to be effective in relaying important information to the pilot in a way that traditional cockpit instruments could not provide.

Furness was working at the Wright-Patterson Air Force base in Ohio in the early 1980s and sums up his early work by saying, "I was trying to solve problems of how humans interact with very complex machines." The result

Figure 1. Starting in the 1960s, high-performance jet fighter planes such as the F-16, shown here, required a different kind of interface than the traditional instrument dashboard. An F-16 fighter jet requires a pilot to simultaneously monitor the status of fifty onboard computer systems while safely flying the plane at supersonic speeds.
Left image: © Jason Smith | Dreamstime.com.
Right image: © Photawa | Dreamstime.com.

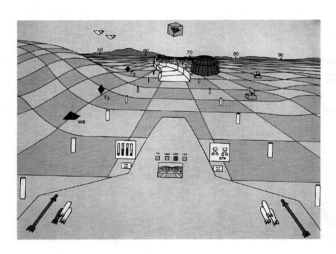

Figure 2. Early 3D graphic displays provided jet pilots vital feedback regarding their current flight status that could be quickly interpreted and responded to.
Photo courtesy of Dr. Thomas Furness.

of this early exploration with computer-based flight simulations was a device called the Super Cockpit, which surrounded a pilot with not only a simulated view of the outside world but also a virtual representation of the plane's instrumentation itself. The pilot could manipulate these virtual controls by using hand gestures. Three-dimensional spatialized sound also played an important role in providing useful navigation information.[8]

In September 1981, Furness along with some other team engineers activated an early prototype of the Super Cockpit. He described this first experience by saying, "I felt like Alexander Graham Bell, demonstrating the telephone. We had no idea of the full effect of a wide-angle view display. Until then, we had been on the outside, looking at a picture. Suddenly, it was as if someone reached out and pulled us inside."[9] One of Furness' early discoveries was that when a displayed field of visual information exceeded 120 degrees, it invoked a subjective sense of immersion, of being fully present. Ivan Sutherland had also worked on immersive virtual displays at the University of Utah. Both scientists are considered to be the first inventors of virtual reality technology.

When his early immersive simulations work with the Super Cockpit was declassified, Furness' work with interactive virtual reality systems attracted media attention early on. After his first interviews with national media, public fascination with the possibilities of virtual reality became "show business."[10] Virtual reality made a strong appearance in the press and mainstream media during the early 1990s. It inspired a short-lived television series, *Wild Palms,* and several feature films, including *Lawnmower Man, The Net, Virtuosity, Johnny Mnemonic, Hackers,* and *Strange Days.*

Furness himself began to consider what applications there might be for this new technology in areas beyond electronic cockpit simulations. He began to think of this virtual worlds technology in terms of applications in

Figure 3. A young Air Force Lieutenant, Tom Furness, demonstrates two early versions of the Virtual Cockpit in 1967 to 1968.
Photos courtesy of Dr. Thomas Furness.

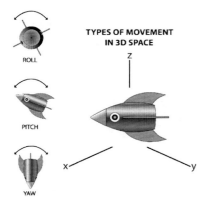

Figure 4. 3D coordinates—yaw, pitch, and roll. Illustration by Kirsten Adams.

scientific visualization, prosthetic devices for the handicapped, manufacturing, education, and entertainment. After a period of planning, he decided to leave the Air Force, and he collaborated with the University of Washington in Seattle, Washington, to establish a research lab for developing knowledge about virtual worlds technology and its applications, and transferring that knowledge to industry.[11] This center, known as the Human Interface Technology Lab, was created in 1989 and has been one of the leading research laboratories for virtual worlds technologies.

While games and gaming consoles have approached world-building from the standpoint of entertainment, the Human Interface Technology Lab has been concerned with industrial, educational, and medical applications of this technology. There are some fundamental concepts associated with virtual worlds technologies that have emerged from research and development at the Human Interface Technology Lab and elsewhere.

Virtual Worlds Concepts

1) The **virtual world** consists of a three-dimensional computer-generated space created to accommodate a task or activity, whether it is a game, scientific visualization, simulation, or physical enhancement. You will often hear the expressions *virtual world*, *virtual reality*, and *VR* used interchangeably. The term applied to the construction of virtual environments is called *world-building*. A virtual world does not have infinite size, but it is given mathematically defined boundaries and borders.

    A virtual world contains **three dimensions** that define the location of points and objects within the world. These dimensions are x (width), y (height), and z (depth). Movement of objects within a 3D space is described using the terms **yaw** (object nose point pivots side to side), **pitch** (object nose point pivots up and down), and **roll** (object tilts left or right). Movements of objects within a 3D space can include any one or a combination of these.

2) There are two kinds of virtual worlds: **nonimmersive** and **immersive**.

    Nonimmersive virtual reality is experienced through a flat screen display and is like viewing events through a window. Examples of these are 3D video games like *Doom, Quake, Myst, Halo,* and

World of Warcraft—and computer-assisted design (CAD) architectural models. You are able to see various perspectives and camera angles of a scene or object but always remain "outside" of the action, looking through a screen.

Immersive virtual reality seeks to create a *perceptual envelope* so compelling and responsive that the person experiencing it feels as if they are actually *present* in the synthetic digital environment. Although it can be argued that a well-designed movie, play, or novel can totally capture an audience's attention, an immersive 3D world makes specific use of a number of perceptual modeling techniques to enhance the illusion of presence, of actually *being there*. In order to create this quality of presence, a number of interrelated VR technologies are required.

Stereoscopic displays have been around since the beginning of photography, when it was discovered that by shooting the identical scene from two slightly different angles, and allowing a viewer to see both images superimposed on one another, the illusion of 3D can be created. It's an impression of depth that can't be obtained from a single image alone. Stereo images were used in nineteenth century Victorian-era stereoscopic viewers as well as in mid-twentieth century 3D horror movies such as *House of Wax* and *Creature from the Black Lagoon*. This same approach is used in immersive virtual reality, where two small digital screens are presented, one for each eye, in a stereoscopic viewing device called a *head-mounted display,* or HMD.

A similar principle is applied to the representation of sound, where the illusion of a 360-degree acoustic environment can be created by applying different signals to each ear in a stereo headset. Sophisticated applications of stereo or binaural signals can make sound appear to be coming from behind, above, or in any other position surrounding the listener. This ability to shape the acoustic environment is referred to as *spatialized sound.* Together, the application of spatialized sound and stereoscopic imagery greatly enhances the illusion of immersion and presence within a virtual world.

Immersive VR also refers to the direct responsiveness of a virtual world to the user's gestures and body movements. As microprocessor speeds have increased, so has the ability of computers to handle an increasing amount of data input. Initially instructions were input to computers by way of punch cards, followed by keyboards, the electronic mouse, joystick, and finally voice commands as well as gestures. The goal in virtual worlds is to maximize the effectiveness of increased processing speeds by enabling the user to look around, fly, communicate, pick up objects, and receive useful feedback within a virtual environment. This kind of sophisticated response to user input requires that the computer interpret the body movement of a user and feed that changing position data back to the computer so that it can update the visual display of information. In virtual worlds terminology,

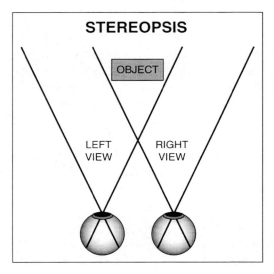

Figure 5. Stereoscopy: Two separate views of the same object creates an illusion of depth. Illustration by Kirsten Adams.

the ability for a computer to interpret user movements and display these changes in real-time is known as *position tracking*. Several devices have been developed to allow a user to engage with an immersive virtual world using position tracking.

1) The *head-mounted display* (HMD) was first introduced by Ivan Sutherland in 1968 at the University of Utah using a bulky contraption called the *sword of Damocles*. This is a device that mounts on the head and provides stereoscopic views through two eye screens and can represent spatialized sound through built-in earphones. As a user changes the position of his or her head or body, the first-person viewpoints and sound envelope adjust correspondingly to these movements in a virtual world. Newer versions include a microphone that allows the user to input voice commands.

2) The *dataglove* is an interactive device that was developed for use in virtual environments by Jaron Lanier, Scott Fisher, and others. The virtual world user puts on the dataglove, which in turn is equipped with sensors that record the positions of the user's "real hand" and converts that information into movements of a "virtual hand" in the 3D world. The virtual hand lets users push virtual buttons, pick up virtual objects, and give gestured commands for walking, running, or flying.

3) The *datasuit* is an extension of the dataglove, in the sense that users put on a wearable position-sensing system that tracks the movements of their entire body. In this way an entire human body can be represented in 3D space.

Since the Human Interface Technology Lab opened its doors at the University of Washington in 1989, it has been exploring many different practical applications for virtual worlds technology beyond its obvious uses for entertainment and interactive storytelling. Here are a few examples of a wide range of innovative projects carried out by the HIT Lab over the past decade.

Treatment of Phobias

Because virtual reality technology can simulate real-world scenarios, various approaches have been designed to place people in situations where they may experience intense fear without having to risk any authentic danger. For example, a person who fears heights can approach a virtual cliff or a virtual window in a tall skyscraper. Those who experience severe anxiety while flying can face their terror in a realistic simulation of an airplane taking off and landing. In one recent experiment conducted by cognitive psychologists, a woman who was called "Miss Muffet" by researchers, who had a long history of arachnophobia (fear of spiders), was placed in a virtual kitchen environment called *Spiderworld* where she encountered spiders hiding in cupboards or dropping from the ceiling on a web. After twelve one-hour sessions the woman's fear of spiders was greatly reduced. As evidence of this, Miss Muffet, who had previously experienced terrifying nightmares of spiders, was able to scold a large cigar-smoking spider in one of her dreams for scaring her. He responded, "Don't feel bad, lady; we scare everyone."[12] She was also eventually able to hold an actual live spider, a large tarantula, in her hand.

Figure 6. A stereoscopic head-mounted display (HMD) and datagloves track a user's movements and map them in real-time with a virtual hand and point of view in an immersive digital 3D display. Photo courtesy of NASA/Langley.

Figure 7. Cognitive psychologist Dr. Hunter Hoffman uses virtual worlds technology to treat phobias, in this case arachnophobia, or the fear of spiders. By using increasing levels of exposure over time to immersive, anxiety-provoking situations, Hoffman is able to alleviate fearful reactions in his clients.
Photo by Stephen Dagadakis, UW, copyright Hunter Hoffman, University of Washington, Seattle.

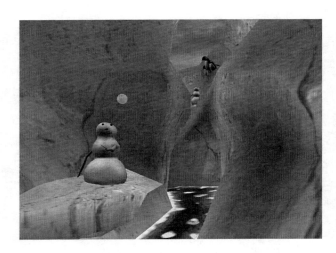

Figure 8: *SnowWorld* is an immersive virtual environment where burn patients can be effectively distracted from painful skin treatments by shooting snowballs at a variety of winter-themed targets—such as snowmen and igloos, while listening to soothing music. Image by VR worldbuilder Ari Hollander, www.imprintit.com, copyright Hunter Hoffman, University of Washington, Seattle.

Dr. Hoffman describes his approach to treatment of phobias using virtual worlds technology:

"Gradual exposure to a virtual spider helps spider phobics habituate their fear and anxiety. Tactile augmentation, the final step in the therapy, involves having patients reach out and touch a virtual spider with their virtual hand in SpiderWorld. When their virtual hand touches the virtual spider, their real hand simultaneously touches a furry toy spider. Their brain unifies the sensory inputs, giving them the illusion of physically touching the virtual spider. At first this is very anxiety provoking, but gradually they get used to it and it no longer makes them so anxious. After 10 hours of VR exposure therapy, most patients show clinically significant reductions in their fear of spiders."

Pain Management

In another virtual environment, hospital patients with painful body burns are immersed in a virtual environment called *SnowWorld*. Hoffman explains how an interactive game within *SnowWorld* works in a hospital setting:

"During burn wound care and physical therapy, patients fly through an icy 3D canyon and shoot snowballs at snowmen, igloos, penguins, and woolly mammoths. The mammoths trumpet angrily when pelted by snowballs thrown by the patient (by pushing the mouse button). Patients can look around by moving their head and shoot snowballs by pressing a mouse button. They hear sound effects and see animated reaction of the virtual objects (e.g., snowmen shatter into 3D pieces when hit by snowballs). And patients listen to the soothing music of Paul Simon in the background."

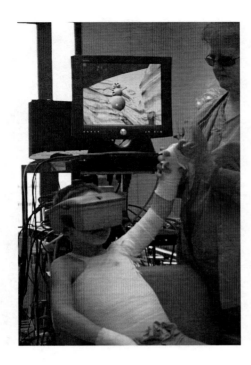

Figure 9. Photo and copyright by Hunter Hoffman, University of Washington, Seattle.

According to Hoffman's research, these patients were effectively able to reduce the amount of pain they were experiencing while playing this game in a therapeutic process called "VR pain distraction."[13] It was found that this approach works as well as strong pain relievers, such as morphine, in reducing the experience of pain in burn patients undergoing skin treatments.

Hoffman explains the following example of pain distraction therapy in the photograph shown in Figure 9.

"A six year old boy suffered 3rd degree burns on over half of his body, after accidently pulling a pot full of boiling water and spaghetti onto himself. Pain during physical therapy is often severe to excruciating and can limit how far the patient can stretch. Immersive virtual reality pain distraction is a technique developed in a collaboration between VR researcher Hunter Hoffman from the University of Washington Human Interface Technology lab, and pain psychologist Dave Patterson from Harborview Burn Center in Seattle. Burn patients report large (35-50%) reductions in how much pain they experience during medical procedures while in virtual reality. Interacting with the virtual world such as SnowWorld (see below) helps take their mind off their pain."

Collaborative Virtual Reality

One important aspect of immersive VR research at HIT Lab has been the development of *distributed virtual environments,* or the ability of immersive virtual worlds to be shared simultaneously by several people over a computer network. In an early experiment in 1994, HIT Lab partnered with the Fujitsu Research Institute in Japan to create a collaborative virtual environment called *GreenSpace.* In this experiment, which was made open to limited public involvement, participants in Seattle and Tokyo donned virtual reality headsets and datagloves. Participants in Tokyo were surrounded by a virtual log cabin with a window overlooking Mt. Rainier, whereas those in the United States found themselves in a traditional Japanese home with Mt. Fuji in the background. Together, the virtual collaborators, whose faces were visible to one another, picked up computer-generated paddles with their datagloves and herded flying "insects" into virtual holes.

The Magic Book

One innovative interface for immersive virtual worlds by the HIT Lab is the Magic Book. This device looks and reads like a book, but when viewed using a head-mounted display, it can either show 3D objects or allow the user to actively enter and explore a 3D world. In this case, the user can experience information from three different levels: (1) as printed text, (2) as 3D objects, or (3) as a participatory 3D environment.

Figure 10. The Magic Book brings 2D and 3D worlds together into one interactive interface. Human Interface Technology Lab, University of Washington.

Figure 11. Dr. Tom Furness views an early prototype of the virtual retinal display (VRD) in the 1990s, where a digital image can be "painted" on the retina of the eye, much like a miniature television tube. Human Interface Technology Lab, University of Washington.

One of Dr. Furness' current projects is the creation of a Virtual Worlds Society, with the goal of putting sophisticated world-building software tools in the hands of a wider range of users and collaborators around the world. The intent is to build interactive 3D environments for a wide variety of purposes—such as scientific visualizations, ecosystem modeling, educational games, and psychotherapy.

Wireless Retinal Scanning: The Next Generation of VR?

One of the most innovative ideas to come out of the HIT Lab is the *virtual retinal display,* or VRD, which is now being developed and sold by Microvision, Inc., in Bothell, Washington. In this technology, very precisely modulated laser light paints images on the retina of the human eye, much like a cathode ray tube scans electronic images onto a television screen. A miniature device referred to as a micro-electro-mechanical system (MEMS) controls the extremely rapid horizontal and vertical movement of a mirror roughly the size of the head of a pin to scan tiny laser images on the retina. The laser light is safe to view and creates images whose resolution, transparency, and perceived size can be adjusted.

Over the past few years, Microvision has developed lightweight retinal scanning devices that can be used for many different purposes. Physicians are able to continually view a display of their patient's vital signs while they perform a surgical procedure. Pilots can see displays of aircraft speed, altitude, GPS location, and terrain without looking down at their instrument panel. Technicians can review heads-up schematics as they complete electronic diagnostics. Information in the form of text, graphics, images, and real-time data can be superimposed on the eyes' view of the actual world—a type of information-*augmented* reality.

Recently, Microvision has developed the ability to display full-color retinal-scan images, which opens up many possibilities for future forms of information design and entertainment. One can imagine a wireless, stereoscopic, lightweight, full-color retinal display device with stereophonic sound that would permit users to communicate with others in shared virtual worlds over a network, as well as augment their work and life experience within an information-enhanced environment. As one of the pioneers in VRD technology, Microvision may be leading the way to a distributed worlds-based communications network.

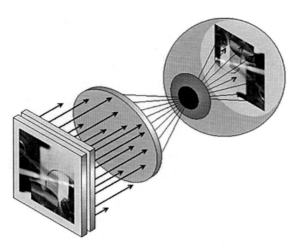

Figure 12. In traditional flat screen video displays, the eye views information that is being scanned onto a flat screen.
Courtesy of Microvision, Inc.

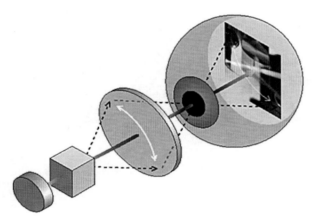

Figure 13. Virtual retinal display technology makes use of modulated laser light that scans miniature video images directly onto the eye.
Courtesy of Microvision, Inc.

Virtual Worlds Technology

Most computer displays and interfaces are based on flat screen representations, with icons and drop-down menus, whose functions are activated by mouse clicks, keyboard commands, a trackball, or a stylus. The flat screen display requires either a bulky monitor on a desktop or compels the user to maneuver within the tiny screen real estate available on a laptop, palmtop, or cell phone. Sound is usually localized within individual speakers or headsets.

On the other hand, traditional virtual reality devices such as head-mounted devices (HMD), datagloves, and datasuits have proved to be too bulky, expensive, and slow to attract many computer users. However, a combination of the increasing speed of microprocessors along with electronics miniaturization is now making it possible to create portable virtual display devices that are more powerful and less intrusive.

The lightweight Microvision VRD technology, described earlier in this section, is a strong step in this direction. In a fully developed form, virtual worlds technology could deliver multisensory experiences via wireless connections, and it would eliminate the need to carry handheld computers or be tethered to a desktop monitor.

This portable multisensory simulation device would have the following characteristics:

Visual Display

1) Wireless, lightweight retinal scanning glasses, priced for the consumer, that can be worn anywhere, any time, with continuous Internet connections.

2) High-resolution display that can be scaled in size and positioned spatially—ranging from a private wide-screen CinemaScope to updated electronic text. (Microvision retinal scanning technology is currently able to project screen detail that exceeds the resolution of the human eye.[14])

3) Screen displays are full-color and have adjustable transparency to permit data in the virtual world to be superimposed on a view of the "real world."

4) Displays can be stereoscopic, which permit the representation of real-time 3D virtual environments, avatars, objects, and user interfaces.

Audio Display

5) Sound can be localized or spatial, positioned anywhere within the user's 3D psycho-acoustic field, and delivered through high resolution stereophonic earplugs.

6) A user can provide voice input, for creating text, communicating verbally with others on a network, or delivering commands to the user interface.

Position Tracking

7) A user can interact with a virtual environment and other users on a shared network through the use of mobile *position tracking.*

As described earlier, *position tracking* is the ability of a computer to follow the movements of a computer user in real-time. Without going into a lot of detail here, there are several methods for accomplishing this—optical, mechanical, and magnetic. By capturing body motion in real-time, it allows the possibility of interacting with a computer in a more natural and dynamic way in 3D space, rather than by pointing and clicking on a flat screen. Computer captured actions can also be seen by other participants in a shared virtual world. As in real life, gestures and body language are powerful forms of communication.

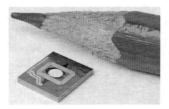

Figure 14. A Micro-Electro-Mechanical System (MEMS) device that provides a way to scan imagery directly onto the eye's retina.
Courtesy of Microvision, Inc.

Figure 15. An example of augmented personal reality: transmitted messages and directions are integrated within a view of the external world.
Courtesy of Microvision, Inc.

Figure 16. A video gamer plays on a virtual screen that appears to be suspended in a space directly front of him. The screen can be scaled in size, and has variable transparency settings.
Courtesy of Microvision, Inc.

Haptic Displays

8) *Haptic* refers to the engagement of virtual touch or kinesthetic sensations delivered through a glove, joystick, or other external device in response to user interactions with objects in a virtual environment (also called *force-reflecting* devices). These are not as well developed as audio and visual displays, but they could be more fully implemented over time in portable virtual display systems.

A portable virtual worlds display system in development by Microvision, Inc., in Redmond, Washington.

The Multisensory Agora

Once these virtual worlds technologies that we've described become available in the future, how will we use them? First, we need to think in terms of creating perceptual environments, where information can be represented using multiple media—text, video, audio, images, graphics, animation, or 3D models. The atmospherics and spatial architecture of these perceptual spaces can be adjusted through virtual lighting, shadowing, color, space, ambient sound, texture, graphic style, historical setting, and so on.

Imagine that this virtual environment is shared among multiple network users. Although they are geographically in different locations, they perceive a common digitally created space—much like an improvisational theater set. Participants are present as 3D avatars, objects, faces on virtual video screens, or as mute, invisible observers. Within this shared three-dimensional communication space, users may engage in voice conversations and can import ideas in any number of available media. Interaction can range from a one-to-many formal classroom model to free-form participation and improvisation. Participants can present or discuss mathematical, scientific, musical, architectural, artistic, literary, political, or theatrical ideas using a wide array of digital media tools available in this information-augmented virtual space.

This is the electronic twenty-first century version of the ancient Greek agora, a virtual commons for human interaction and the exchange of multisensory ideas. One could think of many different electronic agoras, each attracting a different group of participants based on common interests, professions, and pursuits. The mobile virtual worlds device would also serve as an entertainment medium, providing high-resolution access to movies, books, plays, and games.

Information Modeling in Three-Dimensional Space

Within this shared network environment there are methods available for working with time and space in a flexible way.

Space and Time

1) Three-dimensional virtual environments will allow the movement of the user's perspective (the camera) to any part of the simulation. If a character is represented by an avatar, first-person and third-person perspectives are available.

2) Objects and virtual scenarios are *scalable*—events in a scene can be observed from a global (macroscopic) view to a detailed (microscopic) view.

3) The physics or overall context of a 3D virtual space can be altered, including gravity, viscosity, density, object attraction, object repulsion, time acceleration, time deceleration, time reversal, time pausing, instant replay, and so on. These time/space devices would be useful for representing scientific, mathematical, or storytelling/dramatic concepts.

4) Graphic displays of complex information such as stock trends, monetary flow, disease distribution, weather systems, or the time/space structure of a collapsed star could be represented accurately and efficiently within a 3D information environment. This multisensory real-time modeling of complex information streams was introduced in the first Virtual Cockpit, as described earlier, and continues to be a strength of virtual worlds simulations.

5) As seen in the HIT Lab's GreenSpace prototype in the 1990s as well as the current massively multiparticipant online environments like *EverQuest, World of Warcraft, Second Life,* or *Eve Online,* shared networked virtual spaces can be used for many forms of online collaboration and communication.

It should be noted that many of the features in this description of the *ultimate display* can be found in new generations of video game consoles, such as Microsoft's Xbox Live, or Playstation 3 *Home*, where game participants can talk to each other over the Internet while their avatars interact or play games in virtual worlds. Fully interactive environments, where first-person gamers can roam freely within large 3D landscapes or cities, are now common. Also, as mentioned earlier, multiparticipant Internet role-playing games are beginning to solve the difficult technical challenges of managing thousands of networked participants who simultaneously inhabit the same virtual world. In many ways, the video game industry is taking the lead in creating the digital narrative and interactive spaces of the future.

Thomas Furness has given a lot of thought to the technical, social, and creative aspects of virtual worlds technologies during his distinguished career in the field. His ideas are visionary and thought provoking, as shown in the next few pages. Interestingly, Furness sees some of the most significant virtual worlds discoveries taking place not in the laboratory, but in the video game design studio and living room.

"I think that the community that is going to create the economy of scale that will drive the prices down, and truly get widespread use of these devices, will be the computer gaming community . . . We're beginning to see some trends in the direction that involve whole body interaction with these games, and particularly I'm talking about the [Nintendo] Wii. The Wii is such a dramatic change in thinking from the old hand controllers we were using in the past, which required quite a transformation—you had to learn a whole lot in order to operate these. Now the kids could do that very well, but the old folks didn't do it too well. But if you look at the Wii, it uses natural intuitive interaction in terms of movement—and even the old guys can play it, and have some kind of reasonable competition with the grand kids. But I believe that domain—the computer gaming domain—as it continues to evolve, will use more and more virtual interfaces—we'll see heads-up displays in automobiles, we'll see more augmented reality in surgery, and things like that. There'll be a widespread integration of this technology, without a lot of hype! I think it will just happen, because the underpinnings are there. And all those things that twenty years ago, or even four years ago, that I was envisioning could be done with VR . . . will be."[15]

Furness feels that the biggest boon for virtual reality will be how it fits into the digital convergence of broadband telecommunications, computers, and the telephone, as discussed in earlier chapters. Bringing "high bandwidth to the brain" and the ability to easily share multisensory ideas within shared, interactive 3D environments will also be added to this mix, as portable, wireless, high-resolution display systems begin to appear within the next few years.

"The interface for humans to that ubiquitous channel is going to be a virtual one. When you put [these different media] together, basically what you get is the "virtuphone," a telephone that your wear. And basically now in your home, even through coax, you have the ability to disconnect your head from your body and go places—through what we used to have as television, only television wasn't interactive. Now [this new medium] is going to be completely interactive. You'll go to work with it, you'll play with it, you'll go to school with this new medium [that is] two generations beyond the print medium. We'll be taking ourselves—head and body, because we're going to feel as if we're present—to another place."[16]

One of the leading computer interface scientists to explore the use of fully portable wireless multisensory devices as described by Furness is Steve Mann, who began his work with wearable computers as a student at MIT in the 1970s. As microprocessors and computers have become smaller and more powerful, Mann's gear has also evolved from being heavy and bulky to lightweight and mostly invisible. Mann has actually embedded electronic circuitry in the fabric of his clothing to disguise its presence. His goal is to make computing as natural an extension to human experience as riding a bicycle, a technology which comfortably integrates with a person's mobility over time.

By the late 1990s, Mann had integrated a computer display into a pair of glasses, which superimposed electronic information onto the visual and audio experiences of his everyday life—what he calls *computer-mediated reality*. The computer is invisible except for an interactive controller that Mann carries in one hand. He's able to transmit as well as receive video signals. He's fully mobile, because all information is transmitted over a wireless connection.

Another major change that will occur as we progressively move into these new virtual environments is *how* we communicate with each other. Written text is rapidly becoming one of an integrated suite of digital communications methods that can include video, photography, gestures, voice, 3D models, and collaborative virtual gaming experiences. These new multisensory channels will also change the *style* of what we communicate.

Concerning this, Furness says:

"We will always have different levels of symbols that we use to communicate. The emphasis on symbols, however, can change. We're much more visually oriented today. We're wanting compressed information: bytes, both sound and visual. . . . But new media does not have to replace old media. After all, new technology doesn't necessarily replace old technology. We still have travel even though we have telephones. Radio was not dead after television came on the scene. In fact, in some ways, it's more alive than ever. Also, movies did not die with television. What could happen with a new medium added is a changing emphasis somewhat in the written word. This could dilute attention to reading, but there will be a rediscovery of reading. We'll cycle.

"In the meantime, there will be another kind of reading. We're beginning to see this in fact on the Internet. An *embedded narrative*—using spatial organization of information. In other words, the information you're organizing is narrative, but instead of just text, it will also be visual; a picture, like a cartoon. You look to a particular location to select a visual link to hypertext—you search out the text pieces. This is a new hybrid link of using written textual material along with three dimensional visual worlds. But I do believe we won't end up replacing the written word; we'll end up changing it only to come back to it once again. The written word will, for a time, be de-emphasized. But there will be a reemphasis."[17]

Tom Furness sees digital and communications technology merging in immersive virtual reality. Right now, he feels that the problem with moving in this direction is that the computational resources to make virtual worlds better and "faster" (whereby everything will happen in "real-time" and there won't be any gaps between the user's movements in the real world and those same movements in the virtual world) will take some time to develop. But develop they will, and when they do, our language and the traditional job of the *writer,* the craftsman of printed symbols, will once again take on new dimensions.

"We need to change the term 'writer,'" Furness says. "A writer is thought of as someone who manipulates symbols on a page. In this new age, we really need to call writers, creators."[18]

And what do these virtual worlds creators need in order to express themselves well in this new medium?

"A knowledge of theatrics, of story building and story telling. Also, with multimedia you must describe by pictures and storyboards and not just the written word. They will need to visualize as in movies, allowing the user to fill in the blanks. And then there is the element of interactivity: the consumer is passive in a movie, but if they're suddenly going to be part of it, there's a whole new set of things and no one is an expert on this at this point. You're trying to lead the user, but you're also leaving the user latitude, allowing them alternative pathways and endings."

Furness says one of the problems is that "consumers are terrified about being interactive. They don't know how to do it. Television has generated a civilization of passive observers, spectators. Remember, there was originally an aversion on the part of people to use a computer. We have an inertia we have to overcome. It's the kids who'll be involved {with the new medium} first."[19]

However long it takes, a new medium, a new form of communication and language, and a new form of "literature" have all already emerged. Our big mistake with technology, any technology, is the belief that it will solve all our problems. What technology usually does is solve some problems while creating others. For content creators, new digital technology will open up whole new vistas to explore and extrapolate on while very possibly changing the entire concept of "the word" and just how important it will remain to our culture and our civilization.

Artificial Intelligence and Its Integration into Virtual Worlds

The philosopher Aristotle (fourth century BC) wrote a justification for slavery in ancient Greek society in a treatise called *The Politics.* He said, "There is only one condition in which we can imagine managers not needing subordinates, and masters not needing slaves. This would be if every machine could work by itself, at the word of command or by intelligent anticipation. . ."

In Aristotle's time, this hypothetical notion undoubtedly seemed absurd, and his statement was made for rhetorical purposes. Aristotle couldn't have imagined in his wildest dreams how this level of intelligence, derived from mechanical devices, could actually be achieved. In fact, up until recently, this idea was considered to be in the realm of sheer fantasy. However, slow and erratic strides have been made over the past few decades that have brought significant gains in the development of machines with increasing degrees of *artificial intelligence,* or AI.

AI has traditionally referred to the attempt to recreate human-like learning, reasoning, and self-directed behavior by using computers and specialized software. That is not to say that AI research needs to be limited to human-like intelligence in the future—there may very well be new forms of synthetic intelligence that will emerge from this area of research.

A good example of AI is an Internet search engine, such as *Google, Ask, Yahoo,* or Microsoft's *Live Search,* where keywords can be typed into a textbox to retrieve listings for subject-associated websites. If we submit the keyword *bass* to the search engine, we can expect to receive references to fish, musical instruments, vocal styles, beer, sandals, and individuals whose last name is *Bass.* The speedy information retrieval software is not discriminating and finds every instance of the word *bass* in its database without any understanding of what kind of bass you're looking for. We can refine our inquiry by adding additional terms to the search (such as *bass fishing* or *bass guitar*), but not with the same ease with which we carry on a conversation with someone familiar with our interests. Of course, more sophisticated AI-based search engines can learn your preferences and tastes and discriminate which meaning of the word *bass* you intend, which represents a higher level of synthetic intelligence.

As search engine users know well, a keyword search can yield thousands of Web page results within seconds. The reason for this is that search engines send out an information-gathering software entity called a *spider* that retrieves and tracks information updates and changes on the Web. This retrieved data is processed using sophisticated, mathematically derived algorithms that index and catalog it so that it's current and can be quickly accessed. This automated series of tasks represents a form of AI that retrieves and displays meaningful information millions of times faster than any group of experienced librarians could do on their own. Although this is a very specialized operation, it nonetheless greatly expands our ability to think, discover new concepts, and recall important information. It expands the natural capacities of the human brain.

One of the earliest proposed tests for AI came from Alan Turing, a British mathematician who was instrumental in breaking the notorious Nazi code called Enigma—a feat that strongly contributed to the fall of Hitler's Germany. In 1950 Turing wrote an article called "Computing Machinery and Intelligence" where he described a method for determining whether a computer program possessed intelligence or not. Turing begins his article with an ambitious tone, "I propose to consider the question, 'Can machines think?' This should begin with definitions of the meaning of the terms 'machine' and 'think.'"

He called his proposed AI test the *imitation game,* which originally involved the interrogation of a man and a woman by a questioner via typed commands on a teleprinter. The aim was to see if the questioner could determine which person was a man and which was a woman based on their keyboard responses.

In Turing's mind, the goal for this exercise was as follows:

"We now ask the question, 'What will happen when a machine takes the part of A in this game?' Will the interrogator decide wrongly as often when the game is played like this as he does when the game is played between a man and a woman? These questions replace our original, 'Can machines think?'"[20]

More than half a century since Turing wrote his article, his original test has been slightly modified and is called the *Turing Test.* In the most current version, the questioner is connected by a networked computer to a human being and to a computer running an AI program. The goal of the questioner is to determine which of the respondents is a machine and which is human. If the AI-equipped computer can convince the questioner that it is human in free-form conversation—in other words, if the questioner can't decide which respondent is human and which is the computer—then the machine is intelligent.

As detailed in Chapter 7, Joseph Weizenbaum created his own version of the Turing Test in his simple text chatbot named ELIZA while he was at MIT in the 1960s. The program made use of simple keywords that triggered off a range of automatic responses. Although it is important to note that the program had no understanding of the questions themselves, it created the illusion of genuine caring for the questioner. Weizenbaum was surprised to discover that this simple mimicry of human conversation caused so many people to spend hours typing out messages to ELIZA, much of it highly personal in nature. The key to ELIZA's success was that people acted *as if* they were interacting with a compassionate, intelligent person.

Beginning in 1990, Dr. Hugh Loebner, in conjunction with The Cambridge Center for Behavioral Studies, offered $100,000 for the developer of the first computer that could pass the Turing Test—whose responses in free-form text chat would be indistinguishable from a human respondent's. No AI program has yet passed the Turing Test, but an annual prize of $2,000 is given to the AI program that most closely matches human responses. Dr. Richard

Wallace won the prize two years in a row with his AI program A.L.I.C.E. You can run your own version of the Turing Test using one the world's smartest AI bots, A.L.I.C.E., at **http://alicebot.org/**. Another *chatbot,* Alan, who expands his vocabulary and understanding through online conversations, can be found at **http://www.a-i.com.**

In the many years of discussion following the Turing Test, many questions have come up. Is convincing conversation in text a true measure of human intelligence? What about skills like dancing, intuition, poetry, music, painting, or improvisation? Should the goal of AI research be to actually replicate or just to enhance human intelligence? Is it actually possible for a machine to match the full range of emotional, conceptual, and expressive abilities of human beings?

Marvin Minsky, an engineer and computer scientists who also worked at MIT, made some of the most important contributions to the field of AI to explore answers to these more challenging AI questions, including early work with Turing machines, robotics, neural networks (to simulate human neurons), and a clear description of central problems relating to the creation of self-aware machines. He and fellow engineer John McCarthy started the MIT Artificial Intelligence Lab in 1959. Ever since those beginnings at MIT, Minsky's name has continued to be closely associated with advancements in AI.

AI developed very slowly during its first few decades, and this resulted in the emergence of several core concepts and areas of research. Briefly, some of most important of these include the following:

- **Expert Systems**—Attempts to organize the knowledge of human experts based on "if-then" rules of logic. "If you have a temperature, a headache, and a runny nose, then you may have an infection." An expert system relies on a **knowledge base**—based on information you supply, the program consults a database of information that matches your question or inquiry and then draws a conclusion. Expert systems work best where they're limited to sharply defined subjects such as automobile maintenance, planning and scheduling, diagnosing disease, and troubleshooting specific devices.

- **Pattern Recognition**—A form of AI that looks for key points of reference in a set of data and derives conclusions from those. Used in retinal scanning, finger scanning, facial scanning, and data mining to determine overall trends and future developments.

- **Fuzzy Logic**—A type of AI that is used for interpreting complex changing data and arriving at approximate conclusions. For example, in weather reports, fuzzy logic would predict a 30% chance of rain, which is more accurate than saying 100% or 0% chance of rain. Fuzzy logic is used in handheld video cameras to adjust for jiggling and create a stable image—the built-in circuitry figures out what should and should not move in an image and stabilizes the picture accordingly.

- **Neural Nets**—AI that attempts to emulate neurological processes in humans and animals.

- **Natural Language Processing**—AI programs that recognize and understand human speech and generate speech from text to communicate with humans.

- **Robotics**—Intelligent robots are often used for situations not accessible to humans, such as the Chernobyl nuclear plant or the Pathfinder Mars mission.

Artificial Intelligence in Video Games and Massively Multiplayer Online Games

As noted earlier by Thomas Furness, many of the most exciting developments in AI are taking place in the competitive arena of game development. Game players are continually pushing the expectations for increasingly challenging and interesting AI in video games. Because the stakes are high and the competition for successful games is fierce, new and exciting forms of AI have been making their appearance in the video game marketplace.

A traditional approach to AI in games can be seen in earlier scenarios where events or behaviors take place in response to the player's actions. An example of this simple form of AI can be seen in the following example of pseudocode:

```
If (a player enters the crypt)
    Then (start the spooky music and initiate the zombie attack)
Else
    Wait
```

An AI Milestone: Deep Blue Defeats a World-Class Chess Master

A key milestone in the evolution of AI took place in 1997, when a chess-playing computer called *Deep Blue*, designed at IBM's Thomas J. Watson's Research Center, beat world chess champion Garry Kasparov in a chess match by 3.5 games to 2.5 games. It was the first time that a world champion chess player was beaten by artificial intelligence.

Kasparov's silent computer opponent was impressive; it contained 500 coprocessors performing up to a trillion calculations and capable of analyzing 200 million moves per second. Deep Blue drew from a knowledge base consisting of the strategies and moves from chess masters in games over the previous 100 years, including those of Kasparov himself! An account of the match from IBM's research lab describes the gameplay: "[Deep Blue] . . . was able to produce 'brilliant' moves, including the famous moment in Game Two when it unexpectedly offered an exchange of pawns instead of simply advancing its queen to an apparently overwhelming position. This move jarred Kasparov, who later described it as brilliantly subtle. For its creators and many of its fans, Deep Blue had, for a moment, used its incredible processing power and the accumulated knowledge of computer scientists and chess champions to engage in something resembling 'thought.'"[21]

As AI evolved in games, more complex behavior began to emerge. An early pioneer in the use of intelligent character behavior is Valve Games, developer of the game *Half-Life 2,* which was released in November 2004. This was a science fiction–themed 3D first-person shooter game that received numerous awards, including special recognition for its use of AI. As an example, enemy alien characters in this game seem to have instincts for self-preservation, which sets it apart from earlier first-person shooters. Their willingness to attack the player is based on multiple factors taken together:

- **The player's health**
- **The enemy's health**
- **Where the player is going**
- **How many fellow enemies are close by**

In more recent AI-based games like Will Wright's *Spore,* Peter Molyneux's *Fable II,* and Bioware's *Mass Effect,* player decisions have long-term consequences in terms of how the game will end. In *Fable II,* for example, the player may decide to act selfishly or with good deeds, and the character will change appearance accordingly—either becoming a villain or a virtuous hero. Other characters in the game will also respond accordingly—regarding the player either with fear and contempt or with adoration, based on his or her acquired reputation in the game.

Figure 17. *Fable II* by Lion's Head Studios uses a specialized application of artificial intelligence to allow a player to make choices that result in a variety of possible consequences and endings as the game unfolds.
Courtesy of Lionhead Studios and Fable II.

Ben Goertzel, a researcher in the field of AI, has recently claimed that what he calls *artificial general intelligence* (AGI) may find a home for rapid development in virtual worlds environments such as *Second Life.* Currently, semi-intelligent nonplayer characters take on a variety of limited roles in virtual worlds as virtual pets, shop owners, wildlife, and job recruiters. In this case, artificial intelligent agents (often referred to as nonplayer characters, or NPCs) will be programmed to learn their behaviors and develop personalities through interactions with thousands of virtual world participants— they will become progressively more intelligent over time. Goertzel says, "When the AGIs reach human-level intelligence, they will be part of the human social network already. It won't be a matter of "us versus them"; in a sense it may be difficult to draw the line."[22] This is still science fiction, of course, but his idea is intriguing.

The Future of Virtual Worlds Technology

Ray Kurzweil is one of the world's most prolific and respected inventors. When he was in high school, he developed a computer program that analyzed the work of the world's most famous music composers and then recreated new melodies based on their styles. He invented the first flatbed scanner, as well as the first optical character recognition program capable of electronically reading any typographic style. Later, with pop singer Stevie Wonder, he developed the first synthesizer that could realistically reproduce the sound of pianos and other acoustic instruments. More recently he developed software for translating the human voice to text, as well as AI software to assist in making stock market decisions. Because of his unique background, Kurzweil has a good track record for predicting future technological trends.

In a public presentation,[23] Kurzweil described the future of virtual reality, and he predicted that, beginning around 2010, fully wireless virtual worlds will become increasingly available as a means of communication. "By 2010 our primary visual display will be contact lenses or glasses that write images directly on your retina . . . we will have ubiquitous very high bandwidth (Internet) connections at all times, and electronics will be very small, will be flexible, and will be in our clothing, and our eyeglasses, and we will walk around online, all the time. All the computation and communications resources will be in our clothing. We'll have augmented reality at all times. We'll have full immersion visual/auditory virtual reality so that we can have a meeting like this with a group of a couple hundred people or an encounter with one person, at least visually and auditorly with a sense of full immersion, by the end of this decade."

In short, part of Kurzweil's prediction for the second decade of the twenty-first century is that virtual reality will become an umbrella for a wide variety of media experiences—for information access, communication, work, games, and other forms of interactive entertainment. This matured form of digital convergence will be built around continuous wireless connections to the Internet, as well as computer hardware resources and displays that are lightweight,

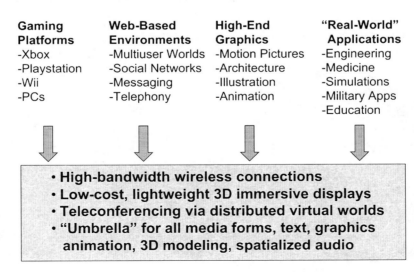

Current Trends in Virtual Worlds Technologies

Gaming Platforms	Web-Based Environments	High-End Graphics	"Real-World" Applications
-Xbox	-Multiuser Worlds	-Motion Pictures	-Engineering
-Playstation	-Social Networks	-Architecture	-Medicine
-Wii	-Messaging	-Illustration	-Simulations
-PCs	-Telephony	-Animation	-Military Apps
			-Education

- **High-bandwidth wireless connections**
- **Low-cost, lightweight 3D immersive displays**
- **Teleconferencing via distributed virtual worlds**
- **"Umbrella" for all media forms, text, graphics animation, 3D modeling, spatialized audio**

Figure 18. Current trends in virtual worlds technologies.

portable, and almost invisible. Wireless cell phones are early versions of this technology, which currently deliver games, stock listings, weather reports, email, voice communications, and images.

Figure 18 shows some of the applications and current trends in virtual worlds technology. These trends seem to be converging toward the development of lightweight, nonintrusive, networked, highly interactive display devices that will enable users to remain connected via networked three-dimensional virtual communities. Kurzweil's future projections anticipate this kind of convergence beginning to take place around the year 2010.

The second part of Kurzweil's prediction regarding virtual reality is that this spatial computing environment represents a place where human and machine intelligence will coevolve over time. Computers will gain the ability to interact intelligently with humans, and humans will derive the benefits of enhanced memory, information access, electronic processing, and networking. Kurzweil describes this gradual development by saying, "We'll be spending a lot of our time in virtual environments, which will not emerge overnight as competitive with real reality, but over time virtual reality will become more and more compelling."[24]

The Future of World-Building and the *Ultimate Display*

In this textbook we've discussed how early computer pioneers such as Vannevar Bush (Memex), J.C.R. Licklider (networking), Norbert Wiener (cybernetics), and Douglas Engelbart (computer interface devices) were keenly aware of the computer's potential for expanding, augmenting, and amplifying human intelligence. Within virtual worlds, emerging powerful computer systems and software are providing enhanced information environments that are beginning to fulfill this potential. This developing merger between humans and machines has profound social implications, as Kurzweil indicates in his prediction for the year 2040.

> "If you meet an individual in 2040, typically I believe you'll be interacting with someone who has significant and profound non-biological thinking processes going on. Some of those could just be augmenting or adding new connections to improve our memory and speed up our thinking processes, and to expand our human-like thinking. It could also mean intimately connecting human thinking with non-biological forms of intelligence. Some of that hasn't been invented yet, and it will take on many different forms. But you will have significant non-biological processes going on in the human brain. And the power of that will grow."[25]

If Kurzweil's prediction for the future of virtual worlds technology is correct, what form will this enhanced human-computer hybrid relationship take? In 1965 Ivan Sutherland, an early computer graphics pioneer and virtual reality theorist, described what he felt would be the *ultimate display.* "The ultimate display would . . . be a room within which the computer can control the existence of matter. A chair displayed in such a room would be good enough to sit in. Handcuffs displayed in such a room would be confining, and a bullet displayed in such a room would be fatal. With appropriate programming such a display could literally be the Wonderland into which Alice walked."[26] Sutherland's idea of three-dimensional worlds that could simulate reality, including objects with

Figure 19. An advanced virtual reality interface would function much like this photo simulation, and have the following characteristics:
© Dmitroza | Dreamstime.com.

tangible, physical properties, was later taken up in Gene Roddenberry's Star Trek television series in the holodeck. The holodeck was used by the space-faring crew of the Starship Enterprise for entertainment, problem solving, and confronting psychological fears or uncertainties in hyper-realistic simulations.

1) Electronics are embedded and invisible.

2) The interface can be engaged through gesture, voice, and thought commands.[27]

3) A retinal display via contact lenses provides a projected image that is scalable and has variable transparency. Spatialized audio and haptic feedback is also integrated to create three-dimensional multisensory images.

4) Multisensory concepts can be created, transmitted, accessed, and shared via a wireless connection, providing three-dimensional social networking capabilities.

5) An array of intelligent agents assist in a variety of tasks, such as information access, time management, virtual worlds communication, and problem solving.

Although the advanced virtual reality simulations represented by the *ultimate display* and *holodeck* remain science fiction, the movement toward fully immersive virtual spaces as a common ground for human-computer interaction will inevitably find its way into the mainstream, much like the palmtop computer or cell phone. Virtual worlds simulations will become more compelling by integrating good storytelling techniques, effective information design, alluring architecture or landscapes, interactivity, and enhanced human communication. It is probable that virtual worlds design will incorporate many of the lessons learned in twentieth century entertainment media such as movies, TV commercials, print graphics, animation, Web design, music videos, and computer games to strongly engage human attention and enhance interaction with computer processes. This is largely unexplored territory—the principles of world-building are still being developed.

Figure 20 shows a big-picture view of a possible direction virtual worlds development may take over the next decade. It shows a convergence of increasingly high-performance delivery platforms, expanding network capabilities, and an increasing influence of AI. It indicates a progressive merging of technology-enhanced experiences with our personal and social lives.

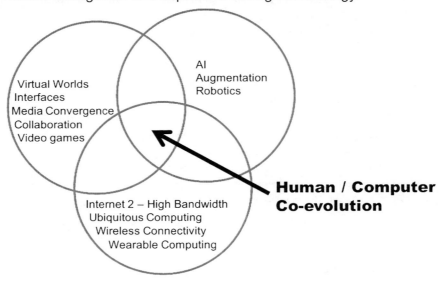

Figure 20. Social impact of virtual worlds technologies.

For the first time in history, we're gaining the ability to represent ideas in the form of multisensory simulations that have great flexibility and precision. These simulations simultaneously communicate on multiple levels—intellectual, aesthetic, social, and emotional—and can be presented across a universal publishing medium, the Internet and the World Wide Web. Back in 1991, Howard Rheingold in his book *Virtual Reality* predicted the direction of this development by saying:

"The cyberspace experience is destined to transform us in other ways because it is an undeniable reminder of a fact we are hypnotized since birth to ignore and deny—that our normal state of consciousness is itself a hyperrealistic simulation. We build models of the world in our minds using the data from our sense organs and the information processing capabilities of our brain. We habitually think of the world we see as 'out there,' but what we are seeing is really a mental model, a perceptual simulation that exists only in our brain. That simulation capability is where human minds and digital computers share a potential for synergy."[28]

Endnotes

[1]Ray Kurzweil, "The Human Machine Merger: Why We Will Spend Most of Our Time in Virtual Reality in the Twenty-first Century," KurzweilAI.net,
http://www.kurzweilai.net/meme/frame.html?main=/articles/art0141.html.

[2]BNET Business Network, "Stephen Hawking's Remarks Gives Giant Boost to Brain/Computer Interface Maker IBVA Technologies," September 10, 2001,
http://findarticles.com/p/articles/mi_m0EIN/is_2001_Sept_10/ai_78034436.

[3]Colin Greenland, "A Nod to the Apocalypse: An Interview with William Gibson," *Foundation,* no. 36 (Summer, 1986): pp. 5–9.

[4]Pamela McCorduck, *Machines Who Think: A Personal Inquiry into the History and Prospect of Artificial Intelligence* (A K Peters, Ltd., 2004), p. 81.

[5]Ivars Peterson, "Looking-Glass World: Learning to Assemble the Machinery of Illusion—Virtual Reality," *BNET Business Network,* January 4, 1994,
http://findarticles.com/p/articles/mi_m1200/is_n1_v141/ai_11747951/pg_2.

[6]Anne Eisenberg, "Moving Mountains with the Brain, Not a Joystick," *The New York Times,* June 8, 2008, http://www.nytimes.com/2008/06/08/technology/08novel.html?_r=2&partner=rssnyt&emc=rss&oref=slogin&oref=slogin.

[7]Oliver Grau, "Ancestors of the Virtual, Historical Aspects of Virtual Reality and Its Contemporary Impact," September 2000, http://www.unites.uqam.ca/AHWA/Meetings/2000.CIHA/Grau.html.

[8]Rita Cipalla, "The Brave World of Virtual Reality," *Smithsonian News Service,* http://www.dreammerchant.net/feature_dec99.htm.

[9]Dr. Thomas Furness, interview with the authors, July 16, 2008.

[10]Ibid.

[11]Ibid.

[12]Hunter Hoffman, "VR Therapy for Spider Phobias," HIT Lab,
http://www.hitl.washington.edu/research/exposure/.

[13]Hunter Hoffman, "VR Pain Control," HIT Lab, http://www.hitl.washington.edu/projects/burn/.

[14]Casey Tegreeve, chief technology officer of Microvision, interview with the authors, July 9, 2002.

[15]Dr. Thomas Furness, interview with the authors, Michael Korolenko and Bruce Wolcott, July 16, 2008.

[16]Dr. Thomas Furness, interview with the author Michael Korolenko, October, 1993.

[17]Dr. Thomas Furness, interview with the author Michael Korolenko, September 22, 1995.

[18]Dr. Thomas Furness, interview with the author Michael Korolenko, September, 1995.

[19]Ibid.

[20]Alan Turing, (1950) "Computing Machinery and Intelligence" *Mind* 59, 236, 433–60.

[21]IBM Research website, "Deep Blue Technology,"
http://www.research.ibm.com/know/blue.html.

[22]Ben Goertzel, "AI Meets the Metaverse: Teachable AI Agents Living in Virtual Worlds," October 18, 2007, http://www.kurzweilai.net/meme/frame.html?main=/articles/art0710.html.

[23]Ray Kurzweil, "The Singularity Is Near," keynote talk at Extropy Institute's EXTRO-5 conference in San Jose, June 15, 2001. Available online at http://www.kurzweilai.net/meme/frame.html?main=/articles/art0235.html, Part 4.

[24]Ibid.

[25]Ibid.

[26]Ivan Sutherland, "The Ultimate Display," *Proceedings of IFIP Congress* (Washington, DC: Spartan Books, 1965).

[27]Darren Waters, "Brain control headset for gamers", BBC News, February 2008, http://news.bbc.co.uk/2/hi/technology/7254078.stm,

[28]Howard Rheingold, *Virtual Reality* (New York: Summit Books, 1991), p. 387.

Chapter 9
The Hall of Reflection: Tomorrowland Revisited

"Gentlemen, progress has never been a bargain. You've got to pay for it. Sometimes I think there's a man behind a counter who says, 'All right, you can have a telephone; but you'll have to give up privacy, the charm of distance. Madam, you may vote; but at a price; you lose the right to retreat behind a powder-puff or a petticoat. Mister, you may conquer the air; but the birds will lose their wonder, and the clouds will smell of gasoline!'"[1]

Jerome Lawrence and Robert E. Lee, *Inherit the Wind*

"There is more to life than increasing its speed."

Gandhi

"We don't stop with asking what a tool does. We ask about what kind of people we become when we use it."

Amish farmer in a conversation with Howard Rheingold

We are in a period where multinational corporations strongly influence our lives, our wants and needs, our images of ourselves, and our ideas about the future. It's not surprising, because these same corporations own most of the media subsidiaries that supply us with much of the information about the world around us—television, movies, books, magazines, newspapers, and radio stations. Former *Los Angeles Times* editor Ben Bagdikian reported in 2004 that five corporations own most of the media industry in the United States.[2] Interestingly, our common vision of the future during the first decade of the twenty-first century is, for the most part, pessimistic. It is being framed by our limited resources, an increasing population, a global environment in crisis, and a fragmentation of society along the lines of class, politics, race, religion, and values. Entering into this scenario is the rapid deployment of new telecommunication technologies that hold out both a promise of independence and a threat of absolute control.

So, in this, our final chapter, we look once again at social issues, the implications of new technologies, and just why the future isn't what it used to be.

Considering Alternative Futures: Past and Present

In the early 1970s author Alvin Toffler coined the term *future shock*. Serving as the title of Toffler's book, the idea behind *Future Shock* was that once upon a time, any obvious change took centuries to be observed. During the past 150 years, change had to be faced decade to decade. And now, according to Toffler, **change itself** is accelerating. One only had to look at the quickly changing technology to realize that there was much in Toffler's theory: We went from vacuum tubes to transistors to integrated circuit chips in a period of less than fifty years. Since Toffler's book first came out, the rate of acceleration has increased to a point where our own future now seems like an alien civilization. The frantic growth of both the use of computers and the Internet has changed the very landscape of our culture. The things we value, from family to relationships to our natural living environment, are coming under

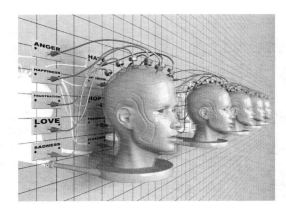

Figure 1. Cybernetic extensions.
© Yannis Ntousiopoulos | Dreamstime.com.

increasing stress from technological acceleration itself. The dystopian dreams of the twentieth century as described by Forrester, Huxley, Orwell, and Bradbury and seen in films like *The Forbin Project, Silent Running, Blade Runner, The Matrix,* and *V for Vendetta* now seem too close to reality for comfort. The days of seeing a nightmarish vision like *Fahrenheit 451* in the film of the same name and walking out into a world still filled with idealism (circa 1967) belong to a vanished era. The future continues to beckon as it always has but ominously and with great foreboding.

Since the early 1980s and the beginning of the so-called computer revolution, our accelerated pace has surpassed the warnings of Toffler's future shock. We feel adrift, as if finding ourselves in a foreign land without the familiarity of a common language, customs, or even a shared worldview with the people around us.

Not only in books and movies do we find a world where the percentage of people between the ages of eighteen and twenty-four years who read for pleasure is in rapid decline because of the impact of interactive entertainment, as anticipated in Ray Bradbury's *Fahrenheit 451.*[3] It is no longer only in works of fiction where our fuel supply is quickly dwindling, where our values have been completely uprooted, where news has become entertainment and entertainment has become news, and where one angry individual with Internet knowledge can shut down an entire corporation.

We need to have the courage to face head on some of the major personal and social issues that have come along with the technological revolution we continue to experience. We need to temper our pessimism with ongoing honest and open communication about how we might successfully navigate through the perilous waters these challenging times present to us. Ironically, we will need the assistance of the very technologies that challenge us in order to do this. It isn't within the scope of this book and website to find long-term solutions, but to present an introductory overview of some of the topics we should be looking at more closely relating to the impact of telecommunications technology on society and open up areas for future discussion.

Although Moore's Law (see Chapter 5) inexorably takes us on a digital thrill ride that doubles computer processing speeds every two years, we need to take time to collectively paddle out of the whitewater of change for some introspection. Hence the name of this chapter's pavilion—*The Hall of Reflection: Tomorrowland Revisited.* World's Fairs have traditionally provided public spaces where possible futures based on current technologies can be introduced and considered. In the past centuries, these public exhibitions as visions of the future have been largely influenced by nationalistic ambition and pride, or by corporations wanting to steer the public in directions that will benefit their bottom line. The Internet holds a promise of mobilizing the collective intelligence from people all over the planet and bringing it to bear on a range of problems, and we need that intelligence more than ever. So while we raise a number of social and personal issues relating to the communications revolution, we simultaneously are hoping to find ways in which computer social networks may potentially help us bootstrap ourselves out of our current crisis. We need to discover ways in which we can most appropriately and successfully forge a healthy relationship with the technology genie that we let out of the bottle.

Redmond, Washington, is the home of Microsoft, and it has one of the highest population percentages of computer and Internet technology users in the world. It is also the home of Jay Parker, CDP, and Hilarie Cash, PhD, counselors who co-manage the Internet/Computer Addiction Services center. One of their primary specialties is video game and Internet addictions. They care for some of the worst-case scenarios of technology dependency and are on the front lines in the struggle to find appropriate relationships with twenty-first century gadgets and their associated social networks. In a recent interview, Parker summed up his view of how the new telecommunications landscape is affecting us socially and personally.

"When I think about the computer industry and where we are in 2008, I liken it very much to the automobile industry of 100 years ago. So think back 100 years. Henry Ford has a desire to make a cheap, available car for every American family, and that was his goal; the same goal that Bill Gates had [for computers] when he started Microsoft. The same set of goals, 100 years apart. . . But as visionary as Henry Ford was 100 years ago, there was no way that he envisioned in 1908, that 40,000 Americans would die a year in his invention. No way did he see airbags, DUI laws, freeways, even red lights—and a bunch of other things that we take for granted."

"Well, Bill Gates created this wonderful industry, and created this availability of every person not just in this country, but worldwide, to have access to the Internet and a computer. No way did he envision that Sean Wooley, seven years ago, would be playing EverQuest for thirty-six straight hours, have a psychotic break, and blow his brains out. . . He could not envision predators on the computer, he could not envision marriages blowing up because of infidelity created through a chatroom on the computer."

"I think just looking at it historically, from a sociological standpoint, between the automobile industry and the computer industry, I think that's about where we are now. I think we're at about 1912, maybe 1920. People didn't see cars in any negative light in 1920. People still see the computer as harmless, as positive, as educational. As a culture, we still don't see that there's a downside."[4]

In this last chapter, we'll describe what we consider to be five challenges of the future, areas where telecommunications technologies will continue to impact our lives in profound ways. Our hope is to provide some background to these issues and pose some questions about them to generate an ongoing conversation about what our personal and collective future relationship with novel twenty-first century technologies should be. And although there are more social issues related to technology use than can be adequately presented here and there are no simple "right answers," it's a start.

Five Technology-Based Social Challenges of the Future

- The Digital Divide
- Intellectual Property versus *Open Source* Information—Is the Internet a Tollway or a Freeway?
- Privacy
- Transhumanism and the *Singularity*
- Technology Dependence and Addiction

We will also explore the importance of choosing sustainable technology futures that ensure long-term health for ourselves and our planet.

Challenge #1: The Digital Divide

We are in an era of information haves and have-nots. This is the essence of the term *digital divide*. Although there are many who agree that "information must be free," the reality is that the more affluent tend to own the media in general. Television, motion pictures, radio, books, and games are owned and created by a few. There are now technological tools created by the computer revolution that enable individuals to produce their own content. An example is high-definition digital video cameras, which just a few years ago were beyond the reach of ordinary people. Now they have come down in price so that they are, in fact, affordable to educational institutions and individuals for under $6,000.

However, there are those who cannot even afford the least expensive computer, let alone the cost of Internet access and the ability to create content for the Web, video, or any other medium. The benefit of online access is a surfeit of information unthought of even ten years ago. However, if we have become the "global village" that Marshall McLuhan wrote and dreamed of, there are literal villages and towns and cities throughout the world that cannot participate in this vision.

As early as 2002, the research paper "Unveiling the Digital Divide" (regarding the situation in Canada) by G. Sciadis noted, "Many variables, including income, education, age and geographical location, exert significant influences on household penetration of both ICT (Information Communication Technology) and non-ICT commodities."[5] According to Sciadis, the divide exists between the following groups: socioeconomic (rich/poor), racial (majority/minority), generational (young/old), or geographical (urban/rural). A central concern of the digital divide issue is how to ensure that everyone has equal access to all the benefits of online digital information, which include government documents, news, online purchases, genealogies, and entertainment.

As an example of the digital divide, the Statistics Bureau of Canada in 2007 showed a dramatic difference in Internet and computer use between more affluent and less affluent Canadians. In part, their report states, "The vast majority (91%) of people in the top quintile (more than $95,000) used the Internet. This was almost twice the proportion of 47% for the lowest quintile (less than $24,000). This gap in use has narrowed slightly since 2005."[6]

Worldwide, approximately 1 billion people, or 800,000 villages, lack any kind of electronic communications technology, including the telephone. In 2004, 3 out of 100 Africans used the Internet versus 1 out of every 2 Americans or Europeans. More than eight times the number of Internet users are in the United States versus the continent of Africa. The area of strongest growth has taken place in cell phone access to the Internet, especially in China, Africa, and the former Soviet Union.[7]

South Asia has 23% of the world's population but represents only 1% of the total number of Internet users. The Sustainable Development Department of the United Nations summed up the characteristics of the most common Internet user by saying, "The typical Internet user worldwide is male, under 35 years old, with a university education and high income, urban based, and English speaking."[8]

The Internet provides access not only to useful knowledge but also increasingly to primary livelihood needs: employment, education, communications, travel schedules, maps, and products. As Internet users gain the multiple benefits of online access, the digital have-nots are left further behind.

Recently, some of the major telecommunications companies such as Comcast and AT&T have been lobbying for a "tiered" form of broadband Internet services where increased prices are charged for special forms of content—multimedia, streaming video, conferencing, voice-over the Internet (VOIP), and high-speed wireless connections. However, some groups and companies object to what they consider a socially stratified Internet where the wealthy have special privileges and those who can't afford the expanded information delivery systems are left behind—what they see as an undemocratic digital divide between the haves and have-nots. These groups support the idea of "net neutrality," where online services should be a public utility, like water or electricity, that is universally available to everyone at a uniform rate.

Google, the company that created the well known Google search engine and other online applications, officially supports net neutrality on its Web site, by claiming that everyone should have equal access to content on the Internet and should not be discriminated against by large Internet broadband providers such as AT&T and Comcast. They claim that without net neutrality, the availability of full Internet services would be restricted to those users who could afford it – which is discrimination based on personal wealth.[9]

On the other hand, David Cohen, the executive vice president of Comcast, sees net neutrality as excessive government regulation of free enterprise and technological innovation:[10]

"It is a sad and perverse truth that, so long as some people will build networks, other people will try to regulate them. For the past several years, we have been fighting off proposals for 'network neutrality,' a term that I prefer not to use because it is inherently misleading. The term has been kicking around for several years, and it never means the same thing twice. It is the sheep's clothing donned by those who want to regulate the Internet for their own purposes."

Key Questions

Should we be planning for a global communications infrastructure so that everyone, regardless of race, gender, income, age, or geographical location, has equal information access capabilities?

Is this idea economically feasible or desirable?

Do you support *net neutrality,* or are you opposed to it?

Challenge #2: Intellectual Property versus Open Source Information—Is the Internet a Tollway or a Freeway?

In the prologue to Shakespeare's play *Romeo and Juliet*, the entire plot of the story is given away by the narrator, who introduces the spoiler in part by saying:

> "Two households, both alike in dignity,
> In fair Verona, where we lay our scene,
> From ancient grudge break to new mutiny,
> Where civil blood makes civil hands unclean.
> From forth the fatal loins of these two foes
> A pair of star-cross'd lovers take their life"

The fact is, various dramatic interpretations of *Romeo and Juliet* had been around for at least 125 years before William Shakespeare penned his version of the story in 1595. Elizabethan audiences were very familiar with the story—they wanted to see what William Shakespeare would do with it. Shakespeare's interpretation and delivery of the story is what we remember today. Just like Shakespeare did in his own time, new enterprising playwrights can take his original play and put their own spin on it, because it is part of the *public domain.* When a work is in the public domain, it is not copyright protected, which means that other creative minds can freely borrow from it for their own purposes in a process that's called a *remix* in the popular vernacular of the Web.

This was not always true, however. Up until the mid-1700s, copyright was retained for a period of fourteen years past the original date of publication. In 1769 some Scottish publishers laid claim to Shakespeare's work as well as other literary works in the public domain, declaring that they could retain copyright-protected ownership forever. Five years later, in 1774, this verdict was reversed in the English House of Lords, a decision that has been referred to as the birth of *free culture.*[11] Afterward, Shakespeare's work was once again openly available for use in the public domain.

The terms *intellectual property* (IP), *franchise,* and *brand* are often used to describe privately owned ideas or creations in much the same way that real estate titles designate sections of land for private possession. These legal concepts regarding the protection of ideas for exclusive use or sale have gained increasing traction in the digital information age. This is a recent development, and not everyone agrees that this is a step in the right direction.

Lawrence Lessig is a copyright expert who teaches law at Stanford University. He's also a strong proponent of limiting the length and extent of intellectual property ownership. He's at the vanguard of a growing *open source* movement that wants to preserve the Internet as a location for the free exchange of ideas, not strictly a marketplace for their commercialization. The term *open source* refers to the practice of making an author's work available to the public for further embellishment or expansion by others.

Lessig describes the growth of the Disney Corporation,[12] one of the greatest instigators of intellectual property legislation, which benefited early on from numerous public domain resources for their own creations—among them, *Alice in Wonderland, Cinderella, Snow White, Beauty and the Beast,* and *Pinocchio:*

> "[In] 1928, my hero, Walt Disney, created this extraordinary work, the birth of Mickey Mouse in the form of Steamboat Willie. But what you probably don't recognize about Steamboat Willie and his emergence into Mickey Mouse is that in 1928, Walt Disney, to use the language of the Disney Corporation today, 'stole' Willie from Buster Keaton's 'Steamboat Bill'.

> "It was a parody, a take-off; it was built upon Steamboat Bill. Steamboat Bill was produced in 1928, no [waiting] 14 years—just take it, rip, mix, and burn, as he did to produce the Disney empire. This was his character. Walt always parroted feature-length mainstream films to produce the Disney empire, and we see the product of this. This is the Disney Corporation: taking works in the public domain, and not even in the public domain, and turning them into vastly greater, new creativity. They took the works of . . . the Brothers Grimm, who you think are probably great authors on their own. They produce these horrible stories, these fairy tales, which anybody should keep their children far from because they're utterly bloody and moralistic stories, and are not the sort of thing that children should see, but they were retold for us by the Disney Corporation. *Now the Disney Corporation could do this because that culture lived in a commons, an intellectual commons, a cultural commons, where people could freely take and build. It was a lawyer-free zone.*

"It was culture, which you didn't need the permission of someone else to take and build upon. That was the character of creativity at the birth of the last century. It was built upon a constitutional requirement that protection be for limited times, and it was originally limited. Fourteen years, if the author lived, then 28, then in 1831 it went to 42, then in 1909 it went to 56, and then magically, starting in 1962, look—no hands, the term expands." (Current copyright has been expanded from fourteen years for new works in the early twentieth century, to the life of the author plus seventy years.)

"Eleven times in the last 40 years it has been extended for existing works—not just for new works that are going to be created, but existing works. The most recent is the Sonny Bono copyright term extension act. Those of us who love it know it as the Mickey Mouse protection act, which of course [means] every time Mickey is about to pass through the public domain, copyright terms are extended. The meaning of this pattern is absolutely clear to those who pay to produce it. The meaning is: No one can do to the Disney Corporation what Walt Disney did to the Brothers Grimm. That though we had a culture where people could take and build upon what went before, that's over. *There is no such thing as the public domain in the minds of those who have produced these 11 extensions these last 40 years because now culture is owned.*"

The Internet and the public who uses it have strongly benefited from the open source movement. Here are a few examples, among many:

- Tim Berners-Lee created an early version of the World Wide Web for his employer, the CERN particle physics lab in Switzerland. His World Wide Web software made possible the creation of Web documents that could link to one another across a computer network. Rather than commercializing his idea, Berners-Lee gave away his software to be freely used as a public benefit, earning him a reputation as the "patron saint of the Internet."

- Linus Torvalds was a twenty-three-year-old student at the University of Helsinki when he came up with a plan to build a network operating system used to manage the functions of a server and client computers on a network because he was unable to afford a license fee for the commercial network software UNIX. In 1991 he released his code to the Internet, asking for help from other programmers around the planet. Over time he built up a committee of volunteers who helped manage the development of Linux, a free open source network operating system that is now used by numerous computer hardware vendors as well as many computer users around the world. Another important and widely used open source network operating system software is GNU, created by Richard Stallman.

- John Carmack and John Romero, developers of the popular 3D first-person shooter games *Doom* and *Quake,* released open source code for their game engine so that users could create their own *mods,* or versions of the game. This decision resulted in the creation of a loyal, dedicated fan base—and turned out to be a smart business decision. This unusual, although successful, practice was later picked up by other game developers.

- Larry Wall released the Perl scripting language in 1987, an open source application that's used to complete numerous network-based tasks, notably interactive forms, online questionnaires, and polls.

- Sun Microsystems, a major Silicon Valley computer hardware and software company, released Open Office in 2000, a productivity suite that has similar functionality to the programs in Microsoft Office. It's available for free download on the Web.

Other corporations, including Google, IBM, and even Microsoft, have recognized the value of open source concepts, and they have incorporated some of these in the development of their own business practices. A recent development has taken place to provide an alternative to traditional copyright.

Lessig's intention has been to develop an alternative to the ironclad intellectual property laws while allowing authors to derive benefit for their works. As a result, he created the Creative Commons licenses with support from the Harvard Law School and the Stanford Law School for Internet Society. As described on the Wikipedia entry for *Creative Commons:*[13]

"The Creative Commons licenses enable copyright holders to grant some or all of their rights to the public while retaining others through a variety of licensing and contract schemes including dedication to the public domain or open content licensing terms. The intention is to avoid the problems current copyright laws create for the sharing of information.

"All these efforts, and more, are done to counter the effects of what Creative Commons considers to be a dominant and increasingly restrictive permission culture. In the words of Lawrence Lessig, founder of Creative Commons and former Chairman of the Board, it is 'a culture in which creators get to create only with the permission of the powerful, or of creators from the past'. Lessig maintains that modern culture is dominated by traditional content distributors in order to maintain and strengthen their monopolies on cultural products such as popular music and popular cinema, and that Creative Commons can provide alternatives to these restrictions."

Not everyone is a fan of Lessig's ideas or the Creative Commons approach to copyright, however. John Dvorak, in his column for PC Magazine Online, said of the Creative Commons concept in a recent article:[14]

"If I write something on my blog . . . and decide not to cover it with the general copyright notice, I can simply say that it is in the public domain and be done with it . . . I don't need a middleman—a Creative Commons Commissar—to approve my decision. And yet there is this perception that I do . . . That's what's bothersome. Creative Commons trying to insert itself as another layer into a system that already protects content developers like me to an extreme. I mean my grandkids will own all my writing exclusively until 75 years after I'm dead, unless I sell all the rights to someone else. What more do I want from copyright?"

The debate over the *free culture* movement versus *intellectual property* is not over, and it remains a central, hotly disputed issue on the Internet. Will the Internet be a freeway or a tollway?

Key Questions

Where do you stand on the issue of the private ownership of ideas?

Do think that the slogan "information wants to free," as we assume in a public, spoken conversation—should also be applied to all Internet communication?

Do you think copyright protections should be reduced to fourteen years, as they were before the twentieth century, or should they remain the same—seventy years past the death of the author?

Challenge #3: Privacy

Back in the 1980s and 1990s, the Internet was much like the Wild West. The computer networks were patchwork quilts of different operating systems and hardware gear that often didn't communicate well with each other. Security was often nonexistent or lax. The terms *hacker* and more notoriously *cracker* are applied to programming jockeys who are able to write clever software *hacks* to solve a variety of purposes. An example of a clever and useful hack was email, created by MIT graduate and computer programmer Ray Tomlinson, who wrote the initial email software back in 1971. There are also network crackers, who much like Wild West outlaws, break into secure computer networks to carry out pranks, steal private information, or shut down entire local area business or government networks.

Among the most infamous of these network outlaws was Kevin Mitnick. Mitnick, using the nickname *BugBear,* broke into the computer networks of more than thirty-five large international corporations and other organizations over a period of thirteen years. These included such well known technology names as Nokia, Motorola, Novell, and Sun Microsystems. They claimed that he caused more than $300 million in lost revenue.[15] His hacking activities put him on the FBI's most wanted computer criminals list. Mitnick assumed new identities and continued his hacking from different geographical locations, always one step ahead of the FBI.

Figure 2. Privacy Concerns. © Nikolai Sorokin | Dreamstime.com.

He was finally caught when he hacked his way into the Lawrence Livermore Lab and crossed paths with a determined and skilled young computer expert named Tsutomu Shimomura. Through Shimomura's efforts, Mitnick's location was traced via the Internet to his apartment in Raleigh, North Carolina. There he was arrested by the FBI, who'd previously spent years trying to track him down.

Mitnick used two approaches to his illegal network cracking—his computer and network programming skills and an approach known as "social engineering," which he describes as "Lying on the phone—manipulating or conning information out of people over the telephone."

His motivation? Mitnick says, "I saw myself as an electronic joyrider having a great time on the information superhighway.I felt like I was James Bond behind a computer. It was a big game to me; I was just having a blast. *It was an invasion of privacy—going and getting access to other people's information is obviously a gross invasion of privacy, and it is wrong.* I was an accomplished computer trespasser; I don't consider myself a thief."

After his release from prison, Mitnick began a new career as a computer security consultant to raise awareness of what security threats are, how the bad guys operate, and what you can do to protect yourself. It's the adage: "It takes a thief to catch a thief."

Mitnick's story highlights an important aspect of our new "wired" life in the twenty-first century—our lives in this new electronic landscape are potentially an open book. Mitnick considered his invasion of other people's privacy wrong. However, information derived from our computers, cell phones, credit cards, club cards, public Web cameras, legal transactions, and bank accounts all give away personal and private information about ourselves. If privacy is important to us, it needs to be given consideration and protected in a deliberate and strategic way.

Here are some areas to consider when thinking about your personal privacy.

Data Mining

The term *data mining* refers to the process of extracting electronic information about your electronic purchases, your online website surfing habits, your email contacts, and what search terms you use when you use a search engine. Your personal information access habits and profile are worth money to marketing firms and product manufacturers. When surfing the Web, be conscious of the fact that all of your transactions can be tracked and that you may be "shedding" vital contact information to marketing companies building database dossiers of your searching and purchasing behaviors. This information gathering is done through the use of *cookies,* or software programs that track your online activity and transmit that information back to a host company. Also be aware that all online email, surveys, and political petitions are information that may be openly available, potentially forever, on the net.

Grocery stores and buying warehouses provide special price savings in return for your willingness to swipe a club card revealing your recent purchases at the checkout cash register. More sophisticated tracking systems involve placing your index finger into a cradle where your fingerprint is read by a scanner. This associates your personal identity with store purchases and is directly stored on centralized databases whose records can be sold, in turn, to other marketing companies.

Related to these privacy concerns is the growing problem of identity theft. Numerous situations have come up where e-commerce databases have been hacked into or private information has been obtained by criminals who then charge credit cards up to their limits or empty bank accounts. With this in mind, the importance of protecting your personal data becomes more important every day.

Radio Frequency Identification Chips

Radio Frequency Identification, or RFID, is a growing form of automatic identification and tracking. The RFID system consists of a portable wireless device that transmits information to an RFID reader when it passes through an electromagnetic field, for a variety of purposes. This technology first appeared in the 1980s, when stores used RFID devices to mark merchandise before it was purchased to prevent shoplifting.

New RFID chips, which are smaller, more powerful, and cheaper, are now used to keep track of pets, people, merchandise, and even motor vehicles. They can be read from a distance and in many different kinds of weather conditions.

As costs continue to drop for these devices, they will begin to appear everywhere. Larger companies like Wal-Mart are beginning to use them to track even smaller merchandise as it moves from the shelves as a way to keep track of current inventories. The European Economic Community, which has been using a common currency among its participating nations, has plans for embedding RFID chips as small as a fiber into euro bank notes. This makes

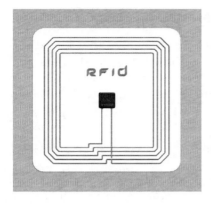

Figure 3. RFID chip. © Magann | Dreamstime.com.

possible the tracking of currency flows and activity, which would be useful to law enforcement agencies and economic planners and as a deterrent to counterfeiters. Medical organizations are considering the use of RFID marker chips with diagnostic information that would provide instant information about patients with diabetes, drug allergies, or other medical vulnerabilities as they enter a hospital or doctor's office.

Civil liberties groups have expressed concerns that large numbers of integrated RFID chips in public locations could create the conditions for a system of real-time surveillance of everyone's personal, financial, legal, and medical status.

Government Surveillance

Currently, the hundreds of databases that track medical, financial, personal, and legal information are owned by a variety of businesses and government agencies. These separate databases rarely communicate or coordinate information with one another. This has been changing with the implementation of new surveillance initiatives such as the Total Information Awareness program, which was originally administered by Admiral John Poindexter but later disbanded by the U.S. Congress in 2003. The continuing concerns about this intelligence program are described Jay Stanley of the American Civil Liberties Union.[16]

> "Technology that tracks the things we do is rapidly spreading throughout American life—through electronic passes, Web-enabled cash registers, location-tracking cell phones, and of course, surveillance cameras—leaving more and more records of activities in some database or other.

> "It will soon be possible to combine information from different sources to recreate an individual's activities with such detail that it is equivalent to being followed around with a video camera. As bad as privacy invasions are, they become far worse when they're all put together into one big picture of our life. Although TIA's implementation has been limited by Congress, research into the tool itself is continuing, and there is a danger that, once perfected, the power to monitor Americans' lives on a mass scale will emerge in some other way."

Related to this is an increasing use of surveillance cameras for law enforcement. As anyone can see by going into electronics stores, video cameras are becoming smaller and cheaper and can deliver better quality than ever before. Back in the mid-1990s some cities in England began using video cameras to view "high crime" areas on city streets. The town of Lynn used sixty remote miniature video cameras whose signals were transmitted back to the local police headquarters. This resulted in a crime reduction to 1/70 of what it had been before the surveillance program. The savings in cost to the police department in reduced police patrols paid for the video equipment within a few months.[17] Hundreds of thousands of surveillance cameras are now installed throughout England. David Brin, who wrote the book *The Transparent Society,* argues that because everything we do, whether we're a common citizen, a corporation, or a public official, is coming under the public eye, we are all becoming accountable because we are all equally "transparent."[18]

Key Questions

The FBI, law enforcement, and intelligence agencies have legitimate concerns about needing surveillance technologies to prevent crime and other potential threats to U.S. citizens, but how many of our personal freedoms and Constitutional rights are we willing to relinquish in the name of increased "security"?

In other words, when do we reach the point of diminishing returns, when security concerns trump individual freedoms?

Challenge #4: Transhumanism and the Singularity

Ray Kurzweil is one of the world's most prolific and respected inventors. When he was in high school, he developed a computer program that analyzed the work of the world's most famous music composers and then recreated new melodies based on their styles. Later, with pop singer Stevie Wonder, he developed the first synthesizer that could realistically reproduce the sound of pianos and other acoustic instruments. He invented the first flatbed scanner, as well as the first optical character recognition program capable of electronically reading any typographic style. More recently he developed software for translating the human voice to text, as well as artificial intelligence software to assist in making stock market decisions. Because of his unique background, Kurzweil has a good track record of predicting future technological trends.

According to Ray Kurzweil, *we can expect to witness as much technological change in the next ten to fifteen years as we experienced in the previous century.* In Kurzweil's accelerating model of change, the twenty-first century will bring in the equivalent of 20,000 years of progress at today's rate. Kurzweil makes a compelling case for his conclusions—they're based on consistent statistical trends of invention and change dating back to the nineteenth century. From his perspective, several major factors are driving this accelerating rate of technological change:

Moore's Law: This concept was discussed earlier in the textbook, but it bears repeating here because of its central role in defining the pace of technological change. Gordon Moore was one of the inventors of the first integrated circuit and eventually became chairman of Intel. In the 1970s Moore predicted that microprocessor speeds would double every twenty-four months while microprocessor costs would remain constant. This "law" is derived from the consistent historical fact that transistors and circuits have become progressively smaller, and more of them can be placed simultaneously onto silicon chips. In addition, increased storage capacity and faster Internet connection speeds are rapidly increasing the amount of information that is available and widely distributed. This accelerating rate of information processing and communication corresponds with an increasing pace of new discoveries and technological breakthroughs. The *rate of change* itself is speeding up.

Kurzweil describes three sources of major technological transformation taking place around us, which he describes as the *GNR revolution.*

- **G** stands for *Genomics,* or the understanding of how the DNA molecule, which exists in every living cell, controls biological processes. This term is often used interchangeably with *biotechnology*—the ability to directly edit and reprogram the genetic instruction book of life for humans and other living organisms. Since the mapping of the human DNA molecule was completed, many important discoveries have been made about human origins, disease, and methods of identity authentication.

- **N** is for *Nanotechnology,* or the capacity to manipulate atoms and molecules, providing low-cost, efficient methods of microscale manufacturing. One long-term goal for nanotechnology is to be able to create new materials with specialized properties, such as strength, resistance to high temperatures, flexibility, or conductivity. Another goal is to create self-replicating devices called *nanobots* that would be able to carry

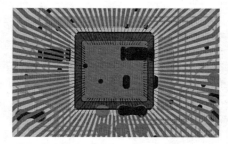

Figure 4. A microprocessor, the engine of Moore's Law.
© Rene Drouyer | Dreamstime.com.

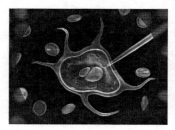

Figure 5. Genetic engineering.
© Magann | Dreamstime.com.

out a wide number of unusual tasks, such as clearing the arteries of fatty deposits, scanning the brain, or cleaning up pollution.

- **R** is for *Robotics,* or information technologies—or as Kurzweil says, "artificial intelligence at a human level." Over time, computing will be small scale, embedded in everything from clothing to eyeglasses, and largely invisible. "Everywhere" wireless computing will augment, expand, and enhance human experience. Kurzweil predicts that the ability to scan the brain down to the molecular level and translate biological events into digital information will open the way for true human intelligence modeling. *Biorobotics* will provide ways in which mechanical devices will be integrated with organic, living processes. These entities may be able to eventually reproduce like a form of living matter.

What these three technology domains have in common is the fact that they are all digital information–based sciences. Although biology, materials science, and computing have traditionally evolved independently, they now share a common digital language of 0s and 1s. This common language makes it possible for these disciplines to "talk" to one another in ways that were never dreamed of until just a few years ago.

For example, one possible application of GNR convergence was first introduced by IBM scientists in 1993 in the form of a tiny device called a quantum corral, a miniature area 14 nanometers wide surrounded by a spiky ellipse of iron atoms. Potentially the corral can store binary information in the form of 1s and 0s.

The idea is to make use of the cold-causing rhinovirus, which contains information embedded in its RNA strand consisting of 7,000 nucleotides. This information could be harnessed as software to drive the atomic-scale device. USC professor Larry Smarr describes the concept, "The quantum corral stores data. Rhinovirus executes a program. Design a nanophotonic interface between them and, in principle, you've got a computer only 100 times bigger than a silicon atom!"[19]

Smarr summarizes the convergent character of this *bioinfonanotechnology* device by saying, "Today, the corral is considered an engineered device, while rhinovirus is viewed as a biological entity. Within the nano arena, though, the distinction is meaningless. Both are nanomachines, one built on a substrate of metal, the other on a substrate of organic molecules."[20]

The Singularity

According to a futurist philosophy called *Transhumanism,* the GNR revolution is leading us to a point in time where profound technological change will come about so quickly that we will move into an event called the *singularity,* which is projected to take place sometime around the year 2030, in which any meaningful prediction about the future will become impossible. This is the approximate predicted time that forms of artificial intelligence will surpass human intelligence and biologically based intelligence will take a progressively diminished role in day-to-day decision making. Although the Transhumanists see this as a profound historical event, they don't think of it as a negative development. They anticipate this as a time when accelerating GNR advances will allow us to greatly enhance our intelligence, cure sickness, delay or reverse aging, develop abundant energy resources, solve world hunger, and protect the environment, and where the natural evolutionary process will become consciously directed for the first time. As University of Texas biochemist Angela Belcher has stated, "What would take millions of years to evolve on its own, takes about three weeks on the bench-top."

Science journalist and filmmaker Chip Walter sums up a transhumanist view of the singularity by saying:

". . . we will have evolved into another species. We will no longer be Homo sapiens, but Cyber sapiens—a creature part digital and part biological that will have placed more distance between its DNA and the destinies they force upon us than any other animal. And we will have become a creature capable of steering its own evolution ("cyber" derives from the Greek word for a ship's steersman or navigator—*kybernetes*). The world will face an entirely new state of affairs.

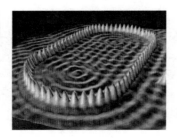

Figure 6. IBM scientists created the "quantum corral," made up of iron atoms on a copper substrate, that potentially could store information and execute it using software instructions derived from a biological entity, a rhinovirus, making it a *bioinfonanotech* device—a blending of biology, atomic level engineering, and computation. Reprint courtesy of International Business Machines Corporation, copyright © 2007 International Business Machines Corporation.

Why would we allow ourselves to be displaced? Because in the end, we won't really have a choice. Our own inventiveness has already unhinged our environment so thoroughly that we are struggling to keep up. In a supreme irony we have created a world fundamentally different from the one into which we originally emerged. A planet with six and a half billion creatures on it, traveling in flying machines every day by the millions, their minds roped together by satellites and fiber optic cable, rearranging molecules on the one hand and leveling continents of rain forest on the other, growing food and shipping it overnight by the trillions of tons—all of this is a far cry from the *hunter-gatherer*, nomadic life for which evolution had fashioned us two hundred thousand years ago."[21]

Part of the transhumanist claim is that human beings have been technologically enhancing their existence for many centuries, from the wheel to the pacemaker, and gradually pulling themselves away from the random forces of evolution. The difference now is that the pace has quickened. Transhumanists make the case that these anticipated technical and social changes will not be experienced as an alien invasion but as a friendly and beneficial development. For example, the Google search engine is a "large scale deployed artificial intelligence system"[22] that didn't exist a few years ago. Today it is seen as a useful and helpful ally by millions of Internet users who connect to Google every day for a wide variety of purposes. The World Wide Web, for that matter, wasn't invented and broadly distributed until 1993, and it has transformed the entire world.

In the area of artificial intelligence alone, Ray Kurzweil has predicted that by 2020, a standard desktop computer will have the computing capacity of the human brain. By 2029, a desktop computer will have the processing power of 1,000 human brains.[23] Kurzweil concedes that software will lag a few years behind the hardware in terms of creating human-like intelligence, but he concludes, "By the end of this century, I don't think there will be a clear distinction between human and machine. We can expand the capacity of our brains by a factor of thousands or millions, and, by the end of the century, by trillions."[24]

Not everyone is in support of the transhumanists, however. Critics view transhumanism as another chapter in the long history of utopian ideologies, claiming that applied science and new gadgetry will save our civilization from decline. The singularity has been jokingly referred to as the *techno-rapture*. One notable skeptic is the cofounder and chief scientist at Sun Microsystems, Bill Joy, who has publically debated Kurzweil on this topic. In his essay titled "Why the Future Doesn't Need Us,"[25] Joy says:

"If our . . . extinction is a likely, or even possible, outcome of our technological development, shouldn't we proceed with great caution?"

Another staunch critic of the transhumanist movement is author Bill McKibben, who sees the results of biotechnology research as mostly benefitting the wealthy, who may choose to biologically engineer their own children at a stage in their development where they will be unable to give their consent. His argument is that while future parents could potentially benefit from enhancing the intelligence, musical talent, and athletic ability of their children, they are also making decisions that are irreversible, and potentially damaging. Furthermore, continuing upgrades and new enhancements could make these genetic alterations obsolete.[26]

Key Questions

What do you see as the best and worst possible future outcomes in the quickly evolving relationship between humans and new GNR technologies?

Do you consider yourself taking a pro or con position regarding the singularity?

Do you agree or disagree with the transhumanist perspective?

Challenge #5: Technology Dependence and Addiction

"The addictive nature of the Internet takes our time and energy away from more communal activities. Like a powerful drug, the Internet snatches our minds from our homes, transporting them into the nowheresville of cyberspace, where time and space have no meaning. The Internet of course is not a family activity."

Clifford Stoll

"When we Spock parents gave our kids television in the 50s, that was a profound evolutionary step. We created the electronic consumer society. When we are giving our kids computers, we are unwitting agents of another profound evolutionary step."

Timothy Leary

The topic of our relationship with technology and its impact on society has generated a wide variety of science fiction stories, opinions, and heated arguments. This section provides a sampler of the wide variety of perspectives, both contemporary and historical, that this topic has generated, and we supply quotations that we believe are excellent summaries of key ideas that have been brought forth into the discussion over the past decades.

In 1909 the British author E.M. Forster wrote a short science fiction story for the November issue of the *Oxford and Cambridge Review* titled "The Machine Stops."[27] In it, he creates a world in which humanity no longer lives on Earth's surface, but underground, where they communicate with one another through a ubiquitous device called the Machine. The story concerns a mother named Vashti, who spends all of her waking hours in a small room, communicating to thousands of contacts she knows, rehashing derivative ideas and lectures. Her son Kuno lives on the other side of the planet and wants to visit her in person, not just through the electronic video conferencing connection provided by the Machine. Meanwhile, the story implies that some sort of human instigated event has made the surface of the Earth uninhabitable—physical travel across long distances is rare or strongly discouraged. The following section of Forster's "The Machine Stops," provides a dark scenario of a retro-futuristic Internet, written seventy years before the modern day Internet was invented.

Introduction to "The Machine Stops" by E.M. Forster, 1909

Imagine, if you can, a small room, hexagonal in shape, like the cell of a bee. It is lighted neither by window nor by lamp, yet it is filled with a soft radiance. There are no apertures for ventilation, yet the air is fresh. There are no musical instruments, and yet, at the moment that my meditation opens, this room is throbbing with melodious sounds. An armchair is in the centre, by its side a reading-desk—that is all the furniture. And in the armchair there sits a swaddled lump of flesh—a woman, about five feet high, with a face as white as a fungus. It is to her that the little room belongs.

An electric bell rang.

The woman touched a switch and the music was silent.

"I suppose I must see who it is", she thought, and set her chair in motion. The chair, like the music, was worked by machinery and it rolled her to the other side of the room where the bell still rang importunately.

"Who is it?" she called. Her voice was irritable, for she had been interrupted often since the music began. She knew several thousand people, in certain directions human intercourse had advanced enormously.

But when she listened into the receiver, her white face wrinkled into smiles, and she said:

"Very well. Let us talk, I will isolate myself. I do not expect anything important will happen for the next five minutes—for I can give you fully five minutes, Kuno. Then I must deliver my lecture on 'Music during the Australian Period'."

She touched the isolation knob, so that no one else could speak to her. Then she touched the lighting apparatus, and the little room was plunged into darkness.

"Be quick!" She called, her irritation returning. "Be quick, Kuno; here I am in the dark wasting my time."

But it was fully fifteen seconds before the round plate that she held in her hands began to glow. A faint blue light shot across it, darkening to purple, and presently she could see the image of her son, who lived on the other side of the earth, and he could see her.

"Kuno, how slow you are."

He smiled gravely.

"I really believe you enjoy dawdling."

"I have called you before, mother, but you were always busy or isolated. I have something particular to say."

"What is it, dearest boy? Be quick. Why could you not send it by pneumatic post?"

"Because I prefer saying such a thing. I want—"

"Well?"

"I want you to come and see me."

Vashti watched his face in the blue plate.

"But I can see you!" she exclaimed. "What more do you want?"

"I want to see you not through the Machine," said Kuno. "I want to speak to you not through the wearisome Machine."

"Oh, hush!" said his mother, vaguely shocked. "You mustn't say anything against the Machine."

"Why not?"

"One mustn't."

"You talk as if a god had made the Machine," cried the other.

"I believe that you pray to it when you are unhappy. Men made it, do not forget that. Great men, but men. The Machine is much, but it is not everything. I see something like you in this plate, but I do not see you. I hear something like you through this telephone, but I do not hear you. That is why I want you to come. Pay me a visit, so that we can meet face to face, and talk about the hopes that are in my mind."

She replied that she could scarcely spare the time for a visit.

The story represents a world in which a continuous mediated relationship with the omnipresent Machine has largely replaced authentic contact with the natural earth and physical connections between human beings. In fact, the intimate bond with technology is preferred over direct contact with other people, even close family members.

Two decades later, in 1931, another British science fiction author, Aldous Huxley, wrote *Brave New World,* a literary combination of fear and cynicism reacting to the advent of Nazism and the Soviet totalitarian state. The new "god" was Henry Ford, and cultural ideology was founded on mass production and consumption. Total control was levied by social conditioning and a "feel good" drug, Soma. In *Brave New World,* the state provided continual pleasure as a substitute for freedom. The *feelie movies* were a form of distraction and entertainment. In Huxley's world, citizens could go into a movie theater, take a hold of two knobs while viewing the movie, and when the movie ran, they would experience everything either the hero or heroine sees, hears, smells, and feels.

This work is provocative because it was one of the first mentions of immersive virtual reality and the parallels that developed between Huxley's *Brave New World* and our reality. Consider Soma and feelie movies compared with the artificially created worlds of television, cyberspace, virtual reality, raves, and the widespread use of Prozac and *smart drugs* medicating and distracting the population. Audiences today are willing participants in sensory manipulation. Pleasure, discomfort, and hunger can be triggered by powerful media images.

One element that is the life blood of media is that it is rarely one-dimensional or stand-alone. Since the earliest combination of film and sound, or print and pictures, media has been constantly fused. The future continuum of this trend is profound. The human urge for escape and ecstasy fuels this progression. It is the quest to eliminate the interface between human and hardware, a theme that we've seen running through the history of computers and virtual worlds technology. Although the dystopic futures portrayed by Forster and Huxley do not match our current circumstances, there is a strong element of resonating truth in them and important messages for us today.

Living with Technopoly

The early fascination with technology and the idea of progress in the United States can be seen in the work of Alexis de Tocqueville, whose descriptions of the North American character can be found in his book *Democracy in America,* which was published in 1835.

> "America is a land of wonders, in which everything is in constant motion, and every movement seems an improvement. The idea of novelty is there indissolubly connected with the idea of amelioration. No natural boundary seems to be set to the efforts of man; and what is not yet done is only what he has not yet attempted."[28]

Much later, Neil Postman, who was skeptical of this tendency in American society to uncritically accept new technologies and the changes they inevitably bring to society, described North American society as a *technopoly,* which he defined as "the submission of all forms of cultural life to the sovereignty of technique and technology."[29] He expanded on this idea by saying:

> "Technopoly is a state of culture. It consists in the deification of technology, which means that the culture seeks its authorization in technology, finds its satisfactions in technology, and takes its orders from technology. This requires the development of a new kind of social order, and of necessity leads to the rapid dissolution of much that is associated with traditional beliefs. Those who feel most comfortable in Technopoly are those who are convinced that technical progress is humanity's supreme achievement and the instrument by which our most profound dilemmas may be solved."[30]

Along with this unremitting march of progress, sustained by the immense material resources of the North American continent over the past two centuries, has come a progressive separation and isolation from the natural biological ecosystems of the planet, according to Jerry Mander, author and former advertising executive who describes this process as the "madness of the astronaut":

> "Our entire society has begun to suffer the madness of the astronaut; uprooted, floating in space, encased in our metal worlds, with automated systems neatly at hand, communicating mainly with machines, following machine logic, disconnected from the earth and all organic reality, without contact with a multidimensional, biologically diverse world and with the nuances of world views entirely unlike our own, unable to view ourselves from another perspective, *we* are alienated to the nth degree. Like the astronaut, we don't know up from down, in from out. Our world and our thought processes are confined to technical boundaries. All invention, if achievable, becomes plausible, and even desirable, since it is part of the commitment we have already made, even if the commitment leads logically to reorganizing our genes, our trees, and our skies, and possibly abandoning the planet and life itself."

Unlike the transhumanists, Mander sees our evolving (and accelerating) relationship with computers and related devices as ultimately a diminishment of our experience with the "real" world. Talking about video games Mander states:

> "Computer video games are good training for the faster world. When we play a video game, our goal is to merge with the computer program. The electronic symbols on the screen enter our brain, pass through our nervous system, and stimulate the fight-or-flight reaction that still lives within us and that expresses itself here through our hands. . ."

> "A skillful video-game player stimulates the computer program to go faster, and as the cycle (computer program to nervous system to hands to machine to computer program) speeds up, the player and the machine become connected in one fluid cycle; aspects of each other. Over time, and with practice, the abilities of the human being develop to approximate the computer program. Evolution is furthered by this kind of interaction, but this is a notably new form of evolutionary process. Where evolution once described an interaction between humans and nature, evolution now takes place between humans and human artifacts. We coevolve with the environment *we* have created; we coevolve with our machines, with ourselves. It's a kind of in-breeding that confirms that nature is irrelevant to us."[31]

Despite the concerns expressed by Jerry Mander and Neil Postman in the 1990s, the actual use of Internet-based or entertainment-based media has been steadily climbing. In 2009 it is estimated that American teenagers and adults will spend 3,555 hours and spend $1,023.69 per person on various electronic media experiences.[32] This represents approximately sixty-five days watching television, forty-one days listening to music, a week of Internet viewing, and a week reading magazines and newspapers. In the year 2000 the average number of viewing hours per person totaled 3,333.

A quickly growing category of media entertainment is in video game use. In 2005 a study by the Jack Myers Media Business Report showed that 62% of males and 47% of females played video games over the previous week. Male gamers played an average of an hour and six minutes a day, and female gamers played an average of forty-two minutes.[33] More telling statistics show that the video game industry is now taking in more than twice the revenue ($18.85 billion in 2007) of the Motion Picture Association of America's estimated box office sales for 2007 ($9.6 billion).[34] Another recent statistic published by the Entertainment Software Association is that 63% of parents whose children play video games think the games have a positive influence on their children's lives.[35]

Video game designer Lorne Lanning, who was the creative director for the Oddworld game franchise, whose titles included *Abe's Oddysee, Munch's Oddysee,* and *Oddworld: Strangers Wrath,* feels that video games are given a bad rap by people who've never played them or who misunderstand them. He feels that video games have an enormous potential for teaching a new way of communicating and exploring ideas that can't be matched by traditional print media.

"I think video games are the most powerful medium yet on the planet. They just haven't matured yet to point where that's recognized, or where the content has really made that happen. But is not about so much the content that determines the power of the medium. The power of the medium ultimately is determined by its ability to captivate, and for how long a duration. So what's the dosage that's capable in this medium? Video games beat everything else right now. The kid who can't spend ten minutes with a book will spend 150 hours on one *Final Fantasy* game."[36]

Marc Prensky is a consultant, public speaker, and advocate for a major overhaul of the U.S. educational system to accommodate the major technological shifts that are taking place. He believes that students who have been raised with cell phones, instant messaging, Internet access, digital music players, interactive video games, and so on, act and think differently than people who were raised before the introduction of this wide array of digital devices. This has created a special challenge to educational institutions, which traditionally have delivered instruction from a "sage on the stage" and text-based materials to passive learners. Prensky states, "Our students have changed radically. Today's students are no longer the people our educational system was designed to teach."[37]

Prensky explains this technology-based divide as consisting of two groups, the *digital immigrants* and the *digital natives.* Those who adopted digital technologies later but still carry many predigital communication habits, like paying for online merchandise by check, calling to confirm the receipt of email, or being unwilling to use instant messaging, are part of the older generational newbies, or *immigrants. Natives,* on the other hand, navigate through the wide variety of digital devices and thumb-typed messages effortlessly. Natives are accustomed to multitasking, social networking, and scanning written materials for keywords rather than reading every line of text. Immigrants tend to work sequentially from beginning to end on discrete tasks and consider entertainment trivial and work a serious endeavor. He sums up this situation by saying "...our Digital Immigrant instructors, who speak an outdated language (that of the pre-digital age), are struggling to teach a population that speaks an entirely new language."[38] Prensky advocates the increased use of interactive games, discussions, and social simulations in the classroom to move away from traditional didactic teaching models to more collaborative, relational ones.

Although Marc Prensky and others, such as MIT's Henry Jenkins and James Gee of the University of Wisconsin, see video games and simulations as potentially powerful tools for engaging and teaching new generations of students, others see a darker side to interactive communications technologies that needs to be taken into account.

Dr. Hilarie Cash is a mental health counselor and author specializing in Internet and video game addiction. She's cofounder of the Internet/Computer Addiction Services counseling center in Redmond, Washington—which is also the home of Microsoft, the software giant. She's a pioneer in the field and a "go to" expert on the topic, appearing in the *New York Times, Washington Post,* National Public Radio, BBC, and Fox television. She's author of the book *Video Games and Your Kids: How Parents Stay in Control.*

Figure 7. Computer addictions.
© Zulla | Dreamstime.com.

In a recent interview with the authors, she described how she initially became involved in video game and addiction work:

"My interest got piqued by having a client in 1994 who came in, and was addicted to a Dungeons and Dragons text-based only game. He didn't say 'I'm addicted'—he came in because he was depressed, and his marriage was falling apart. And in the course of working with him, it dawned on me what was going on. I knew he was playing with a lot of other gamers—I suggested I could run a group for them, and he said no, that just isn't going to work out, and they'll never come in. They're all dropouts—the guys I play with are all dropouts, from work and school, and they live at home with their parents—and they don't have money! You know, they'd never come in. So, it just was shocking, and awakened my curiosity about the phenomenon."[39]

Cash thinks that it's a growing problem and not generally recognized, although she pointed out that both South Korea and China have both designated video game addiction as their number one health problem! She explains her concern, based on many years of counseling addicted Internet users and gamers:

"I think the problem is serious and growing. I think Internet behavior and computer behavior with video game play, is highly addictive. It's interactive, it elevates the dopamine and opiates in the brain, and can easily create an addictive response. And by so doing, they get very hooked in whatever it is they're interested in—whether it's the video games or pornography, chatting, web surfing, gambling, buying and selling, all these activities—people get deeply engaged with them and can fairly easily become addicted to it, unless they understand the problem, and are willing to implement the kinds of limits and boundaries that they need to implement."[40]

She describes the major characteristic features of video game addictions by saying:

"The signs and symptoms have to do with people spending increasing amounts of time—in the addictive activity, whatever it is—in this case we're talking about video games. So the person wants to play more and more, and as they do that, they begin retreating. Their world shrinks down more and more, because they're less engaged in the rest of life. So they may have had physical activities to stay fit, they may have had friends, they might be married and have family that they live with—or just be living at home. But they begin withdrawing from those relationships, and spending less and less time with those real world relationships, as the time they devote to their online activities and online relationships grows."[41]

Finally, Cash provides some advice to parents who are facing game and Internet addiction challenges:

"I think it's extremely important that parents understand that for a developing child, their brain is getting wired according to the activities that the child engages in. So if you want your child to be a normal, healthy child, who is able to have good healthy relationships with family members, and with friends; a child who will later on be able to date and create their own healthy families; a child who has got all of the both emotional and intellectual resources that they need to be successful out in the working world—then parents need to understand that they have to keep video gaming, computer and Internet time very limited. Because if they let that get out of control, then their child's brain will get wired in a way that will have some negative consequences..."[42]

Disengaging from the Media

Finally, among the many social transformations brought about by new technologies, there is an ever accelerating pace and an exponential increase of information in the form of news, deadlines, email, and unexpected interruptions—along with a disquieting feeling that events are spinning out of control and that there is no time left to think or reflect.

Professor Mara Adelman teaches at the Department of Communications at Seattle University in Seattle, Washington, and has spent much of her career exploring how people use communications technology and find an appropriate relationship to it in their lives. She came to realize that what is missing is the ability of people to find time in their busy lives to carve out time for themselves—and if they do, the problem is how the personal time could be used to best restore a sense of balance and a psychological "shelter from the storm." She teaches a class called "Restorative Solitude" in which one of the assignments is to completely disengage from all electronic media for several days. Here is her account.[43]

Professor Adelman's Class Experiment: Disengaging from the Media

I've spent most of my life researching and teaching how people *connect*. And a couple of years ago I was invited to teach any course I've ever wanted to teach. So I decided to teach a course on how to help people *disconnect*. The name of the course was 'Restorative Solitude,' and I was interested in what Phillip Koch calls 'engaged disengagement'—intentional, conscious effort to disengage from the power of [communications devices], and to spend some time alone.

So, I decided to teach this course on restorative solitude. And I think there are several parts to this notion of "no time to think." One is, I do think that solitude is critical in terms of quality. The absence of self-consciousness, the absence of having to be accountable in responding to people around you. I think the second aspect of this is voluntary simplicity. I think it's very difficult to find time to think, unless you've made some kind of conscious decision to simplify your life—materially, in terms of the ways you want to spend your energy, whether it's shopping, or going to theater, the practice of your own private life. Then the third thing is the contemplative practice—whatever that is—whether it's body contemplative practices, yoga, or meditation—in terms of enhancing the quality of our time to think and the quality of our attentiveness ... In fact some of those skills—focus, observation—are really being lost.

Well one of the experiments was very interesting. [My students] had to spend a week in which they couldn't engage in any kind of mediated communication. So there are no cell phones, telephones, Internet, television, radio—they had to turn it off. There was a protest in the class—and that discussion was so interesting! The students felt that seven days was more than they could handle. And of course if they had to use the Internet for work, or for emergencies, fine—but they were to enter the spirit of the assignment. So they were to inform their parents, and their friends, that they were going to participate in this period of "disengagement." Seven days was too long, so we negotiated among ourselves for four days. They felt that four days—they could do it.

"Fine, that's the spirit of the assignment, we'll do it for four days." And I had no idea of what to expect. Now I must say that prior to this assignment, each student had kept a week long log of their media usage—and what was going on before, during and after they get on the Internet, their cell phone, and they saw some interesting patterns. So that set them up for the amount of time they spend in media and communication—what propels it, what motivates it, what are the consequences of it. So, they were ready for this assignment.

What I didn't expect were some of the outcomes that came back from four days. First of all, I have to say that there was a lot of pressure from families and friends, not to do the assignment! I had one irate parent say, "I want my child in constant contact." And the students felt a lot of normative pressure from their colleagues to stay engaged—you know, "I can't call you, I can't text message you..." So there was that realization.

Number two, there was a realization of how liberating the four days was for them—how unbelievably liberating! How much time they had, and the quality of the time they had. One person said, "I got into my car, and it was the first time I heard the engine—and realized that it needed to be fixed!" There were some profound things that emerged as well. And I think this experience was very transformative.

My main purpose was to give them hope that there was a sense of agency around technology. They could make small choices—Do they have to answer that phone in the middle of a conversation? Do they have to have the TV going while they're eating dinner? Do they have to check their email fifteen times a day?

What kind of boundaries do they need to put into place for themselves?

In both the work of the computer addiction therapist, Hilarie Cash, and in Mara Adelman's Restorative Solitude class, the goal is the same. How do you find a balanced relationship with the ever-increasing number of information streams, distractions, video games, social networks, and new hi-tech gear moving through our lives? A 24/7 schedule has suddenly imposed itself on many people whose lives are involved with information technologies. How do you set boundaries and claim space for yourself and your psychological well-being?

Key Questions

Are you in control of your daily use of electronic media, or are you its servant?

Is your relationship with electronic media a positive one, or is it a source of anxiety?

Do you feel that you might be spending excessive amounts of time on the Internet or playing video games, at the expense of real-world friendships or personal health?

Forecasting the Future

"Science Finds, Industry Applies, Man Conforms"
1933 Chicago World's Fair motto

"People Propose, Science Studies, Technology Conforms"
Donald A. Norman, *Things that Make Us Smart*

As we discussed in earlier chapters, looking at the prognostications of Jules Verne, Charles Robida, and Alvin Toffler, we can predict with a certain degree of accuracy what the future will bring based on current trends, our imagination, and our own initiative. As Alan Kay, inventor of the first laptop prototype says, "The best way to predict the future is to invent it."[44]

There has yet to be a consensus of how technology will change us. In the mid-twentieth century, Orwell and Huxley wrote of communications media as a mass, omnipresent controller. It stratified the differences between the haves and the have-nots, and it was a tool of oppression.

Imagine the evolution of technology thirty years from now. What will it be? How will it affect the global condition? Now imagine *yourself* thirty years from now. Is the transition dramatic? Probably not. A hype-fueled, media-driven construction of reality, such as the machine behind technology, alters our perception. Where are you in this mix? Technology, often veiled in secrecy behind the scenes, develops at a frenetic pace. On the other hand, human evolution proceeds in small measured increments, as noted by Robert Wilensky of the University of California at Berkeley:

"We've all heard that a million monkeys banging on a million typewriters will eventually reproduce the entire works of Shakespeare. Now, thanks to the Internet, we know this is not true."[45]

A cultural dysfunction is inevitable. The laws can't keep up. Educational structures scramble to implement the tools of the marketplace. Futurists and academia make their fortunes by postulating the world to come based on the tools we have. They use prediction from what is known rather than foresight (such as Huxley's) from what is unknown. How accurate can this be?

Donald A. Norman, a cognitive psychologist and computer interface expert, says:

"In this new age of portable, powerful, fully-communicating tools, it is ever more important to develop a human technology, one that takes into account the needs and capabilities of people."[46]

Norman's work with Apple Computers' advanced technology group was to develop a third generation of technology—computers you will not even see, that just fit naturally into your everyday life:

"On the one hand, I will argue that artifacts of technology can indeed make us smart, that we are in the midst of most interesting times. On the other hand, I will also argue that those in power are primarily driven by their perception of the marketplace, that if we are not careful, Hollywood standards will dominate the information industry—low standards in culture, low standards in content, high standards in glitter, and a price for everything."[47]

Stewart Brand takes a different approach. When Brand considers the impact technology will have on our world, he means it literally. Brand has been a *macro* activist for forty years. In 1968 he founded the Whole Earth Catalog, "a manual of sorts with a hippie-ish, Northern California slant referring to useful tools and products." He pioneered the Internet conference known as the WELL (Whole Earth 'Lectronic Link), which has grown to include more than 9,000 members. In 1988 he founded the Global Business Network, a think tank of consultants and futurists.

Brand is working on a remedy to the ecological fallout of technology. Obviously, the notion that computer technology would lead to a paperless office turned out to be a cruel joke. Let's add to the heap the volumes of software manuals, design guides, and website printouts. Brand hopes for improvement by applying the recycle strategy to technology's by-products.

"There's two ways to go. One is the manufacturer always owns the physical tool and they have to take it back. That makes them design them in such a way so that it's easy to take apart and reuse it and recycle everything. Or you build things so that the basic skeleton is really robust and then you can just keep swapping the high turnover stuff in and out. That way you keep much less material having to move around."

In his book *Amusing Ourselves to Death,* Neil Postman points to two different visions of the future and communications technology's role in it. On one hand, there is George Orwell's dystopia *1984,* where the ever-present eye of Big Brother watches a grim and depressed public through television. On the other hand, there is Aldous Huxley's *Brave New World.* Written originally as a farce in the early 1930s, Huxley's book details a society where people use pills to go to sleep and stay awake, conception is by test tube, people can enjoy "feelie" movies (a version of virtual reality), and advertisements continually blare over sound systems. Postman feels that Huxley's vision, already on its way to becoming a reality in 1960, when he published his essay "Brave New World Revisited," really shows what we have become. We are, in fact, living in a science fiction world, and we need not be watched by the omnipotent eye of television. Instead, we watch television of our own volition. That we live in a consumer culture where people crave instant gratification and where even the "talk" shows on television (which were once sophisticated and urbane in the days of Jack Parr and even the early days of Johnny Carson) have bowed to the lowest common denominator, where the idiocies of Leno have replaced the wit of Parr and Carson. In other words, the final result of all this new technology is that we as a people no longer want to think—we want to be entertained.

Howard Rheingold, a longtime commentator on the computer, the Internet, and our relationship with cyber technologies, doesn't see the future through a glass quite as darkly as Postman. He sees a double-edged sword, implying great promise as well as great danger offered up by the new digital social networks.

> "We temporarily have access to a tool that could bring conviviality and understanding into our lives and might help revitalize the public sphere. The same tool, improperly controlled and wielded, could become an instrument of tyranny. The vision of a citizen-designed, citizen-controlled worldwide communications network is a version of technological utopianism that could be called the vision of 'the electronic agora.'"[48]

The Greek agora of the ancient world, to which Rheingold refers, has been often held up as an ideal democratic institution—a public space where issues of the day are debated and solutions are found through collective wisdom and discussion. Citizen participation in politics was not only encouraged, it was expected. The word *idiot* originally derived from the ancient Greek *idios*—someone who refused to participate in public life, either through laziness or ignorance. However, ancient Greek democracy was not open to slaves, women, or men who lacked property. In Rheingold's view we could do much better through our marvelous communications networks—with the goal of providing all citizens with accurate information and engaging them in stimulating and empowering political debate.

Writer and film critic Richard Schickel has a more cynical view regarding the future of cyber-democracy:

> "Electronic populism is the form our government now takes. Electronic anarchy is the form it will soon assume. In these circumstances traditional governance has long since lost decisiveness. It is largely a showy carapace beneath which a self-perpetuating bureaucracy, alternately impotent and imperious, administers our sacred entitlements ... In another forty years representative democracy, the Age of Reason's most inspiring dream, may well be the road kill of three hundred million sputtering, muttering, stuttering Volkscomputers chugging implacably down the information superhighway, intent on their own mindless agendas."[49]

In his book *The Lost World,* Michael Crichton expresses another less than utopian prediction of humanity's migration to cyberspace.

> "Personally, I think cyberspace means the end of our species . . . because it means the end of innovation," Malcolm said.

> "This idea that the whole world is wired together is mass death. Every biologist knows that small groups in isolation evolve fastest. You put a thousand birds on an ocean island and they'll evolve very fast. You put ten thousand on a big continent, and their evolution slows down. Now, for our own species, evolution occurs mostly through our behavior. We innovate new behavior to adapt. And everybody on earth knows that innovation occurs only in small groups. Put three people on a committee and they may get something done. Ten people, and it gets harder. Thirty people, and nothing happens. Thirty million, it becomes impossible. That's the effect of mass media—it keeps anything from happening. Mass media swamps diversity. It makes every place the same. Bangkok or Tokyo or London: there's a McDonald's on one corner, a Benetton on another, a Gap across the street. Regional differences vanish. All differences vanish. In a mass-media world, there's less of everything except the top ten books, records, movies, ideas. People worry about losing species diversity in the rain forest. But what about intellectual diversity—our most necessary resource? That's disappearing faster than trees. But we haven't figured that out, so now we're planning to put five billion people together in cyberspace. And it'll freeze the entire species. Everything will stop dead in its tracks. Everyone will think the same thing at the same time. Global uniformity."[50]

Our best long-term hope is in the long-term survivability of our children, now being born into a fully technological and digitally connected world. The hope is that they maintain their humanity, their wisdom, and their love of Mother Earth, the natural world that sustains and protects us all.

Faye Ellman's 5-year-old daughter, Mala, had her first computer class recently. After school, her mother asked her what she had done, and she said, "First I was on one computer and played on a drawing program, then I exited myself and moved to another computer that had funny games, and then we got online." Mrs. Ellman was impressed. "On the very first day!" she exclaimed. "What did you do online?" Mala looked at her quizzically. "We took our partner's hand and walked back to our classroom," she said.[51] *New York Times,* November 4, 2000.

In one wistful scenario, and perhaps the most optimistic of all, San Francisco poet Richard Brautigan wrote a short poem in 1967 called "All Watched Over By Machines of Loving Grace" about a future world in which advanced artificial intelligence plays an important role, but lingers respectfully in the background, serving human and planetary needs.

This beautiful poem, written during the long ago Summer of Love by someone who was part of a movement to make poetry and information "free", could not be used to end our textbook due to increasingly complex and restrictive intellectual property laws. This is one example of the types of labyrinths we are facing now and will continue to face as we move towards our shared technology-driven future.

Endnotes

[1] Jerome Lawrence and Robert E. Lee, *Inherit the Wind* (New York: Bantam Books, 1985), p. 83.

[2] Ben Bagdikian, quoted in "Media Reform Information Center: Links and Resources on Media Reform," http://www.corporations.org/media/.

[3] National Endowment for the Arts, "To Read or Not To Read," executive summary, November 2007, http://www.nea.gov/research/ToRead_ExecSum.pdf.

[4] Jay Parker, interview with authors Michael Korolenko and Bruce Wolcott, July 6, 2008.

[5] G. Sciadis, "Unveiling the Digital Divide" (regarding the situation in Canada) 2002, http://www.statcan.ca/english/research/56F0004MIE/56F0004MIE2002007.pdf, p. 4.

[6] Statistics Canada, "Canadian Internet Use Survey," June 12, 2008, http://www.statcan.ca/Daily/English/080612/d080612b.htm.

[7] The Internet Telecommunication Union, "ITU Internet Reports: The Internet of Things," November 2005, http://www.itu.int/wsis/tunis/newsroom/stats/The-Internet-of-Things-2005.pdf.

[8] Murali Shanmugavelan, "Information Technology in Developing Nations," *SDdimensions*, June 2000, http://www.fao.org/sd/cddirect/cdre0050.htm.

[9] Eric Schmidt, "A Guide to Net Neutrality for Google Users," 2008, http://www.google.com/help/netneutrality.html.

[10] David L. Cohen "Reconsidering Our Communications Laws: Ensuring Competition and Innovation," Testimony before the Committee on the Judiciary, June 14, 2006, http://judiciary.senate.gov/testimony.cfm?id=1937&wit_id=5417.

[11] Lawrence Lessig, "Free Culture," lecture at the Open Source Convention 2002, http://www.oreillynet.com/pub/a/policy/2002/08/15/lessig.html?page=1.

[12] Ibid.

[13] Wikipedia, the free encyclopedia,"Creative Commons," http://en.wikipedia.org/wiki/Creative_commons.

[14] John Dvorak, "Creative Commons Humbug," *PC Magazine*, July 18, 2005, http://www.pcmag.com/article2/0,1895,1838244,00.asp.

[15] Kevin Mitnick, interview with Ed Bradley, "Kevin Mitnick: Cyberthief," CBS News, *60 Minutes*, October 20, 2004, http://www.cbsnews.com/stories/2004/10/20/60II/main650428.shtml?source=search_story. Video available on YouTube, http://www.youtube.com/watch?v=8_VYWefmy34.

[16] Jay Stanley, "ACLU Sounds the Alarm on Data Mining," Civil Liberties Newsletter, Spring 2003, p. 4.

[17] David Brin, "The Transparent Society," *Wired Magazine* no. 4.12, 1996, http://www.wired.com/wired/archive/4.12/fftransparent_pr.html.

[18]Ibid.

[19]Larry Smarr, "Nano Space: The New Space Race is the Battle For More and More Control Over Less and Less", *Wired Magazine* no. 11.06, June 2003. http://www.wired.com/wired/archive/11.06/nano_spc.html.

[20]Ibid.

[21]Chip Walter, *Thumbs, Toes, and Tears*, (New York: Walker & Company, 2006), p. 212.

[22]Rodney Brooks, "The Future of AI," Web interview, http://www.singinst.org/summit2007/podcasts/brooks/.

[23]Ray Kurzweil, "Ray Kurzweil Predicts the Future," *NewScientist*, November 21, 2006, http://www.newscientist.com/channel/opinion/science-forecasts/dn10620-ray-kurzweil-predicts-the-future.html.

[24]Declan McCullagh, "Kurzweil: Rooting for the Machine," *Wired Magazine* no. 8.04, November 3, 2000, http://www.wired.com/science/discoveries/news/2000/11/39967.

[25]Bill Joy, "Why the Future Doesn't Need Us", Wired, Vol. 8, April 2000. Full text available at http://www.wired.com/wired/archive/8.04/joy.html.

[26]Bill McKibben, quoted in David Gelernter, "The End of Human Nature," *Wired Magazine* no. 11.05, May 2003, http://www.wired.com/wired/archive/11.05/play.html?pg=3.

[27]E.M. Forster, "The Machine Stops," 1909, http://brighton.ncsa.uiuc.edu/prajlich/forster.html.

[28]Alexis de Tocqueville, *Democracy in America*, translated by Henry Reeve (D. Appleton and Company, 1904), p. 471.

[29]Neil Postman, *Technopoly* (New York: Alfred A. Knopf, 1992), p. 52.

[30]Ibid., p. 71.

[31]Jerry Mander, *In the Absence of the Sacred: The Failure of Technology and the Survival of the Indian Nations*, (San Francisco, Sierra Club Books, 1991), p. 65.

[32]U.S. Census Bureau's Statistical Abstract of the United States: 2009, "Media Usage and Consumer Spending," http://www.census.gov/prod/2006pubs/07statab/infocomm.pdf.

[33]Jack Myers, "Gaming Medium Growing in Pervasiveness, Not Fully Tapped," AdRants, December 2005, http://www.adrants.com/2005/11/gaming-medium-growing-in-pervasiveness.php.

[34]PC World, "Game Sales Beat DVDs, Box Office in 2007", July 5, 2008, http://www.pcworld.com/article/147984/game_sales_beat_dvds_box_office_in_2007.html.

[35]Entertainment Software Association, "Industry Facts," 2008, http://www.theesa.com/facts/index.asp.

[36]Lorne Lanning, interview with the authors, San Luis Obisbo, CA, 2002.

[37]Marc Prensky, "Digital Natives, Digital Immigrants," MarcPrensky.com, 2001, http://www.marcprensky.com/writing/Prensky%20-%20Digital%20Natives,%20Digital%20Immigrants%20-%20Part1.pdf.

[38]Ibid.

[39]Hilarie Cash, video interview with authors Michael Korolenko and Bruce Wolcott, July 6, 2008.

[40]Ibid.

[41]Ibid.

[42]Ibid.

[43]Mara Adelman, video interview with author Bruce Wolcott, August, 2008.

[44]Alan Kay, "The Quotations Page," Quotation #1432, http://www.quotationspage.com/quote/1423.html.

[45]Robert Wilensky, excerpt from a speech at a 1996 conference, Professor Emeritus, College of Engineering and Computer Sciences, http://www.eecs.berkeley.edu/Faculty/Homepages/wilensky.html/.

[46]Donald A. Norman, "About the Author", MIT Press web site, URL: http://mitpress.mit.edu/e-books/HAL/chap12/author.html.

[47]Donald Norman, "An academic discovers the realities of design", Seminar on People, Computers, and Design, Stanford University, December 2, 1994.

[48]Howard Rheingold, *The Virtual Community: Homesteading on the Electronic Frontier*. (Reading, Massachusetts: Addison-Wesley, 1993) p. 14.

[49]Richard Schickel, "American Heritage Magazine", Volume 45, Issue 8, December 1994, URL: http://www.americanheritage.com/articles/magazine/ah/1994/8/1994_8_57.shtml.

[50]Michael Crichton, *The Lost World*, (Ballantine Books, 1996), p. 339.

[51]Enid Nemy, "Metropolitan Diary", New York Times, November 4, 2000, URL: http://query.nytimes.com/gst/fullpage.html?res=9C00E3D61E3DF937A15752C0A9669C8B63.